CULTURE, POLITICS AND CLIMATE CHANGE

Focusing on cultural values and norms as they are translated into politics and policy outcomes, this book presents a unique contribution in combining research from varied disciplines and from both the developed and developing world.

This collection draws from multiple perspectives to present an overview of the knowledge related to our current understanding of climate change politics and culture. It is divided into four sections – Culture and Climate Change Communication, Media as Actors and Contributors to Climate Politics and Policy, Climate Politics and Policy, and Emerging Research in Climate Politics and Policy – each followed by a commentary from a key expert in the field. The book includes analysis of the challenges and opportunities for establishing successful communication on climate change among scientists, the media, policy-makers, and activists.

With an emphasis on the interrelation between social, cultural, and political aspects of climate change communication, this volume should be of interest to students and scholars of climate change, environment studies, environmental policy, communication, cultural studies, media studies, politics, and sociology.

Deserai A. Crow is an Assistant Professor in the Environmental Studies Program, Center for Science and Technology Policy Research and Center for Environmental Journalism at the University of Colorado, USA.

Maxwell T. Boykoff is Fellow in the Cooperative Institute for Research in Environmental Sciences (CIRES) and an Assistant Professor at the University of Colorado, USA.

CULTURE, POLITICS AND CLIMATE CHANGE

How information shapes our common future

Edited by Deserai A. Crow
and Maxwell T. Boykoff

Routledge
Taylor & Francis Group
LONDON AND NEW YORK

earthscan
from Routledge

First published 2014
by Routledge
2 Park Square, Milton Park, Abingdon, Oxon, OX14 4RN

and by Routledge
711 Third Avenue, New York, NY 10017

Routledge is an imprint of the Taylor & Francis Group, an informa business

British Library Cataloguing in Publication Data
A catalogue record for this book is available from the British Library

Library of Congress Cataloging-in-Publication Data
Culture, politics and climate change : how information shapes our common future / edited by Deserai A. Crow and Maxwell T. Boykoff.
     pages cm
  Includes bibliographical references and index.
  1. Climatic changes – Public opinion. 2. Climatic changes – Political aspects. 3. Mass media and the environment. 4. Environmental responsibility. I. Crow, Deserai A., 1975–
  QC903.C87 2014
  304.2′5–dc23   2013036830

ISBN13: 978-0-415-66148-5 (hbk)
ISBN13: 978-0-415-66149-2 (pbk)
ISBN13: 978-0-203-07340-7 (ebk)

Typeset in Times New Roman
by HWA Text and Data Management, London

For Jason, Anderson, and Josephine.

D.C.

In memory of Carl M. Moore.

M.B.

'This important new book explores the cultural politics of climate change. With dispatches from the front lines of diverse fields and geographies, the authors provide some of the first maps of this fast evolving landscape underlying some of the most important decisions humanity will make in the 21st century.'

Anthony Leiserowitz, Yale University, USA

'Climate change is the most important environmental challenge we face yet there has been little political action to address the problem. This volume examines the reasons for inaction, by considering different cultural and ethical perspectives and how the media plays a role in translating and presenting scientific information. It provides the most comprehensive assessment available, by leading experts in the field.'

Raymond Bradley, University of Massachusetts, Amherst, USA

'If you can't keep up with the fire hose of daily information and communication about climate change, much less make sense of what it all means and what it tells us about not just our climate, but also about our culture, the media, and the politics that choreograph our dance around the burning question of what to do about the problem, then I recommend you find a comfortable chair, step back from the heat, and read this book. Here are some great people trying to sort out the complex terrain of media and culture that lies between our everyday lives and the "grand stage" of climate change politics and policy-making. It is not all pretty, but it is helpful, and therefore hopeful.'

Susanne Moser, Susanne Moser Research & Consulting, Stanford, USA

'The only thing more complex than the climate system is the tangle of meanings we've wrapped around it. The varied perspectives gathered in this important book go a long way toward unsnarling the cultural politics of climate change—the first step in weaving the stories and policies we'll need to move forward.'

Jean Goodwin, Iowa State University, USA

'From citizens' perspectives over the "old" and "new" media all the way to politics and decision-making – Crow and Boykoff's volume is an excellent example of a societal turn in the analysis of climate change, and deals with its most pressing issues.'

Mike Schafer, University of Zurich, Switzerland

CONTENTS

FIGURES

TABLES

CONTRIBUTORS

Alison Anderson is Professor in the School of Government and Society, and Director of the Centre for Culture, Community, and Society at the University of Plymouth, UK. She also holds an adjunct professorship in the School of Social and Political Inquiry, Monash University, Australia. Alison is Editor of *Environmental Communication: A Journal of Culture and Nature* (Routledge) and the author of numerous publications on media, politics, and the environment.

Maxwell T. Boykoff is Fellow in the Cooperative Institute for Research in Environmental Sciences (CIRES) at the University of Colorado, and an Assistant Professor teaching in Environmental Studies, while serving as Adjunct Faculty in Geography. Max is also a Senior Visiting Research Associate in the Environmental Change Institute at the University of Oxford.

Mark B. Brown is a Professor in the Department of Government at California State University, Sacramento. He teaches courses on modern and contemporary political theory, democratic theory, and the politics of science, technology, and the environment.

Grace Chau has recently received her M.Sc. from the School for Conflict Analysis and Resolution, George Mason University and currently interns at the NIH (National Institutes of Health) Office of the Ombudsman, Center for Cooperative Resolution (CCR). She adopts a narrative approach to conflict analysis and resolution, and focuses on the role of culture in conflicts, climate change, and organizational conflicts.

Sara Cobb is a Professor at the School for Conflict Analysis and Resolution (S-CAR) at George Mason University, where she was also the Director for eight years. She teaches and conducts research on the relationship between narrative and violent conflict; she is also the Director of the Center for the Study of Narrative and Conflict Resolution at S-CAR that provides a hub for scholarship on narrative approaches to conflict analysis and resolution.

Deserai A. Crow is an Assistant Professor at the University of Colorado Boulder in the Environmental Studies Program, Associate Director of the Center for Environmental Journalism, and is on the faculty of the Center for Science and Technology Policy Research. She holds a Ph.D. in environmental policy from Duke University's Nicholas School of the Environment and Earth Sciences, a masters in Public Administration from the University of Colorado Denver's School of Public Affairs, and a B.A. in journalism from the University of Colorado Boulder.

Jason Delborne is Associate Professor of Science, Policy and Society in the Department of Forestry and Environmental Resources at North Carolina State University. He conducts research on highly politicized scientific controversies, including agricultural biotechnology, nanotechnology, biofuels, natural gas, climate change, and environmental toxics. He holds a Ph.D. in Environmental Science, Policy, and Management from the University of California, Berkeley and an A.B. in Human Biology from Stanford University.

Dallas J. Elgin is a doctoral candidate in public affairs at the University of Colorado Denver's School of Public Affairs. His doctoral dissertation focuses on the role of resources and strategies among supporters and opponents of climate policies. Dallas' research interests include climate and energy policy, theories of the policy process, and policy analysis. He holds a B.S. in Political Science from Florida State University and has more than five years of professional research and analytical experience within the public and private sectors.

Cheryl Hall teaches political theory in the Department of Government and International Affairs at the University of South Florida. Her early research focused on rethinking concepts of reason and passion in political theory. Following her growing concern with climate change and biodiversity loss, she began working in environmental political theory. She is interested in the interconnected roles that values, habits, emotions, deliberation, imagination, stories, culture, and structures play in encouraging or discouraging action to foster more sustainable ways of life.

Mike Hulme is Professor of Climate and Culture in the Department of Geography at King's College London. His most recent book is *Exploring Climate Change Through Science and In Society* (Routledge, 2013). From 2000 to 2007 he was the Founding Director of the Tyndall Centre for Climate Change Research, based at the University of East Anglia.

Dan M. Kahan is the Elizabeth K. Dollard Professor of Law and Professor of Psychology at Yale Law School. He is a member of the Cultural Cognition Project, an interdisciplinary team of scholars who use empirical methods to examine the impact of group values on perceptions of risk and related facts, including ones relating to climate change. The Project's research has been featured in articles published in a variety of peer-reviewed scholarly journals.

Edward Maibach is a University Professor at George Mason University, and the Director of Mason's Center for Climate Change Communication. Leveraging three decades of experience as a communication and social marketing practitioner and scholar, Ed's research focuses on public engagement in climate change mitigation and adaptation. Ed currently co-chairs the Engagement & Communication Working Group of the National Climate Assessment Development and Advisory Committee, and he previously served as Associate Director of the National Cancer Institute, Worldwide Director of Social Marketing at Porter Novelli, and Chairman of the Board for Kidsave International.

Doreen E. Martinez is a trained sociologist and active applied community researcher of Mescalero Apache, Mexican, and Dutch descent. Her ancestral and community life ground her interests and academic work. Academically, she is a transnational Indigenous epistemologist who studies issues of voice and representation. As an ethnographic researcher, her work focuses on cultural beliefs, traditions, and applications of "meaning making" through comparative cultural racial and gendered ways of knowing/ness.

Mark S. Meisner is the Executive Director of the International Environmental Communication Association (http://theieca.org). He has experience as a teacher, editor, information technology consultant, media analyst, and administrator of cultural programs. His areas of expertise include environmental communication, information technology, media, climate change/global warming, sustainability, and environmental thought.

Matthew C. Nisbet. is Associate Professor of Communication at American University, Washington, D.C. where he studies the role of media and communication in environmental politics and debates over science policy. Since 2002, he has authored more than 70 peer-reviewed studies, chapters, and monographs. Nisbet has been a Visiting Shorenstein Fellow on Press, Politics, and Public Policy at Harvard University's Kennedy School of Government, a Health Policy Investigator at the Robert Wood Johnson Foundation, and a Google Science Communication Fellow. He currently serves as a member of the National Academies Roundtable Committee on Public Interfaces in the Life Sciences.

Matthew Paterson is Professor of Political Science at the University of Ottawa. His research focuses on the cultural political economy of global environmental change, in particular of climate change. He is also currently working as a Lead Author on the Intergovernmental Panel on Climate Change, working on the chapter on international cooperation for the fifth assessment report.

Adrienne Russell is an Associate Professor of Emergent Digital Practices, co-Director of the Institute for Digital Humanities at the University of Denver, and researcher with the MediaClimate team. She is the author of numerous articles and book chapters on the digital-age evolution of activist communication and journalism.

William Schroeder is the Commander of the Air Force Special Operations Command's tenth Combat Weather Squadron. He is responsible for preparing Special Operations Weather Team (SOWT) forces for rapid global deployment to conduct environmental reconnaissance and austere weather operations in permissive, non-permissive, and/or politically sensitive areas in support of Special Operations Command forces. Previously, he served as a Strategic Communication Fellow at the Pentagon, developing engagements for senior Air Force leaders.

Vanessa Schweizer is an Assistant Professor in the Centre for Knowledge Integration at the University of Waterloo in Canada. She studies decision-making under uncertainty and how information gains credibility in such contexts. Her research includes scenario analysis in the context of climate change and the influences of political conflict on climate change attitudes. Previously, she held appointments with the National Center for Atmospheric Research, the Interdisciplinary Research Unit on Risk Governance and Sustainable Technology Development at the University of Stuttgart, and the Committee on the Human Dimensions of Global Change at the National Research Council.

Joe Smith is Senior Lecturer in Geography at the Open University specializing in the politics of consumption, the history of environmental thought, and media and environment. Joe has advised on over 30 hours of BBC broadcasting and runs seminars for senior media people on environmental and development issues (www.citizenjoesmith.wordpress.com @citizenjoesmith).

Johannes Stripple is Associate Professor of Political Science at the Department of Political Science, Lund University, Sweden. His recent research has covered European and international climate policy, carbon markets, renewable energy, climate adaptation, carbon sinks, energy scenarios, and governmentalities around climate change, carbon, and the earth system.

Bruno Takahashi is Assistant Professor of Environmental Journalism and Communication at Michigan State University with a joint appointment in the School of Journalism and the Department of Communication. He is also the Research Director of the Knight Center for Environmental Journalism at Michigan State University. He received his B.S. in communication from the University of Lima, Peru, and his M.S. and Ph.D. in environmental science from SUNY ESF. His research interests include media coverage of environmental affairs, environmental journalism practices, environmental behavior change, risk communication, and the links between media and policy.

Matthew Tegelberg is an Assistant Professor in the Department of Communication Studies and Multimedia at McMaster University and a researcher with MediaClimate, a transnational network of media scholars that studies global media coverage of climate change. He has written on cultural tourism, media representations of indigenous peoples, and environmental communication.

Christopher M. Weible studies policy processes and environmental policy. He is currently an Associate Professor at the School of Public Affairs at the University of Colorado Denver. He received his Ph.D. in Ecology with an emphasis in Environmental Policy Analysis from the University of California Davis. He earned a masters in Public Administration and a Bachelor of Science in Mathematics and Statistics from the University of Washington.

Dmitry Yagodin is a doctoral candidate specializing in journalism and media studies at Tampere University, Finland. He is also a member of the Finnish Graduate School for Russian and East European Studies at Helsinki University's Aleksanteri Institute. His doctoral research focuses on journalism and the political blogosphere in Russia. His work includes contributions to the MediaClimate research team.

ACKNOWLEDGEMENTS

We acknowledge the hundreds of scholars whose work inspired this book. The idea for this work emerged from the 2012 International Conference on Culture, Politics, and Climate Change held in Boulder, Colorado USA. Over 300 scholars from at least 19 countries attended and presented important and innovative interdisciplinary work related to the many facets of the cultural politics of climate change. The works presented in this book were presented at the conference and coalesced into a volume that we are proud to produce. We would especially like to thank the scholars who have contributed to this volume for their patience in fielding editorial questions, responding to peer reviews, and contributing important work that will push the field of climate change scholarship into emerging areas of inquiry.

Because this book was born of the International Conference on Culture, Politics, and Climate Change, it is important to thank the many people who made the conference possible. The planning and organization could not have been successful without the Center for Environmental Journalism at the University of Colorado Boulder, the primary sponsor and cheerleader for the event. Co-Directors Len Ackland and Tom Yulsman were invaluable sources of support, as were the staff members who helped in its production: Sheri Hay, Vince Calvo, Penny Bates, and Doña Olivier. Our faculty advisers also included Rick Stevens and Kathleen Ryan, who we would like to thank for their invaluable advice, review of paper abstracts, and support in planning the conference. We also thank Ben Hale and Nabil Echchaibi for reviewing paper proposals. We thank Aditya Ghosh and Marisa McNatt for their initial help to identify strong conference papers for potential inclusion in the edited volume. We also thank Lydia Dixon, Ph.D. candidate and conference planner extraordinaire. Her work was vital to the success of the conference.

Sponsors for the International Conference on Culture, Politics, and Climate Change included the Cooperative Institute for Research in Environmental Sciences (CIRES), the Committee on the History and Philosophy of Science, the Institute for Arctic and Alpine Research (INSTAAR), Journalism and Mass Communication, the Environmental Studies Program, the Environmental Center, the Vice Chancellor for Research, and Ads a2b, all at the University of Colorado Boulder. Additionally, we would like to thank the International Environmental Communication Association for its sponsorship.

We also thank our fellow scholars, whose peer reviews improved the chapters and cohesion of this book. These reviewers include: Karen Akerlof, Elizabeth Albright, Bob Brulle, Lydia Dixon, Mike Goodman, Lauren Hartzell Nichols, Katharine Hayhoe, Elizabeth Koebele, Adrianne Kroepsch, Alex Lockwood, Kate Manzo, Lucy McAllister, Mark McCaffrey, Marisa McNatt, Matt Nisbet, Shawn Olson, Sam Randalls, Rebecca Schild, Kanmani Venkateswaran, and Xi Wang.

Finally, we acknowledge those who directly contributed to the production of this volume. We would like to thank Olga Baysha for her assistance preparing our proposal. Louisa Earls, Ashley Irons, and Helen Bell at Routledge-Earthscan deserve many thanks for making this process relatively pain-free and for encouraging what we feel is important scholarship. Lastly, but integrally, we thank Ami Nacu-Schmidt with the Center for Science and Technology Policy Research, for her work designing the book cover and preparing the manuscript for publication.

This book is a true collaboration from inception to publication and we thank all of those who have contributed to its content and form.

Deserai A. Crow
Maxwell T. Boykoff

INTRODUCTION

Deserai A. Crow and Maxwell T. Boykoff

"Our Common Future" was the name of the 1987 Brundtland Commission report from the United Nations World Commission on Environment and Development. This report was the culmination of a nearly four-year process that focused attention on notions of sustainable (and unsustainable) development: population, poverty, gender equity, food security, conservation, and energy, among others. As it sought to chart "recommendations for a sustainable course of development," the report also provided an influential re-framing of these connected webs through the considerations of challenges and opportunities at the human-environment interface.

In the new millennium, addressing political and policy problems in an increasingly complex world relies heavily on communication, interpretation, and use of information. Never has this been truer than when we discuss the politics and policy processes related to the promulgation of comprehensive climate policies globally. 'Politics' here are considered as the contestation of policies and elections, through social relations infused with power, authority, and varying perspectives. Politics has been variously defined as Harold Lasswell described: the determining process of "who gets what, when, and how." 'Politics' involve proposals, ideas, intentions, decisions, and behaviors, with a focus on *processes* that prop up, challenge, lurk behind, support, and resist explicit actions (Boykoff, 2010). 'Policy' then refers to the codified and formal articulations of political goals through the creation of legislation, regulations, programs, and the corollary processes that create such policies. Politics, of course, inform and influence the creation of policies but they are distinct processes and see varying outcomes. By distinguishing between 'political/politics' and 'policy' in this way, we can more capably then unpack and examine varied influences that expand as well as constrict the spectrum of considerations for ongoing climate politics, deliberations, and governance. We center our considerations of 'Politics and Policy' through contributions in Part III of this volume.

Concurrently, our culture and values inform how we assess, comprehend, and communicate about complex issues such as climate change. We know that scientific papers, policy evaluations, and media representations are not viewed simply as reified markers of culture, but rather windows into the processes that contribute dynamically to the formation and maintenance of cultural identity as well as the cumulative characteristics of society (Maleuvre, 2004). This communication of information then is engaged by non-nation-state actors (NNSAs) (e.g., media), institutions, and other stakeholders in the political process (Moser & Dilling, 2007). Recognizing these key dimensions, we situate this cross-disciplinary endeavor into a theoretical framework described as 'cultural politics of climate change': dynamic and contested spaces where various 'actors' battle to shape public understanding and engagement with decision-making. These negotiations in the construction of 'information' are critical inputs to what becomes public discourse on today's climate challenges. Ron Lembo has written that, "discourses are understood to work normatively, ordering, organizing and regulating everyday life in ways that reach beyond the power of values or even ideologies" (Lembo, 2000, p. 54). As we focus on the high-stakes, high-profile, and highly-contested case-study of 'climate change,' corollary studies from varied disciplines examining representational practices and public discourses in other human-environment issues like nanotechnology (e.g., Anderson et al., 2013), stem cells (e.g., Leydesdorff & Hellsten, 2005; Leydesdorff & Hellsten, 2006; Nisbet et al., 2003), and agricultural biotechnology (e.g., Brossard & Nisbet, 2007; Hellsten, 2002) inform these considerations as well. To get into the contours of these influences, we center our considerations of 'culture and values' through contributions in Part I.

And then there is the obvious point that most citizens around the world typically do not read peer-reviewed literature, nor do they read policy documents or negotiate international treaties. Instead, to learn about climate change and gain climate information, people in the public arena turn to media communications – television, newspapers, radio, digital, and social media – to link formal science and policy with their everyday lives. Thus, media are an important source through which information is constructed, disseminated, and consumed. Yet, media influences have been changing over time as well: traditional media outlets have faced newfound challenges (Boykoff & Yulsman, 2013; Crow & Stevens, 2012; Siles & Boczkowski, 2012) while shifts to digital and social media tools – such as weblogs (e.g., Merry, 2010; Meyers, 2012), Facebook, Twitter, Digg, Reddit, YouTube (e.g., Kavoori, 2012) – have recalibrated who has a say and how these claims circulate (Baek et al., 2012; Cacciatore et al., 2012; Graham et al., 2013). Media organizations themselves have worked to adapt to these changing conditions and researchers have increasingly sought to make sense of the shifts (e.g., Horan, 2013; Nielsen, 2012; Zhu & Dukes, 2013) and their implications (e.g., Jacobson, 2012) in various cultural, political, social, and environmental contexts (e.g., Adams & Gynnild, 2013; Dutton, 2013; Schuurman, 2013).

Media representations – from news to entertainment, from broadcast to interactive and participatory – are critical links between people's perspectives and experiences, and the ways in which dimensions of climate change are discussed at a distance between science, policy, and public actors. Together, these media are constituted by a diverse and dynamic set of institutions, processes, and practices that together serve as 'mediating' forces between communities such as science, policy, and public citizens. Mass media have limits in terms of potential conduits to attitudinal and behavioral change. Nonetheless, as unparalleled forms of communication to a wide audience, it remains vitally important to examine the ways in which media representations and symbols are produced, interpreted, and consumed, thus influencing a spectrum of possibilities for governance and decision-making. In short, the multifarious contributions that mass media make to public discourse deem it worthy of careful reflection and scrutiny.

Most broadly, references to 'media' include television, films, books, flyers, newspapers, magazines, radio, and internet. They involve publishers, editors, journalists, content producers, and members of the communications industry who produce, interpret, and communicate texts, images, information, and imaginaries. The dance that ensues involves the creation and dissemination of information and the effects that such information has on policy outcomes that attempt to address issues of societal importance such as climate change. Media are frequently referenced as mechanisms for change, usually as a tool through which stakeholders influence policy outcomes by informing public opinion or influencing legislators (Arnold, 1990; Jones & McBeth, 2010; Kingdon, 1995; Sabatier & Jenkins-Smith, 1993; Zaller, 1992), or an influence on policy agendas and policy definitions by raising the salience of certain issues above others (Baumgartner & Jones, 2009; Jones & Baumgartner, 2005).

While media are just one means by which information is created and disseminated, they are certainly a powerful one. As such, media messages function as important interpreters of climate information in the public arena, and shape perceptions, attitudes, intentions, beliefs, and behaviors related to climate change (Boykoff, 2011; Hmielowski et al., 2013). Studies across many decades have documented that citizen-consumers access understanding about science and policy (and more specifically climate change) largely through media messages (e.g., Antilla, 2010; O'Sullivan et al., 2003). We work through analyses of 'communication and media' through contributions in Part II of this collection, bridging between Parts I and III.

Culture, politics, and climate change

Taken together, connections between media information and policy decision-making, attitudes, perspectives, intentions, and behavioral change as negotiated through cultures and values (both individual and collective) are far from straightforward. Coverage certainly does not determine engagement or policy progress; rather, it shapes their possibilities (Boykoff, 2011; Carvalho & Burgess, 2005).

These have been dynamic spaces where claims-makers in the public sphere have been changing (e.g., Baum & Groeling, 2008; Fahy & Nisbet, 2011), and institutions have been also dynamic (e.g., Averyt et al., 2013; Future Earth, 2012). These movements signal substantive changes in how people access and interact with information and who has access. Anthony Leiserowitz has written that these arenas of claims-making and framing are "exercises in power ...Those with the power to define the terms of the debate strongly determine the outcomes" (Leiserowitz, 2005, p. 149). This is consistent with policy scholarship on 'policy images' that determine the venues of jurisdiction and potential policy outcomes of contested issues (Baumgartner & Jones, 2009). These factors have produced mixed and varied impacts: Alissa Quart has warned of dangers of mistaken (or convenient) reliance on '*fauxperts*' instead of 'experts' (2010). These 'experts' are particularly worrying in policy debates since much scholarship points to the influence experts wield and lower barriers to entry for experts in policy processes (Crow, 2010a; Crow, 2010b; Schneider & Teske, 1992). Boykoff (2013) and Boykoff and Olson (2013) – among a growing group of researchers – have examined these dynamics as they relate to public attention paid to 'contrarian' views on various climate issues.

This volume explores the ways in which discursive and material elements comprise the cultural politics of climate change, where discourses are tethered to material realities, perspectives, and social practices (Hall, 1997). Cultural politics refer to dynamic and contested processes behind how meaning is constructed and negotiated. Information flows can confront, avoid, or service power through complex, dynamic, and messy processes. Among actors here, mass media have taken on varied roles, from watch dog to lap dog to guard dog in the public sphere over time (Boykoff, 2011).

The framework for this book is such that we trace the importance of culture on the politics of climate change, then delve into the importance of information in its various forms and contexts, and finally investigate how these two elements help to form the politics of climate change that are witnessed. The book concludes with a discussion of future directions for research and scholarship.

How information constructs climate 'problems'

The prominence and quantity of information available on policy issues is vital to constructing policies to mitigate, adapt to, or respond to climate change. Similarly, the framing, or construction of such media content is vital to understanding public opinion, policy images, and the social construction of policy problems as complex as climate change. Representations of what constitutes 'information' are actually convergences of competing knowledge. These frames draw attention to varying ways that members of the public can (and at times should) make sense of, as well as value, the changing world. Notions of public discourse draw from Maarten Hajer's definition of 'discourse,' as

> an ensemble of ideas, concepts, and categories through which meaning is given to phenomena. Discourses frame certain problems; that is to say,

they distinguish some aspects of a situation rather than others ... discourses provide the tools with which problems are constructed ... [and they] dominate the way a society conceptualizes the world.

(Hajer, 1993, pp. 45–46)

Agendas and those who influence them

Of the important mechanisms by which information is widely distributed, the prominence and salience of information in the public sphere is vital to consider. The distribution of information is most prominently accomplished by media outlets, but is also done by political elites, citizens, and issue advocates. Cohen (1963) famously stated that media "may not be successful in telling its readers what to think, but it is stunningly successful in telling its readers what to think *about*." McCombs and Shaw (1972) coined the term agenda-setting to describe the influence that media have on determining the issues of importance to the public through drawing attention to some issues above others. By covering some issues and ignoring others, media communicate to citizens and to elites what issues are important (McCombs, 2005). It is through this "transmission of salience" (McCombs, 1997, p. 433) that media influence the broad issue agenda within a society. Media coverage of issues, measured by quantity, prominence, and frequency, translates to subsequent placement of those issues on the governmental and public issue agendas (McCombs, 2004).

It is not the information contained in media messages itself that is important to agenda-setting, but rather that the issue in question garnered the attention to begin with and the corollary societal importance placed on the issue (Scheufele & Tewksbury, 2007). The flip side of this – viewed through the lens of cultural politics – deserves our consideration too: in these dynamic, and contested processes behind how meaning is constructed and negotiated, we must not only appraise the portrayals that gain traction in discourses, but also those that are absent from them or silenced (Dalby, 2007; Derrida, 1978). In these ways, agenda-setting and framing processes have important effects on marginalizing some discourses while contributing to the entrenchment of others (Castree, 2004). As Tim Forsyth has stated, "assessments of frames should not just be limited to those that are labeled as important at present, but also seek to consider alternative framings that may not currently be considered important in political debates" (2003, p. 1).

By inference, individuals assume that the issues covered by the media are the most important issues of the day. "Journalists, selecting and highlighting a few stories each day, determine which issues are treated as important in the news" (Paletz, 1999, p. 141). Traditional journalism values focus on truth, transparency, and giving voice to the voiceless (Kovach & Rosenstiel, 2001), but additionally, those that dictate selection of certain issues and events to cover include (1) timeliness of issues in the public arena, (2) significance of stories, (3) prominence (among others) (Keller & Hawkins, 2009). Journalists also often consider pragmatic elements that increase audience interest such as conflict, corruption, celebrity, and similar traits that identify successful stories (Jones, 1999). The issues that gain attention from media are those that are often proposed by advocates, political elites, and even corporations (Cox, 2010; Zaller, 1992), especially as resources are cut from traditional newsrooms and journalists rely increasingly on public relations professionals to educate them and pitch interesting stories. By covering certain issues at the expense of others, media also send signals to one another as to which issues are the most important on a given day, which can influence the media agendas of other organizations and the resulting broader media and public agendas (McCombs, 2004). Through this agenda-setting cycle, the public is informed as to whether or not climate change and similar complex issues are important to their own lives and their communities.

Walter Lippman introduced scholars to the concept of a pseudo-environment, wherein the news media act as a bridge between "the world outside and the pictures in our heads" (as cited in McCombs, 2004, p. 21). This pseudo-environment is constructed by the multitude of daily decisions made by journalists that determine which stories are covered – out of a larger population of stories (see Boykoff & Nacu-Schmidt, 2013) – in the day's news. Some depictions of media actors, including journalists, portray them as powerful gatekeepers, determining which items are placed on the media agenda, and which other items that may also be significant are left off of the media agenda and therefore are not present on the public or policy agendas (Graber, 2006). And amid the dynamism of digital and social media influence, boundaries between who constitute 'authorized' speakers (and who do not) in mass media as well as who are legitimate 'claims-makers' are consistently being interrogated and challenged (Gieryn, 1999; Loosen & Schmidt, 2012).

The pressures of vying for sources, working within government structures, and making do with fewer resources as economic pressures take their toll on traditional United States (US) media (Brainard, 2009; Crow & Stevens, 2012) mean that the simplicity with which we often view media actors is not accurate (McCombs, 2004; McQuail, 2007). They are also comprised of individuals who must negotiate daily deadlines, interactions with sources, and internal organizational and economic pressures to produce media content (see Anderson, 2009; Graber, 2006). The relationships between journalists and government or other elite sources are vital to understanding the complexity with which issues are selected and disseminated daily. Not only do media rely on government sources for much of the information necessary to tell stories, but government sources also depend on media coverage for publicity, positive public opinion, and reelection. The relationship is not one-dimensional but rather inherently complex and muddy.

Sharon Dunwoody has cautioned to not view various modes of media production equally. She said, "because of their extensive reach and concomitant efficiencies of scale, mediated information channels such as television and newspapers have been the traditional channels of choice for information campaigns. But research on how individuals actually use mass media information suggests that these channels may be better for some persuasive purposes than for others" (quoted in Boykoff 2009, p. 2). Furthermore, Cass Sunstein again offered a less rosy picture. He has warned of the likelihood of the 'echo chamber' effect where this interactivity actually walls off users from one another by merely consuming news that mesh with their worldview and ideology (Sunstein, 2007).

Digital and social media and the creation and dissemination of information

An expansive history of communication and media expression begins with the art of rhetoric in ancient Greece and weaves through the centuries of the Roman Empire, the European Middle Ages, and the Renaissance. Over these formative periods, a wide range of activities and modes of communication – performance art, plays, poetry, debate – drew on narratives, arguments, allusions and reports to communicate various themes, information, issues and events (Briggs & Burke, 2005). Organized studies of the art of communications began in these foundational periods for modern expression. However, such growth was limited by a number of competing factors, such as strong state-control over the public sphere, legacies of colonialism, low literacy rates, racial and gender inequalities, as well as ongoing technological capacity challenges (Murdock, 2002). However, it was through conditions during the French Revolution and the First Industrial Revolution in the late 1700s that provided opportunities for media communications – newspapers in particular – to emerge with widespread force (Chapman, 2005). The increasing reach of modern media communications through these channels, technologies, and innovations has led to the contemporary conception of 'mass media.' However, it still was not until the 1920s that scholars actually began to speak of such activities as 'media,' as we do today (Briggs & Burke, 2005). Rapid expansion of modern media communications continued into the twentieth century, and set the stage for the impressive deployment on a mass scale (McQuail, 2005).

In recent decades there has also been a significant expansion from consumption of traditional mass media into consumption of digital and social media. Essentially, in tandem with technological advances, this expansion in communications is seen to be a fundamental shift from broadcast, or 'one-to-many' (often one-way) communications to 'many to many' more interactive webs of communications (O'Neill & Boykoff, 2010; van Dijk, 2006). This movement has signaled substantive changes in how people access and interact with information and who has access. Embedded in this dynamism is the burgeoning influence of digital and social media. And with it comes numerous questions, among them:

- How do digital and social media platforms (e.g., Twitter (Parmalee, 2013)) contribute to agenda-setting in the twenty-first century?
- Does the increase of information content produced by non-journalists lead to lesser ethics, accuracy, or impact of coverage?
- Does increased visibility of climate change in digital/social media translate to improved communication or just more noise (as Neil Gavin calls it, the 'rantosphere' (2009, p. 5))?

- Do these spaces provide opportunities for new forms of deliberative community regarding questions of climate mitigation and adaptation (e.g., Harlow & Harp, 2013; Rogers, 2004) and conduits to offline organizing and social movements (e.g., Jankowski, 2006; Tufekci, 2013)?
- Or has the content of this increased coverage shifted to polemics and arguments over measured analysis? In this democratized space of content production, do digital/social media provide more space for contrarian views to circulate?
- And through its interactivity, does increased consumption of news through digital/social media further fragment a public discourse on climate mitigation and adaptation, through information silos where members of the public can stick to sources that help support their already held views (e.g., Hestres, 2013; Yang & Kahlor, 2012)?

Evidence of media ability to set the agenda from which citizens make personal opinions, change behavior, and which also influences policy outcomes is more powerful for issues where individuals do not have personal experience (McCombs, 2004; McCombs, 2005). Additionally, where we once saw relatively homogenous agendas among media (see McCombs & Shaw, 1972 for example), we now see widely diverging media agendas as a result of digital media (McCombs, 2004). In this digital media age we also see a significant transformation of the concept of media from a 'mass' where a limited number of media outlets communicate to multitudes of citizens, to a transmission from many sources to many citizens. This also involves a change in who is considered a media actor – now citizens are as empowered and capable of producing media images and stories through the use of digital technology as many professional journalists. We have seen a dramatic rise in what scholars call citizen journalism, and with it brings both a populist ability to set media and policy agendas, and a virtually complete lack of knowledge regarding journalistic values and professional norms (Graber, 2006).

Importantly, in policy agendas research, there is significant evidence to support the claim that media shifts in attention precede governmental or legislative shifts in attention (Baumgartner & Jones, 2009). By focusing on certain topics in media coverage, the public, legislative bodies, and individual policymakers become aware of and concerned with those topics.

The construction of messages and our understanding of information

Beyond understanding how certain issues become important to public and policy agendas through the transmission of salience, it is vital to acknowledge the role that media play in helping shape opinions and collective understanding of issues. Considered in this way, representations are manifestations of past themes, resonant tropes, and collective institutional as well as individual memories. Keep in mind, however, that media are not the only actors to actively frame messages.

All humans do this – at the dinner table, in boardrooms, or in written and broadcast content. Sometimes this can be a purposeful or manipulative effort, but often it can be a simple byproduct of attempting to explain complex subjects to people without a background in the issue.

Entman (1989) describes framing as a way in which media explain the salient aspects of complex issues. "To frame," he explains, "is to select some aspects of a perceived reality and make them more salient in communicating text, in such a way as to promote a particular problem definition, causal interpretation, moral evaluation, and/or treatment recommendation for the item described" (Entman, 1993, p. 52). Scheufele (2009) argues that framing helps construct our social reality, and articulates the connections between two important types of frames: individual and media (Scheufele, 1999). Media frames are central organizing ideas or story lines that provide meaning to a complex story (Gamson & Modigliani, 1987). Individual frames, on the other hand, are clusters of information that individuals use to process information (Entman, 1993).

Through these media frames and individual frames, media content can have important, dynamic, iterative, and non-linear effects on public opinion. Moreover, as representational practices populate, construct, and influence public discourse they can fuel rather than quell the highly-contentious and highly-politicized milieu of climate science and governance. By highlighting certain attributes of a policy problem, media, stakeholders, and policymakers can attempt to shape public policy outcomes. Baumgartner and Jones (2009) claim that by shifting attention to new attributes of a problem, stakeholders can successfully expand policy venues and jurisdictions which can in turn shape the scope of the debate and policy outcomes. In so doing, actors can influence policy outcomes. Stone (1997) further supports these claims, with her assertions that certain frames – causal stories in particular – are effective in shaping debates over policy issues.

Information as a resource or tool in the policy process

Information, including the frames used by journalists and other storytellers, can be used as a strategic tool by coalitions of actors seeking policy change. These framed messages, or policy images, can reframe an established issue to accelerate venue expansion, citizen mobilization, and policy change (Baumgartner & Jones, 2009). They can also help shift societal understanding of policy problems so that a new status quo emerges after policy change happens. In doing so, these messages also shift governmental understanding of issues and therefore can shift legal jurisdiction in legislative bodies or in courts. For example, if climate change is considered solely an economic issue, then there is no need for health or environment committees within legislative bodies to debate issues related to the topic. Once the issue of climate policy is reframed to include these environmental and health concepts, committees governing areas of health and environment now have policy jurisdiction (Baumgartner & Jones, 1993) and influence policy outcomes.

In addition to the broader framing and reframing of policy issues that is continually underway in the policy process, coalitions of actors use messages to communicate internally and externally, hoping to consolidate influence and change policies to conform with their beliefs (see Jones & McBeth, 2010; Shanahan et al., 2011). By constructing narratives, framing issues, and describing their opponents, coalitions influence policy outcomes by using messages and media dissemination of those messages as both resources and strategic tools. As resources, media are relied upon to disseminate pre-framed messages (talking points) and analysis by coalitions. As tools, media messages are actively crafted and strategically used to increase coalition influence. Moreover, Arnold has described that there are two policy processes continually at work (1990). One, the visible policy process, is the one we typically see portrayed in media reports, and focused public opinion polls. This is the arena for debate over topics that give rise to significant controversy, media coverage, and citizen activism. There is also a second policy process, an invisible one, in which multitudes of policy issues are debated and passed without media coverage, or with very little, and without notable citizen input or awareness. It is within the visible policy debate that legislators are constrained by constituent desires, ideological and party divides, and the prospect of negative or positive media coverage. However, much policy work is done outside the public eye, in this invisible policy process.

These are the dynamic and power-laden interactions that critically contribute to how climate change is portrayed, deliberated, and discussed in the public arena. In turn, these constructions of 'information' shape the spectrum of possibility at the climate science-policy interface. Together, constructions of meaning – negotiated in the spaces of cultural politics – are shaped by political economic, structural, and institutional as well as cultural and psychological factors, operating simultaneously at multiple scales. It is not enough to simply categorize all media, even mainstream traditional media, as 'mass media' anymore. It is vital to consider the important differences among media in relation to policymaking.

How information shapes our collective future

The communication of information that emerges from our individual and collective cultural values has significant bearing on the attention paid to climate change as well as the direction that political and policy debates take. By drawing attention to certain issues and framing those issues according to specific constructs, legislative bodies may be more or less likely to promulgate comprehensive climate policies, and these contested communication processes also help to determine the focus of such policies, and therefore the success of such policies in addressing climate change.

The chapters presented in this book bring together contemporary scholarship that collectively synthesizes questions related to 1) how cultural values inform and produce bodies of information which we, 2) collectively disseminate, often through the use of media and the decisions of relevant media institutions and actors, and 3) how this information influences the promulgation of climate policy and the relevant climate politics that accompany such policy discussions. These contributions emerged from the 2012 International Conference on Culture, Politics, and Climate Change, held in Boulder, Colorado (please see http://www.climateculturepolitics. org/ for more). This was a cross-disciplinary gathering that explored intersections between culture, politics, and science in order to enhance collective understanding of public policy addressing climate change in various contexts. Contributors to the conference discussions interrogated the many obstacles and opportunities confronting policymakers, media, scientists, and other non-nation-state actors, and focused on how climate change communications influence ongoing cultural and political issues.

Each section of this book tackles one of the three areas outlined above, and offers a commentary to then synthesize the chapters and present additional perspectives on the questions raised by the authors. Through varied approaches, these contributions value the contextual importance of history in shaping present possibilities across different cultural, political, economic, social, and environmental conditions. The book then concludes with a forward-looking section focused on emerging areas of research in climate politics and policy.

Part I. Culture and climate change communication

Part I of this volume presents two cases of the connection between culture, ideas, values, and climate change. Both chapters presented in this section also clearly address how communication about climate change can and does affect individuals and communities. In Chapter 1, Cheryl Hall ponders whether a discourse of 'gloom and doom' is counter-productive, fostering resistance, apathy, or despair instead of hope and motivation to change. She argues that people do need reasonably optimistic stories about the possibilities for a sustainable low-carbon future, but that such stories must also acknowledge any loss that people face in order to be persuasive. In Chapter 2, Doreen Martinez bears witness to the active engagement and challenges that Indigenous cultures are negotiating regarding their constant visible-invisibleness in public climate change rhetoric. She focuses on the naming and identifying of these practices as forms of climate citizenship that promote neocolonial understandings and actions that explicitly and implicitly challenge sovereignty and citizenship of Indigenous communities. The scholarship presented by Hall and Martinez is further explicated by Mike Hulme, who states that "there is clearly something more powerful, more unsettling, about the idea that human actions are persistently altering the momentary weather which all of us experience intimately on a daily basis." Hulme connects these two pieces that each tackles how climate change can be different things, and different ideas, to various audiences.

Part II. Media as actors and contributors to the climate politics and policy

In Part II of this book, we further delve into scholarship related to the dissemination of information and its corollary effects. Chapter 3 investigates the role of both traditional and emergent forms of journalism as it relates specifically to the United Nations climate summits in Copenhagen and Durban. Matthew Tegelberg, Dmitry Yagodin, and Adrienne Russell examine online and traditional newspaper coverage of the 2009 and 2011 UN climate summits in the United States, Canada, and Russia, finding important patterns of coverage and differences in media platform trends. Chapter 4 further tackles issues relevant to journalism practice, specifically a range of factors that appear to inhibit weathercasters from educating their viewers about climate change. Vanessa Schweizer, Sara Cobb, William Schroeder, Grace Chau, and Edward Maibach find that the obstacles fall into three main categories – occupational, interpersonal, and cultural – and exert different influences on weathercaster behavior and views. Chapter 5, then, analyzes a case study of Peru and focuses on the ways in which media coverage of climate change interacts with individual traits of national legislators; and how such interaction influences the design of policies. The results reveal the policy information environment and the issue attributes enable both the media and alternative sources of information such as the Internet to play an important role in how legislators perceive the issue and act upon it. Joe Smith concludes this section by diving deeper into two of the common traits presented in these chapters: the complexity of climate change and the decisions made by media actors to communicate about the topic. He points to the chapters in this section as helping readers understand the processes and potential successes in communicating about climate change in the future.

Part III. Climate politics and policy

Part III advances the previous discussions by presenting studies related to the role of information, stakeholder advocates, and beliefs in politics and policy. The section begins with Chapter 6 wherein Mark Brown interrogates skepticism about climate science. He argues that such distrust can be usefully understood as part of a long tradition of popular suspicion of organized power. He engages Democratic theory to understand the role that distrust in climate science plays in our larger democratic processes. In Chapter 7, Dallas Elgin and Christopher Weible analyze the Colorado climate and energy policy subsystem. Member beliefs between rival coalitions diverge in regard to the cause, severity, and solutions needed to address issues of adaptation and mitigation to climate change. Both coalitions report similar levels of individual and organizational capacity to generate and analyze information and to engage in similar kinds of activities and strategies. In Chapter 8, Jason Delborne explores the institutional and rhetorical strategies employed by public think tanks to navigate the mix of scientific and political controversies surrounding climate change within an institutional context that demands at least the appearance of "objectivity" and "non-partisanship." Matthew Nisbet concludes this section, arguing that it is now important for the environmental movement to be self-reflective because the status quo from the environmental movement and other political actors has helped to contribute to the polarization of the climate debate. Instead, Nisbet argues that they should begin to engage in capacity building, learning, and collaborative processes in order to help change happen and arrive at compromises that create solutions.

Part IV. Emerging research in climate politics and policy

Part IV concludes this volume by looking forward at emerging areas of scholarship related to the culture and politics of climate change. In Chapter 9, Matthew Paterson and Johannes Stripple explore the ways that practices, and the subjectivities that underpin them, have become contested, and governance initiatives aimed at reshaping them have emerged at various scales. As such, climate change governance is revealed as a fundamentally cultural project – relating to the meanings and identities associated with the generation of carbon emissions and efforts to transform societies towards decarbonization. In the book's final chapter, Dan Kahan argues that it is a mistake to believe (or to represent) that either social scientists or science communicators can intuit effective communication strategies by simply consulting compendiums of psychological mechanisms. Social scientists have used empirical methods to identify which of the myriad mechanisms that could plausibly be responsible for public conflict over climate change actually are. Science communicators should now use valid empirical methods to identify which plausible real-world strategies for counteracting those mechanisms actually work. Alison Anderson concludes the volume by tying together these final chapters and future directions of scholarship. She points to the common threads of top-down versus bottom-up governance in climate institutions, along with the important questions as to how public citizens can optimally enter into contentious climate science-policy discussions going forward.

Conclusion

Through the use, production, and consumption of information, the translation of values into political outcomes presents certain opportunities and obstacles. Focusing on cultural values and norms as they are translated into politics and policy outcomes, the volume presents a unique contribution in combining research from multiple disciplines and from both the developed and developing world.

At the end of the day, exposure to more information can help to understand the world around us and enhance decision-making on climate issues. But Susanne Moser has cautioned, "providing information and filling knowledge gaps is at best necessary but rarely sufficient to create active behavioural engagement" (2009, p. 165). Harry Collins and Robert Evans have delineated competing perspectives on information and decision-making (2002). One they spotlight is that of a 'deficit model' approach. This perspective has posited that poor choices and actions are attributed to 'deficits' of knowledge and information to make the 'correct' choice. Applied to climate issues, one adopting this stance may see that any lack of public and policy engagement is attributed to deficiencies in knowledge of climate information. This 'deficit model' logic is often associated with Mertonian norms and ideals of science as an open, universal, and objective practice. Moreover, this notion has also been linked to positivist conceptions of communication where portrayals of climate change are seen as a link in a chain of one-way communications of science-as-tool-to-inform-policy.

However, over the past sixty years or so, this view has been critiqued in a variety of ways. Critics have pointed out that this model has been too simple a characterization of the dynamic and non-linear interactions between science and governance. Naomi Oreskes has remarked, "When trying to communicate broadly – to the public or the press – scientists follow a deficit model that presumes that their audiences are ignorant and need to be 'supplied' with good, factual information … however, the model has failed" (quoted in Boykoff, 2009, p. 2).

Nonetheless, in the policy and public spheres, there have been residual impulses that have emanated from this deficit model view. These have included a stated reliance on 'sound' science in order to make decisions, as well as pursuits to eliminate uncertainty as a precondition for action. Encapsulating these dynamics, Brian Wynne has proclaimed, "So the deficit model is dead – Long live the deficit model!" (2008, p. 23). As such, contributions to this volume work through connections between information and decision-making that emerge through webs of dynamic and interacting processes, conditions, and influences.

In recent decades, there has been a clear surge in engagements with climate change in various segments of popular culture, and influences on public discourse by a range of NNSAs have brought with them new spaces and dimensions of discursive and material struggles. For instance, many businesses have begun to tout voluntary measures of 'carbon neutrality' in their practices while some environmental non-governmental organizations (ENGOs) and pressure groups have pushed for 'carbon taxation.' Similar debates have also involved questions regarding 'carbon offsets' for carbon-unfriendly travel, carbon labeling of food and household products, movements toward 'low carbon diets' by purchasing local goods, the inherent paradoxes of calling on 'clean coal' technologies to reduce GHG emissions, and varying notions of 'peak oil' (e.g., Bettini & Karaliotas, 2013; Goodman & Boyd, 2011). These are 'cultural politics of climate change': dynamic spaces where various 'actors' battle to shape public understanding and engagement; contested places where formal climate science, policy, and politics operating at multiple scales permeate the spaces of the 'everyday.'

As our collective awareness grows regarding the importance of researching, interrogating, and critically analyzing dimensions of how culture and politics shape information on climate change in the twenty-first century, perhaps now is the time for the United Nations Secretary-General to call for and convene a 'World Commission on Culture, Politics, and the Environment.' With burgeoning research areas mentioned briefly here – and featured in this volume you now hold – climate change certainly makes for a powerful case-study, now standing nearly thirty years from this seminal contribution by Gro Harlem Bruntland and colleagues. As information continues to shape 'our common future,' more systematic and coordinated understanding of how information shapes and is shaped by climate science-policy interactionss would be in our collective- and self-interest.

There is undoubtedly much more to write, to research, and to say on these important topics. The chapter authors are able to dig in a bit and the section commentators are able to provide additional insights. However, our contributions here are merely brief and provoking: it is our hope that this volume marks an important and useful contribution to ongoing conversations, interrogations, and systematic queries in culture, politics, and climate change. Through these case-studies, we hope to further elucidate the multi-scale political, economic, cultural, social, and environmental forces that shape and are shaped by information. We hope these efforts continue to illuminate ongoing possibilities for 'our common future.'

References

Adams, P. C. & Gynnild, A. (2013). Environmental messages in online media: The role of place. *Environmental Communication: A Journal of Nature and Culture*, 7(1), 113–130.

Anderson, A. (2009). Media, politics and climate change: Towards a new research agenda. *Sociology Compass*, 3(2), 166–182.

Anderson, A. A., Kim, J., Scheufele, D. A., Brossard, D., & Xenos M. A. (2013). What's in a name? How we define nanotech shapes public reactions. *Journal of Nanoparticle Research*, 15(2), 1–5.

Antilla, L. (2010). Self-censorship and science: A geographical review of media coverage of climate tipping points. *Public Understanding of Science*, 19(2), 240–256.

Arnold, R. D. (1990). *The logic of congressional action*. New Haven, CT: Yale University Press.

Averyt, K., Brekke, L. D., Busch, D. E., Kaatz, L., Welling, L., & and Hartge, E. (2013). Moving forward with imperfect information. In G. Garfin, A. Jardine, R. Merideth, M. Black, & S. LeRoy (Eds.), *Assessment of climate change in the Southwest United States: A report prepared for the national Climate assessment* (pp. 436–461). Washington, DC: Island Press.

Baek, Y. M., Wojcieszak, M., & Delli Carpini M. (2012). Online versus face-to-face deliberations: Who? why? what? with what effects? *New Media & Society*, 14(3), 363–383.

Baum, M. A. & Groeling, T. (2008). New media and the polarization of American political discourse. *Political Communication*, 25(1), 345–365.

Baumgartner, F. R. & Jones, B. D. (1993). *Agendas and instability in American politics*. Chicago, IL: University of Chicago Press.

Baumgartner, F. R. & Jones, B. D. (2009). *Agendas and instability in American politics*, 2nd edition. Chicago, IL: University of Chicago Press.

Bettini, G. & Karaliotas, L. (2013). Exploring the limits of peak oil: Naturalizing the political, de-politicising energy. *The Geographical Journal*, 179(4), 331–341.

Boykoff, M. T. (2009). A discernible human influence on the COP15? Considering the role of media in shaping ongoing climate science. Copenhagen Climate Congress Theme 6, Session 53.

Boykoff, M. (Ed.). (2010). The politics of climate change. London: Routledge/Europa.

Boykoff, M. T. (2011). *Who speaks for the climate: Making sense of media reporting on climate change*. Cambridge: Cambridge University Press.

Boykoff, M. T. (2013). Public enemy no.1? Understanding media representations of outlier views on climate change. *American Behavioral Scientist,* 57(6), 796–817.

Boykoff, M. & Nacu-Schmidt, A. (2013). *Media coverage of climate change/global warming.* Center for Science and Technology Policy Research, University of Colorado. Retrieved: http://sciencepolicy.colorado.edu/media_coverage. Accessed November 10, 2013.

Boykoff, M. T. & Olson, S. (2013). 'Wise Contrarians' in Contemporary Climate Science–Policy–Public Interactions. *Celebrity Studies,* 4(3), 276–291.

Boykoff, M. T. & Yulsman, T. (2013). Political economy, media and climate change – the sinews of modern life. *Wiley Interdisciplinary Reviews: Climate Change,* doi: 10.1002/wcc.233.

Brainard, C. (2009). Science journalism's hope and despair: 'Niche' pubs growing as MSM circles the drain. *Columbia Journalism Review,* February 13.

Briggs, A. & Burke, P. (2005). *A social history of the media: From Gutenberg to the internet.* Cambridge: Polity Press.

Brossard, D. & Nisbet, M. C. (2007). Deference to scientific authority among a low information public: Understanding US opinion on agricultural biotechnology. *International Journal of Public Opinion Research,* 19(1), 24–52.

Cacciatore, M. A., Anderson, A. A., Choi, D-H., Brossard, D., Scheufele, D. A., Liang, X., Ladwig, P. J., Xenos, M., & Dudo, A. (2012). Coverage of emerging technologies: A comparison between print and online media. *New Media & Society,* 14(6), 1039–1059.

Carvalho, A. & Burgess, J. (2005). Cultural circuits of climate change in UK broadsheet newspapers, 1985–2003. *Risk Analysis,* 25(6), 1457–1469.

Castree, N. (2004). Differential geographies: Place, indigenous rights and 'local' resources. *Political Geography,* 23(2), 133–167.

Chapman, J. L. (2005). *A comparative media history: An introduction, 1789–present.* London: Polity Press.

Cohen, B. C. (1963). *The press and foreign policy.* Princeton, NJ: Princeton University Press.

Collins, H. M. & Evans, R. (2002). The third wave of science studies: Studies of expertise and experience. *Social Studies of Science,* 32, 235–296.

Cox, R. (2010). *Environmental communication and the public sphere.* Thousand Oaks, CA: Sage Publications.

Crow, D. A. (2010a). Local media and experts: Sources of environmental policy initiation? *Policy Studies Journal,* 38(1), 143–164.

Crow, D. A. (2010b). Policy entrepreneurs, issue experts, and water rights policy change in Colorado. *Review of Policy Research,* 27(3), 299–315.

Crow, D. A. & Stevens, J. R. (2012). Local science reporting relies on generalists, not specialists. *Newspaper Research Journal,* 33(3), 35–48.

Dalby, S. (2007). Anthropocene geopolitics: Globalisation, empire, environment and critique. *Geography Compass,* 1, 1–16.

Derrida, J. (1978). Structure, sign, and play in the discourse of the human sciences. In J. Derrida, *Writing and difference* (pp. 278–293). Chicago, IL: University of Chicago Press.

Dutton, W. H. (Ed.). (2013). *The Oxford handbook of internet studies.* New York: Oxford University Press.

Entman, R. M. (1989). How the media affect what people think: An information processing approach. *The Journal of Politics,* 51(2), 347–370.

Entman, R. M. (1993). Framing: Toward clarification of a fracturer paradigm. *Journal of Communication,* 43(4), 51–59.

Fahy, D. & Nisbet, M. C. (2011). The science journalist online: Shifting roles and emerging practices. *Journalism*, 12(7), 778–793.

Forsyth, T. (2003). *Critical political ecology: The politics of environmental science*. London: Routledge.

Future Earth. (2012). Research for global sustainability: A framework document. Retrieved: http://www.icsu.org/future-earth/media-centre/relevant_publications/future-earth-framework-document. Accessed November 10, 2013.

Gamson, W. A. & Modigliani, A. (1987). The changing culture of affirmative action. In R. G. Braungart & M. M. Braungart (Eds.), *Research in political sociology* (Vol. 3, pp. 137–177). Greenwich, CT: JAI Press.

Gavin, N. (2009). The web and climate change politics: Lessons from Britain? In T. Boyce & J. Lewis (Eds.), *Climate change and the media* (pp. 129–144). London: Peter Lang Publishing.

Gieryn, T. F. (1999). *Cultural boundaries of science: Credibility on the line*. Chicago, IL: University of Chicago Press.

Goodman, M. K. & Boyd, E. G. K. (2011). A social life for carbon? Commodification, markets and care. *Geographical Journal*, 177(2), 102–109.

Graber, D. A. (2006). *Mass media and American politics*. Washington, DC: CQ Press.

Graham, M., Schroeder, R., & Taylor, G. (2013). Research. *New Media & Society*, 12(3), 1–8.

Hajer, M. (1993). Discourse coalitions and the institutionalization of practice: The case of acid rain in Britain. In F. Fisher & J. Forester (Eds.), *The argumentative turn in policy analysis and policymaking*. Durham, NC: Duke University Press.

Hall, S. (1997). *Representation: Cultural representation and signifying practices*. Thousand Oaks, CA: Sage.

Harlow, S. & Harp, D. (2013). Collective action on the web. *Information, Communication & Society*, 15(2), 196–216.

Hellsten, I. (2002). T*he politics of metaphor: Biotechnology and biodiversity in the media*. Academic Dissertation, Tampere University Press.

Hestres, L. E. (2013). Preaching to the choir: Internet-mediated advocacy, issue public mobilization, and climate change. *New Media & Society*, 1(1), 1–17.

Hmielowski, J. D., Feldman, L., Myers, T. A., Leiserowitz, A., & Maibach, E. (2013). An attack on science? Media use, trust in scientists and perceptions of global warming. *Public Understanding of Science*, April 3, 1–18.

Horan, T. J. (2013). 'Soft' versus 'hard' news on microblogging networks. *Information, Communication & Society*, 16(1), 43–60.

Jacobson, S. (2012). Transcoding the news: An investigation into multimedia journalism published on nytimes.com 2000–2008. *New Media & Society*, 14(5), 867–885.

Jankowski, N. W. (2006). Creating community with media: History, theories and scientific investigations. In L. A. Lievrouw & S. Livingstone (Eds.), *The handbook of new media*, Updated Student Edition (pp. 55–74). London/Thousand Oaks, New Delhi: Sage.

Jones, B. D. & Baumgartner, F. R. (2005). *The politics of attention: How government prioritizes problems*. Chicago: University of Chicago Press.

Jones, C. (1999). *Winning with the news media: A self-defense manual when you're the story*. Tampa, FL: Video Consultants, Inc.

Jones, M. D. & McBeth, M. K. (2010). A narrative policy framework: Clear enough to be wrong? *Policy Studies Journal*, 38(2), 329–353.

Kavoori, A. (2012). *Reading YouTube: The critical viewer's guide*. New York: Peter Lang.

Keller, T. & Hawkins, S. (2009). *Television news: A handbook for writing, reporting, shooting, and editing*. Scottsdale, AZ: Holcomb Hathaway.

Kingdon, J. W. (1995). *Agendas, alternatives and public policies*, 2nd edition. New York: Longman.

Kovach, B. & Rosenstiel, T. (2001). *The elements of journalism: What newspeople should know and the public should expect*. New York: Three Rivers Press.

Leiserowitz, A. A. (2005). American risk perceptions: Is climate change dangerous? *Risk Analysis*, 25, 1433–1442.

Lembo, R. (2000). *Thinking through television*. Cambridge: Cambridge University Press.

Leydesdorff, L. & Hellsten, I. (2005). Metaphors and diaphors in science communication mapping the case of stem cell research. *Science Communication*, 27(1), 64–99.

Leydesdorff, L. & Hellsten, I. (2006). Measuring the meaning of words in contexts: An automated analysis of controversies about Monarch butterflies, Frankenfoods, and stem cells. *Scientometrics*, 67(2), 231–258.

Loosen, W. & Schmidt J-H. (2012). (Re-) discovering the audience. *Information, Communication & Society*, 15(6), 867–887.

Maleuvre, D. (2004). Beyond culture. *Journal of Human Values*, 10(2), 131–141.

McCombs, M. (1997). Building consensus: The news media's agenda-setting roles. *Political Communication*, 14, 433–443.

McCombs, M. (2004). *Setting the agenda: The mass media and public opinion*. Cambridge: Polity.

McCombs, M. (2005). A look at agenda-setting: Past, present and future. *Journalism Studies*, 6(4), 543–557.

McCombs, M. & Shaw, D. (1972). The agenda-setting function of mass media. *Public Opinion Quarterly*, 36(2), 176–187.

McQuail, D. (2005). *Mass communication theory*. Thousand Oaks, CA: Sage Publications.

McQuail, D. (2007). The influence and effects of mass media. In D. A. Graber (Ed.), *Media Power in Politics*, 5th edition (pp. 19–35). Washington, DC: CQ Press.

Merry, M. K. (2010). Blogging and environmental advocacy: A new way to engage the public? *The Policy Studies Organization*, 27(5), 641–656.

Meyers, E. A. (2012). 'Blogs give regular people the chance to talk back': Rethinking 'professional' media hierarchies in new media. *New Media & Society*, 14(6), 1022–1038.

Moser, S. (2009). Costly politics – unaffordable denial: The politics of public understanding and engagement in climate change. In M. Boykoff (Ed.), *The politics of climate change: A survey* (pp. 155–182). London: Routledge/Europa.

Moser S. & Dilling, L. (Eds.). (2007). *Creating a climate for change: Communicating climate change and facilitating social change*. Cambridge: Cambridge University Press.

Murdock, G. (2002). Media, culture, and modern times: Social science investigations. In K. B. Jensen (Ed.), *A handbook of media and communication research* (pp. 40–61). London: Routledge.

Nielsen, R. K. (2012). How newspapers began to blog. *Information, Communication & Society*, 15(6), 959–968.

Nisbet, M. C., Brossard, D., & Kroepsch, A. (2003). Framing science the stem cell controversy in an age of press/politics. *The International Journal of Press/Politics*, 8(2), 36–70.

O'Neill, S. J. & Boykoff, M. T. (2010). The role of new media in engaging the public with climate change. In L. Whitmarsh, S. J. O'Neill, & I. Lorenzoni (Eds.), *Engaging the public with climate change: Communication and behaviour change*. London: Earthscan.

O'Sullivan, T., Dutton, B., & Rayne, P. (2003). *Studying the media*. Bloomsbury, USA: Hodder Arnold.

Paletz, D. L. (1999). *The media in American politics: Contents and consequences*. New York: Longman.

Parmalee, J. H. (2013). The agenda-building function of political tweets. *New Media & Society*, May 22, 1–17.

Quart, A. (2010). The trouble with experts. *Columbia Journalism Review*, July/Aug, 17–18.

Rogers, R. (2004). *Information politics on the web*. Cambridge, MA: The MIT Press.

Sabatier, P. A. & Jenkins-Smith, H. C. (Eds.). (1993). *Policy change and learning: An advocacy coalition approach*. Boulder, CO: Westview Press.

Scheufele, D. A. (1999). Framing as a theory of media effects. *Journal of Communication*, 49(1), 104–122.

Scheufele, D. A. (2009). Agenda-setting, priming, and framing revisited: Another look at cognitive effects of political communication. *Mass Communication and Society*, 3(2&3), 297–316.

Scheufele, D. A. & Tewksbury, D. (2007). Framing, agenda setting, and priming: The evolution of three media effects models. *Journal of Communication*, 57, 9–20.

Schneider, M. & Teske, P. (1992). Toward a theory of the political entrepreneur: Evidence from local government. *The American Political Science Review*, 86(3), 737–747.

Schuurman, N. (2013). Tweet me your talk: Geographical learning and knowledge production 2.0. *Professional Geographer*, 65(3), 369–377.

Shanahan, E. A., Jones, M. D., & McBeth, M. K. (2011). Policy narratives and policy processes. *Policy Studies Journal*, 39(3), 535–561.

Siles, I. & Boczkowski, P. J. (2012). Making sense of the newspaper crisis: A critical assessment of existing research and an agenda for future work. *New Media & Society*, 14(8), 1375–1394.

Stone, D. (1997). *Policy paradox: The art of political decision making*. New York: Norton.

Sunstein, C. R. (2007). *Republic.com 2.0*. Princeton, NJ: Princeton University Press.

Tufekci, Z. (2013). 'Not this one': Social movements, the attention economy, and microcelebrity networked activism. *American Behavioral Scientist*, 57(7), 848–870.

van Dijk, J. (2006). *The network society*. London: Sage.

Wynne, B. (2008). Elephants in the rooms where publics encounter 'science'? *Public Understanding of Science*, 17, 21–33.

Yang, Z. J. & Kahlor, L. A. (2012). What, me worry? The role of affect in information seeking and avoidance. *Science Communication*, 35(2), 189–212.

Zaller, J. R. (1992). *The nature and origins of mass opinion*. Cambridge: Cambridge University Press.

Zhu, Y. & Dukes, A. (2013). *The selective reporting of factual content by commercial media*. University of Southern California working paper, May. Retrieved: http://groups.haas.berkeley.edu/marketing/sics/pdf_2013/zd.pdf. Accessed November 10, 2013.

PART I

Culture and climate change communication

1

BEYOND 'GLOOM AND DOOM' OR 'HOPE AND POSSIBILITY'

Making room for both sacrifice and reward in our visions of a low-carbon future[1]

Cheryl Hall

As concerns about climate change deepen, environmental advocates have been rethinking the common-sense strategy of issuing increasingly dire warnings in hopes of awakening people to the scope of the problem. The worry is that a discourse of 'gloom and doom' is counter-productive, fostering resistance, apathy, or despair instead of hope and motivation to change. Convinced of the importance of framing, many now aim to present positive visions of an attainable, happy green future rather than gloomy pictures of impending peril and sacrifice. In this chapter I argue that people do need reasonably optimistic stories about the possibilities for a sustainable low-carbon future. At the same time, denying that living more sustainably will involve any genuine loss is either wishful thinking or patronizing – and thereby unpersuasive. The argument over whether to depict positive visions or necessary sacrifices is based on a false choice: it will have to be both. The challenge for environmental scholars, journalists, activists, and policy-makers is to help imagine and articulate new possibilities for a greener future without dismissing the value of what must be given up. Indeed, the greatest challenge is to find ways to encourage broad reflection, discussion, and reevaluation of the values, structures, and practices keeping carbon emissions high, instead of either dictating to people what they should care about or taking their values as unchangeable.

The scope of the problem

There is little doubt that climate change is one of the most significant challenges confronting both human and non-human life. Scientists overwhelmingly agree that greenhouse gas emissions from human activities have already begun to alter global temperatures, weather patterns, sea levels, ocean acidity, polar and glacial ice volumes, species extinction rates, and more. To be sure, there is continued uncertainty and debate over exactly how much carbon dioxide and other greenhouse gases we can discharge into the atmosphere without risking temperature increases that would be 'unacceptably dangerous.' Nevertheless, for some time there has been broad international consensus that a temperature increase of more than 2°C above pre-industrial levels represents a risk that would not (or should not) be acceptable. Indeed, as evidence mounts that the effects of any increase in global temperature are more severe than previously expected, some climate scientists now question whether even 2° would be too much. In the words of the 11 scientists who blog at RealClimate,

> We feel compelled to note that even a "moderate" warming of 2°C stands a strong chance of provoking drought and storm responses that could challenge civilized society, leading potentially to the conflict and suffering that go with failed states and mass migrations. Global warming of 2°C would leave the Earth warmer than it has been in millions of years, a disruption of climate conditions that have been stable for longer than the history of human agriculture. Given the drought that already afflicts Australia, the crumbling of the sea ice in the Arctic, and the increasing storm damage after only 0.8°C of warming so far, calling 2°C a danger limit seems to us pretty cavalier.
>
> (Schmidt et al., 2009)

Or in the words of climate scientists Kevin Anderson and Alice Bows, "2°C now represents a threshold not between acceptable and dangerous climate change, but between 'dangerous' and 'extremely dangerous' climate change" (Anderson & Bows, 2010, p. 23).

So what would it take to stay below a 2° increase in temperature? Anderson and Bows reach a blunt conclusion: "(extremely) dangerous climate change can only be avoided if economic growth is exchanged, at least temporarily, for a period of planned austerity within Annex 1 [industrialized] nations and a rapid transition away from fossil-fuelled development within non-Annex 1 nations" (2010, p. 41). Most recently, Anderson has argued that it requires Annex 1 nations to immediately cut their carbon emissions by 10 percent, and then cut another 10 percent *every year* until about 2020, leveling off to reach nearly total decarbonization by 2030. For the sake of global justice, this plan would allow Non-Annex 1 nations – who have neither been responsible for, nor benefited much from, the majority of the carbon dioxide emitted to date – to burn most of the remaining carbon that can safely be burned in order to grow their economies until 2025, when they too must begin reducing emissions by 7 percent each year (Anderson, 2012). Anderson and Bows' assessment of the situation may be starker than many, but it is hardly alone in its basic outlines. Mainstream organizations such as the World Bank, the International Energy Agency, and PricewaterhouseCoopers have all recently issued reports acknowledging that we are currently on track for a 4–6°C increase in global temperature, and that staying below 2°C is now very unlikely without a rapid shift to a low-carbon economy[2] (International Energy Agency, 2012; Potsdam Institute for Climate Impact Research and Climate Analysis, 2012; PricewaterhouseCoopers, 2012). As the PricewaterhouseCoopers Report "Too Late for Two Degrees?" concludes,

> The only way to avoid the pessimistic scenarios will be radical transformations in the ways the global economy currently functions: rapid uptake of renewable energy, sharp falls in fossil fuel use or massive deployment of CCS [carbon capture and storage], removal of industrial emissions and halting deforestation. This suggests a need for much more ambition and urgency on climate policy, at both the national and international level. Either way, business-as-usual is not an option.
>
> (2012, p. 9)

In advanced industrialized countries, accomplishing such transformations will likely require changes in energy use, land use, methods of transportation, residential patterns, agricultural systems, production processes, and levels of consumption, among other things. Lesser developed countries may also need to make some of these changes, as well as to shift away from the goal of industrializing by carbon-intensive means. Since economic growth intensifies ecological destruction more than it reduces it (Brulle, 2010; Rosa et al., 2004; York et al., 2003), accomplishing such transformations will also require significant changes to a global economic system predicated on unlimited growth. Moreover, while new technology will undoubtedly play a role, it will not be sufficient to solve the problem, both because of inherent physical limitations and because, far from counteracting the effects of growth in population and consumption, historically technology feeds such growth (Huesemann, 2006; Huesemann & Huesemann, 2008; York et al., 2003, p. 287). To prevent the most extreme consequences of climate change will thus require significant departures from current ways of life, particularly in industrialized countries – and soon.

In spite of this urgent need for significant transformation, broad and especially deep popular support for community-wide action to prevent further climate change currently does not exist. This is particularly true in the United States, where polling suggests that most people are in favor of taking some action to address climate change, but not at the cost of addressing other problems they consider to be more important. According to January 2013 data from the Pew Research Center for the People & the Press, only 28 percent of citizens surveyed ranked 'dealing with global warming' a 'top priority' for the President and Congress. Out of a total of 21 possible priorities, the goal is ranked dead last, far behind the top priorities of 'strengthening economy,' 'improving job situation,' and 'reducing budget deficit,' with the support of 86 percent, 79 percent, and 72 percent of those surveyed (Pew Research Center for the People & the Press, 2013). A full analysis of the reasons people prioritize climate change so little is beyond the scope of this chapter, but clearly the urgent need for significant transformation is itself a major source of the problem. In the face of enormous challenges that call for big changes – especially changes that require giving something up – people often feel overwhelmed, paralyzed, and reluctant to act. Unfortunately this same need is also the reason that inertia is so dangerous, for the longer we wait to act, the worse the situation gets and the bigger the changes required.

Focusing on frames

It is in this context that environmental scholars and activists are increasingly talking about the importance of framing (Alexander, 2008; Broder, 2009; de Boer et al., 2010; Ereaut & Segnit, 2006; Fletcher, 2009; Maibach et al., 2010; Mann et al., 2009; Miller, 2000; Moser & Dilling, 2007; Nisbet, 2009; Spence & Pidgeon, 2010). This focus indicates a strong sense that 'information' about the state of the environment is not the only thing that matters. More than anything, what matters is how information is interpreted, what meaning it holds for people. The argument for the significance of frames depends on at least four propositions. First, as already noted, the dangers posed by climate change are serious enough that addressing them will likely require making some major changes in the systems, institutions, and infrastructure of many societies. Second, in any society that is at least nominally democratic (and arguably even in societies that are not), making major changes in the systems, institutions, and infrastructure of that society requires at least some level of support from substantial numbers of people. Third, such popular support requires changes in how people think and feel about existing ways of life and the possible alternatives to those ways of life. And finally, changes in how people think and feel about a situation depend in turn on changes in the frameworks they use to interpret that situation.

Frames are commonly understood as "organizing principles that enable a particular interpretation of a phenomenon" (de Boer et al., 2010, p. 502). Emphasizing the shared nature of these principles, Clark Miller says frames are "the perceptual lenses, worldviews or underlying assumptions that guide *communal* interpretation and definition of particular issues" (Miller, 2000, p. 211, my emphasis). As Alexa Spence and Nick Pidgeon (among many others) point out, the key to organizing the interpretation of information is selectivity: "A frame allows complex issues to be pared down and for some aspects of that issue to be given greater emphasis than others in order that particular audiences can rapidly identify why an issue may be relevant to them" (Spence & Pidgeon, 2010, p. 657, citing Nisbet & Mooney, 2007). Finally, Matthew Nisbet connects frames to narratives: "Frames are interpretive storylines that set a specific train of thought in motion, communicating why an issue might be a problem, who or what might be responsible for it, and what should be done about it" (Nisbet, 2009, p. 4). In other words, by highlighting certain aspects of a situation and leaving other elements out of the storyline, frames convey an analysis of a problem and its solution in a condensed format.

Several points about frames are important to stress. First, they are necessarily partial. If one could include everything within a frame, it would no longer be a 'frame.' While frames are necessarily incomplete, though, they are not thereby necessarily untrue, or at least any more so than language in general, which also inevitably condenses, interprets, organizes, and otherwise shapes reality. To be sure, it is possible to frame an issue in a way that violates essential realities of the situation – but this does not mean that all frames of that issue violate essential realities. Finally, frames are unavoidable, particularly in communication. As Nisbet puts it, "there is no such thing as unframed information" (2009, p. 4). The question, then, is not whether to frame, but how.

What's wrong with 'gloom and doom'?

The recent flood of criticism about environmentalism's 'gloom and doom' message can be understood in this context. The contention, whether explicit or implicit, is that gloom and doom is an ineffective frame.[3] Michael Shellenberger and Ted Nordhaus are perhaps the most well-known critics, consistently taking 'environmentalism' itself to task for what they consider to be its narrow and overly negative approach. The two authors bemoan the lack of a 'compelling vision for the future' offered by environmental advocates (Shellenberger & Nordhaus, 2004, p. 30). As they put it,

> Martin Luther King, Jr.'s 'I have a dream' speech is famous because it put forward an inspiring, positive vision that carried a critique of the current moment within it. Imagine how history would have turned out had King given an 'I have a nightmare' speech instead.
>
> (2004, p. 31)[4]

Yet this is precisely what they believe environmental leaders are doing. The reason leaders should not be painting pictures of apocalypse and cultivating fear is because negativity and fear don't work: "Cautionary tales and narratives of eco-apocalypse tend to provoke fatalism, conservatism, and survivalism among voters – not the rational embrace of environmental policies" (Nordhaus & Shellenberger, 2007b, p. 33).

Nordhaus and Shellenberger are hardly alone in arguing that fear is counter-productive. In a blog post asking "Are Words Worthless in the Climate Fight?" Andrew Revkin cites Tom Lowe of the Center for Risk and Community Safety on the obstacles involved in communicating concerns about climate change. Lowe writes,

> In the absence of physical evidence that something bad is going to happen, people tend to 'wait and see'... A common reaction to this stand-off is for risk communicators to shout louder, to try and shake some sense into people. This is what I see happening with the climate change message. The

public are on the receiving end of an increasingly distraught alarm call. The methods used to grab attention are so striking that people are reaching a state of denial. This is partly because the problem is perceived as being so big that people feel unable to do anything about it, partly because the changes associated with impact reduction are unacceptable and/or unviable to many people, and partly because this 'overselling' of climate change attracts strong criticism from a vocal and disproportionately publicized few.

(Revkin, 2007, p. 6)

Lowe's assessment of the ineffectiveness of the 'increasingly distraught alarm call' is repeated in a report by the British Institute for Public Policy Research entitled "Warm words: how are we telling the climate story and can we tell it better?" In the report, Gil Ereaut and Nat Segnit analyze the 'linguistic repertoires' used in British popular media coverage and government communications about climate change. They find that the two most common repertoires are what they call the 'alarmist' repertoire and the 'small changes' repertoire. The 'alarmist' repertoire uses an urgent tone and extreme words, speaks of acceleration and irreversibility, and employs a "quasi-religious register of death and doom" (Ereaut & Segnit, 2006, p. 7). Unfortunately, they argue, this discourse's emphasis on the catastrophic danger entailed in climate change tends to overwhelm and distance people: "the scale of the problem as it is shown excludes the possibility of real action or agency by the reader or viewer. It contains an implicit counsel of despair – 'the problem is just too big for us to take on'" (2006, p. 7). The 'small changes' repertoire attempts to head off such paralysis by encouraging relatively easy actions that ordinary citizens can take to reduce carbon emissions. But it is frequently used in conjunction with the alarmist discourse, thus raising the "unspoken but obvious question: how can small actions really make a difference to things happening on this epic scale?" (2006, p. 8).

While the criticism of 'gloom and doom' is usually offered as a unified reproach, the phrase nevertheless signals two distinct (albeit connected) worries. The first concern is that the picture environmentalists paint of what needs to be done to mitigate climate change is too gloomy: we (especially we Northerners) need to sacrifice our comforts and conveniences, to consume far less than we do, in order to save the planet, the global South, and future generations. From now on our lives must be considerably more restrained than they have been, our quality of life seriously reduced. This account, the critics note, is deeply unappealing. It promises a future devoid of both freedom and happiness. As such, it is virtually guaranteed to be met with serious resistance. The second concern is that the picture environmentalists paint of the present and especially future state of a world threatened by climate change is too frightening and overwhelming: the problem is monumental, the hour late, and the resources few – consequently we're all doomed, because there's little most of us can do to solve the problem. This account, the critics note, is extremely daunting. It elicits both fear and a sense of powerlessness. Building on arguments that fear-based appeals may be ineffective in motivating action (Feinberg & Willer, 2011; Feygina, 2010; Moser & Dilling, 2004; Nordhaus & Shellenberger, 2009; O'Neill & Nicholson-Cole, 2009; Revkin, 2006), critics contend that a discourse of doom is ill-advised.[5] Finally, adding doom to gloom only makes matters worse. For in emphasizing the magnitude and intractability of climate change, the narrative only further undermines any personal willingness people may have to live within limits. Why sacrifice if it won't make any real difference? Thus, the argument declares, a doom and gloom approach backfires, inspiring resistance, despair, withdrawal, and fatalism rather than personal/political action for change.

Alternatives to gloom and doom: hope and possibility

If the concern is that the frame of gloom and doom is ineffective in these ways, then clearly the solution is to tell a more positive, inspiring story. As with the critique of gloom and doom, the proposed alternative has two distinct facets: to replace gloomy images of deprivation and restriction, authors offer a hopeful vision of a happy and free green life, while to replace doom-filled warnings of impending disaster, they provide an empowering description of what we can achieve if we work together (whoever "we" are). Needless to say, although each narrative emphasizes a different corrective, the two are often deeply intertwined.

Frames that focus on the fulfillment that could come from living more sustainably are becoming increasingly common. Juliet Schor is one prominent example, having argued for many years that the ecologically unsustainable levels of production and consumption that Americans in particular engage in do not lead to satisfaction but rather to alienation and exhaustion. In her most recent book, *Plenitude*, she emphasizes that the model she is advocating – working and spending less, creating and connecting more – is "not a paradigm of sacrifice. To the contrary, it involves a way of life that will yield more well-being than sticking to business as usual ..." (Schor, 2010, p. 2). Where Schor merely distances herself from the frame of sacrifice, Steve Vanderheiden explicitly argues against it. He worries that calling on people to sacrifice in order to mitigate climate change will not work, particularly because in this case (unlike in wartime) the sacrifices involved must be permanent. Instead, environmental advocates should challenge the norms presuming that welfare depends upon consumption, and thus that 'living green' conflicts with 'living well.' For example, they should emphasize that reducing competitive consumption and eating sustainable food can increase leisure time, the quality of personal relationships, and the pleasure people find in food (Vanderheiden, 2010, pp. 14–17). These sorts of revisions to existing norms can help to construct a newly attractive 'low-carbon imaginary.'

Frames that focus on the freedom that could come from living more sustainably are somewhat less common, but still significant. Jason Lambacher argues that respecting ecological limits has seemed to require restraining freedom only because freedom has often been defined as having no limits (Lambacher, 2009, p. 2). We might instead understand freedom as the ability to restrain ourselves

(2009, p. 41). If freedom is "the law we give to ourselves," then to live in more ecologically responsible ways is to live more freely (2009, p.38). Richard Dagger also emphasizes freedom as autonomy and self-government. Drawing on Philip Pettit's distinction between option-freedom and agency-freedom, he argues that having more options (for example, more choices of things to buy) doesn't always lead to greater autonomy.

> What matters is that we have options that promote the ability to be self-governing. This means that we must be able to enjoy a reasonably secure sense of the self as something that is not simply the plaything of external forces or the creature of ungovernable impulses.
>
> (Dagger, 2006, p. 212)

In the case of our relationship to the environment, this means learning to curb self-destructive tendencies that threaten the natural systems that support us. Again, if we can learn to do this, we will actually be freer than we are now.

In the case of frames emphasizing human power and agency rather than the doom of a looming catastrophe, the example offered by Nordhaus and Shellenberger is unparalleled. Over and over, the two counsel against apocalyptic narratives that, they argue, engender fear and fatalism. At the foundation of Nordhaus and Shellenberger's argument is the claim that people are more productive and generous when they feel strong and in control of their lives (Nordhaus & Shellenberger, 2007a, pp. 187, 222). If this is the case, then motivating action on issues such as climate change requires focusing on people's strengths and abilities, not their weaknesses. Instead of telling a story about human arrogance and ecological failure, they write, we should tell a story about how humans throughout history have continually overcome obstacles. "The narrative of overcoming helps us to imagine and thus create a brighter future" (2007a, pp. 150–51). The clear implication is that *without* a narrative of overcoming, we will be unable to imagine and create a brighter future. This is why frames must strive to inspire feelings of joy, gratitude, and pride: because those that inspire feelings of regret, guilt, sadness, and fear will not foster the optimistic attitude necessary to solve the problems we face (2007a, p. 153). Thus, environmentalists hoping to mitigate climate change need to switch from a negative frame that emphasizes all the things people need to *stop* doing to a positive frame that focuses attention on our potential to 'unleash human power' and invent new clean energy solutions (2007a, pp. 120, 113).

What could be wrong with hope and possibility?

It *is* important to tell a story about humanity's relationship to the rest of nature that is not just gloom and doom – now more so than ever. To prevent further climate change, people in advanced industrialized countries need to forego current high-carbon, high-consumption ways of life, while people in lesser-developed countries need to forego whatever aspirations they may have to emulate those particular ways of life.[6] The necessary transformations can only be achieved democratically if enough people are willing to support them. But people are rarely willing to change their lives and dreams unless they have a clear idea of how doing so will make a significant and beneficial difference. Hence the need for alternative frames. Since the increasingly dominant global narrative emphasizes the freedom, power, and happiness entailed in a high-carbon, high-consumption lifestyle, environmentalists need to challenge the assumptions of that narrative. That is to say, we need to help people re-imagine what it might mean to be free, powerful, and happy.

At the same time, telling a story that is overly focused on hope and possibility has some limitations. To understand these limitations, notice first that while the authors discussed above all agree on the importance of replacing a gloom and doom frame with a more positive one, they do not agree on the specific individual, social, economic, and political changes necessary to address the problem of climate change. The question is not just how to 'communicate' about the problem; the question is what needs to be *done* about it, and the answers range from reformist to radical. Of course, disagreement is to be expected in the face of any complex situation. My point here is that the limitations of an overly optimistic frame are different depending on the solution the frame suggests.

Consider Nordhaus and Shellenberger first. In spite of their rousing, revolutionary-sounding rhetoric, the two are decidedly reformist in their recommendations. They do not endorse any significant alterations in the economic system, political structure, or culture of consumption in advanced industrialized countries. They explicitly disavow any need for people in these countries to change their everyday behavior (Nordhaus & Shellenberger, 2011, Fourth Thesis secton). They see no need, for instance, for humans to eat lower on the food chain. Nor do they call for a rejection of the imperative of economic growth; on the contrary, they see continued economic growth as crucial. For Nordhaus and Shellenberger, the fundamental solution to the threat posed by climate change is massive public investment in the development of clean energy technology.

The problem with this reformist narrative lies with the solution itself. This frame is cheery, confident, and reassuring, downplaying difficulties and any need for sacrifice. The reason it can do so is because the proposed solution endorses much of the status quo in advanced industrialized countries, including existing institutions, practices, and values. Since this status quo supports a relatively privileged way of life, little sacrifice is indeed called for here. (Or perhaps better put: little sacrifice of the comforts and conveniences of current forms of advanced industrialized life is called for, while the less obvious sacrifices already entailed in this way of life are ignored.[7]) Given the scope of the problem, though, a solution such as the one offered by Nordhaus and Shellenberger is not sufficient. Recall that we are currently on track for an extremely dangerous 4–6°C increase in global temperature, and that the target of remaining below 2°C is now very unlikely without a rapid shift to a low-carbon economy. Recall as well that new technology cannot produce such a shift all by itself – even less so in the short time required – and that economic growth intensifies ecological destruction more than it reduces it. If everything Nordhaus and Shellenberger advocate were done, not only would it not be enough, it could even make the situation worse.

In the case of the reformist story, then, the proposed solution is too shallow to solve the problem. The second story is more radical: it points to deeper transformations, such as changes in consumption, energy use, land use, methods of transportation, agricultural practices, political institutions, and economic systems. In emphasizing what will be gained, though, this frame doesn't adequately account for what must be given up. Instead, the tendency is to argue that people in advanced industrialized countries are not actually benefiting from current ways of life; therefore, it's no great sacrifice (maybe not even a small sacrifice) for them to change how they're living – or for the rest of the world to forsake this ideal.[8] Whereas in the reformist story no sacrifice is involved because no real change is involved, in this story, no (real) sacrifice is involved because the change, while real, is supposed to be entirely for the better.

But it is not effective to maintain that no real sacrifice is or will be involved in forsaking high-carbon, high-consumption ways of life. For even if the alternative is or will be for the better overall – as it may well be – it does not follow that no loss is entailed. People value many different things. Inevitably, some of the things they care about will conflict with other things they care about. A low-carbon lifestyle may indeed offer some genuinely valuable goods, such as better tasting food, more leisure time, or stronger neighborhood communities. But a high-carbon lifestyle also offers some genuinely valuable goods: to mention only one, the ability to travel long distances quickly and easily, and thus to more easily visit far-flung family and friends or experience a wide variety of different cultures first-hand. Because human beings commonly hold multiple, incompatible values, the reality is that living sustainably unavoidably entails both sacrifice and reward – just as living unsustainably unavoidably entails both sacrifice and reward. Ignoring this reality is either inaccurate in its estimation of what people value or patronizing in its suggestion that people are mistaken to value these things. But a frame that is inaccurate or patronizing will not be persuasive. People can see that *some* loss of what they value (or desire) will be involved in moving towards (or staying with) low-carbon, low-consumption ways of life. Although they may not realize what they do or would sacrifice in order to enjoy the comforts, conveniences, and luxuries of current advanced industrialized economies, they do realize what they do or would need to sacrifice to live more sustainably. Even if they reevaluate what matters to them, not everything they have to give up is worthless. Refusing to acknowledge this fact risks a serious loss of credibility with the audience one is hoping to reach.

So the reformist story is optimistic and inspiring in great part because the solution is too shallow, while the more radical story is optimistic and inspiring at least in part because it overlooks or dismisses the losses entailed in living more sustainably. Its solution is deep but the story about it is too shallow. As a result, neither frame is sufficient. In the first case, the story *is* too good to be true; in the second case, it will be *seen* to be too good to be true. To get past this dilemma, environmentalists must embrace the need for a more profound shift away from existing forms of modern industrial life and help rewrite the story about this shift in a way that allows for complexity in people's values and appreciation of the inevitability of sacrifice in *any* way of life. Currently, many environmentalists advise against any discussion of sacrifice on the principle that there is nothing positive about it. Recall Juliet Schor's claim that the model of plenitude is "not a paradigm of sacrifice. *To the contrary*, it involves a way of life that will yield more well-being than sticking to business as usual" (my emphasis). Here, sacrifice and well-being are entirely opposed. Steve Vanderheiden echoes this opposition. We need, he says, to reconcile the goal of 'living well' with the goal of 'living green,' but a frame of sacrifice "treats these as incompatible aims that require the former to give way to the latter" (Vanderheiden, 2010, p. 6). Moreover, "By casting voluntary reductions in personal consumption as a kind of sacrifice, critics of unsustainable consumption forfeit the ability to question the alleged incompatibility between living green and living well" (Vanderheiden, 2010, p. 6).

These arguments rely on a common interpretation of sacrifice as essentially synonymous with deprivation or self-denial. A closer look at the concept, however, reveals a far more complex picture. As defined in the *New Shorter Oxford English Dictionary,* sacrifice is "the surrender of something valued or desired, especially one's life, for the sake of something regarded as more important or worthy, or in order to avoid a greater loss, reduce expenditure, etc." To be sure, then, sacrifice involves foregoing or giving up something one cares about – but only *for the sake of* something else one cares about even more. In this way, sacrifice is decidedly not the same as simple deprivation or self-denial (Meyer, 2010, pp. 14–17). It entails loss, but it also entails gain. Indeed, the point of the concept is that the gain is considered more important than the loss, else the sacrifice would not be undertaken.

Thus, taking seriously the need for some level of sacrifice in moving toward or staying with more sustainable forms of life in no way precludes presenting a vision of how people's lives are or might be better by doing so. On the contrary, it actually depends on such a vision, because there must be *something* positive, some greater value, to inspire the sacrifice in the first place. I suspect that the fundamental concern is the presumption that this greater value must be an altruistic one. The sacrifice involved in 'living green' (if it is a sacrifice) must be undertaken to benefit other people and beings and ecosystems, not oneself. But this needn't be the case. One can sacrifice something that benefits oneself personally (say, the greater convenience of packaged food) for the sake of something else that also benefits oneself personally (say, the better nutrition and taste of food one prepares from scratch). Furthermore, even if one is sacrificing at least in part for the sake of others, to assume that there is no personal value in doing so relies on an overly individualistic view of what counts as a person's well-being. Living well is not just about one's own individual material well-being. It is, or at least certainly can be, about one's physical, emotional, and spiritual well-being and the well-being of anyone or anything else one cares about. A sacrifice made for the sake of a child, a friend, or even a stranger can and often is experienced as part of a 'good life' for oneself. For this reason, recognizing that "voluntary reductions in personal consumption" may involve some sacrifice in no way requires that one "forfeit the ability to question the alleged incompatibility between living green and living well" (Vanderheiden, 2010, p. 6). It merely acknowledges the reality that there are incompatibilities between *some forms* of living green and *some forms* of living well, just as there are incompatibilities between many, if not most, other choices we make about how to live. It is not possible for any of us, individually or collectively, to have everything we want. As a result, any way of life necessarily entails sacrificing some things we value for the sake of other things we value. In the case of living green, those values may well include both an increase in personal material well-being and an increase in other aspects of one's well-being or the well-being of others. The fear that any discussion of sacrifice must inevitably lead to an entirely gloomy picture is unwarranted, and stands in the way of a realistic account of the choices we face in life.

Climate change, framing, and democracy

Stories of gloom and doom about climate change are not sufficient; people need at least some focus on what could be good about a low-carbon life to be inspired to work toward that goal. But frames that highlight only what could be good necessarily dismiss either the seriousness of how much change is necessary or the seriousness of people's perceptions about the many different, even conflicting, things one might care about in life. Stronger frames would give both of these issues their due. In particular, they would acknowledge and respect people's values and honestly incorporate their realistic concerns about giving up at least some things they care about. Stronger frames would help people to re-imagine what it could mean to be happy, free, and powerful without insisting that there is no true happiness, freedom, or power as things stand.

Clearly this is a tall order for any frame. To some extent, the difficulty may point to the limitations of framing itself, especially insofar as it is conceived as a way for knowledgeable 'experts' to communicate complex messages in simplified form to a potentially unreflective or thoughtless public. But the issue is precisely the issue of democracy itself: whether and how citizens in communities (especially large, diverse communities) can collectively decide what is to be done. If a commitment to democratic politics is still possible and desirable in a time of great environmental risk, then framing needs to embody and inspire that commitment. Above and beyond helping to articulate both the need for sacrifice and the rewards it might bring, the most important task for any climate change frame is to encourage all of us to reflect upon, discuss, and reevaluate the values, structures, and practices that are altering the planet's climate. Rather than either dictating to us what we should care about or responding to our values as if they were set in stone, environmental advocates need to tell stories that encourage us to explore our values, identify where they conflict, and consider how and why they might be understood or prioritized differently. That is to say, they/we need to offer frames that help us all to look at our situation differently, to re-think and re-feel what matters to us and why. The urgency of the situation makes it extremely difficult to recommend such a slow, deliberate approach, yet without this work the chances of any democratic transformation seem slight indeed.

Notes

1 This chapter is a condensed, updated, and revised version of my article, "What Will it Mean to be Green? Envisioning Positive Possibilities Without Dismissing Loss," published in *Ethics, Policy & Environment* 16:2, online at www.tandfonline.com/loi/cepe21 (Copyright © 2013 Taylor & Francis Group). I am grateful to the following people for constructive feedback at various stages in my work on this chapter and the larger project of which it is a part: Max Boykoff, Sheri Breen, Mark Brown, Peter Cannavò, Deserai Crow, Ben Hale, Lauren Hartzell Nichols, James Lowe, John Meyer, Zev Trachtenberg, Kerry Whiteside, Justin Williams, Harlan Wilson, Rafi Youatt, and Michael Zimmerman. I am also grateful to two anonymous referees and to additional audience participants at panels at the International Conference on Culture, Politics, and Climate Change and annual meetings of the Western Political Science Association. Finally, I thank the Humanities Institute at the University of South Florida for much appreciated funding in the form of a summer grant.

2 The assessment of the PricewaterhouseCoopers Report is that "the required improvement in global carbon intensity [emissions per unit of GDP] to meet a 2°C warming target has risen to 5.1 percent a year, from now to 2050. We have passed a critical threshold – not once since World War 2 has the world achieved that rate of decarbonisation, but the task now confronting us is to achieve it for 39 consecutive years ... To give ourselves a more than 50 percent chance of avoiding 2 degrees will require a six-fold improvement in our rate of decarbonisation" (2012, p.1).

3 In this chapter, I discuss two opposing frames of climate change, which I call the "gloom and doom" frame and the "hope and possibility" frame. These frames offer different cognitive-emotional evaluations of the prospects for mitigating further climate change. It is important to note that there are other possible axes around which climate change may be framed. As just one example, it could be framed in terms of the kind of problem it is: technical, political, ethical, etc. I thank Lauren Hartzell Nichols for highlighting this point for me.

4 In *Break Through*, Nordhaus and Shellenberger clarify that King in fact began his speech with a nightmare – but that this only shows how important it was to move on to his dream (Nordhaus & Shellenberger, 2007a, pp.2–4).

5 It is important to note that the claim that fear-based appeals are ineffective is disputed. Other research suggests that results depend greatly on whether people are addressed as individuals or as members of a community, as well as whether or not fear appeals are combined with guidance for effective group action (Camill, 2010; van Zomeren et al., 2010; Witte & Allen, 2000).

6 This is decidedly not to say that people in LDCs will need to forego development of systems to support better health, education, housing, transportation, and so forth – only that they must forego those systems that would lock them into high-carbon, high-consumption paths. It is precisely because people in LDCs need room to develop that people in DCs need to reduce their emissions even more dramatically.

7 For more on the notion of unacknowledged sacrifices already being made, see the discussions in several chapters of *The Environmental Politics of Sacrifice* (Maniates & Meyer, 2010).

8 In the passages below, I describe both those who currently live in high-carbon societies and those who do not (yet) as having to sacrifice something: either some of what they already have or some of what they hope to have. Clearly, though, most of the concrete changes in daily life will need to be made by those who live in high-carbon societies.

References

Alexander, R. (2008). *Framing discourse on the environment: A critical discourse approach.* New York: Routledge.

Anderson, K. & Bows, A. (2010). Beyond 'dangerous' climate change: Emission scenarios for a new world. *Philosophical Transactions of the Royal Society A: Mathematical, Physical and Engineering Sciences,* 369(1934), 20–44.

Anderson, K. (2012). Real clothes for the emperor: Facing the challenges of climate change. Retrieved March 20, 2013 from University of Bristol, Cabot Institute website: http://www.bristol.ac.uk/cabot/events/2012/194.html.

Broder, J. M. (2009). Seeking to save the planet, with a thesaurus. *The New York Times.* Retrieved March 4, 2011: http://www.nytimes.com/2009/05/02/us/politics/02enviro.html.

Brulle, R. J. (2010). From environmental campaigns to advancing the public dialog: Environmental communication for civic engagement. *Environmental Communication,* 4(1), 82–98.

Camill, P. (2010). Climate communication: Is fear + collective action a winning strategy? *Global Change: Intersection of Nature and Culture.* Retrieved March 10, 2010: http://www.globalchangeblog.com/2010/03/climate-communication-is-fear-collective-action-a-winning-strategy.

Dagger, R. (2006). Freedom and rights. In A. Dobson & R. Eckersley (Eds.), *Political theory and the ecological challenge* (pp. 200–215). Cambridge: Cambridge University Press.

De Boer, J., Wardekker, J. A., & van der Sluijs, J. P. (2010). Frame-based guide to situated decision-making on climate change. *Global Environmental Change,* 20(3), 502–510.

Ereaut, G. & Segnit, N. (2006). *Warm words: How are we telling the climate story and can we tell it better?* London: Institute for Public Policy Research. Retrieved July 15, 2009: http://www.ippr.org.

Feinberg, M. & Willer, R. (2011). Apocalypse soon? *Psychological Science,* 22(1), 34–38.

Feygina, I. (2010). System justification, the denial of global warming, and the possibility of 'system-sanctioned change.' *Personality and Social Psychology Bulletin,* 36(3), 326–338.

Fletcher, A. (2009). Clearing the air: The contribution of frame analysis to understanding climate policy in the United States. *Environmental Politics,* 18(5), 800–816.

Huesemann, M. (2006). Can advances in science and technology prevent global warming? *Mitigation and Adaptation Strategies for Global Change,* 11(3), 539–577.

Huesemann, M. & Huesemann, J. (2008). Will progress in science and technology avert or accelerate global collapse? A critical analysis and policy recommendations. *Environment, Development and Sustainability,* 10(6), 787–825.

International Energy Agency. (2012). *World Energy Outlook 2012 Executive Summary,* Paris: International Energy Agency. Retrieved April 5, 2013: http://www.worldenergyoutlook.org/publications/weo-2012/#d.en.26099.

Lambacher, J. (2009). Limits of freedom and the freedom of limits: Responding to the extinction crisis with responsibility, restraint, and joy. *SSRN eLibrary* (pp. 1–47). Annual Meeting of the American Political Science Association. Toronto, Canada. Retrieved September 12, 2009: http://papers.ssrn.com/sol3/papers.cfm?abstract_id=1451845.

Maibach, E. W., Nisbet, M., Baldwin, P., Akerlok, K., & Diao, G. (2010). Reframing climate change as a public health issue: An exploratory study of public reactions. *BMC Public Health,* 10(299), 1–11.

Maniates, M. F. & Meyer, J. M. (Eds.). (2010). *The environmental politics of sacrifice,* Cambridge, MA: The MIT Press.

Mann, M., Kinzig, A., Miller, C. A., Schmidt, G., Henson, R., & Nisbet, M. (2009). Is there a better word for doom? *SeedMagazine.com*. Retrieved March 7, 2010: http://seedmagazine.com/content/article/is_there_a_better_word_for_doom.

Meyer, J. M. (2010). A democratic politics of sacrifice? In M. Maniates & J. Meyer (Eds.), *The Environmental Politics of Sacrifice* (pp. 13–32). Cambridge, MA: The MIT Press.

Miller, C. (2000). The dynamics of framing environmental values and policy: Four models of societal processes. *Environmental Values*, 9(2), 211–234.

Moser, S. & Dilling, L. (2004). Making climate hot: Communicating the urgency and challenge of global climate change. *Environment: Science and Policy for Sustainable Development*, 46(10), 32–46.

Moser, S. & Dilling, L. (2007). *Creating a climate for change: Communicating climate change and facilitating social change* Reissue. Cambridge: Cambridge University Press.

Nisbet, M. (2009). Communicating climate change: Why frames matter for public engagement. *Environment Magazine: Science and Policy for Sustainable Development*. Retrieved March 10, 2010: http://www.environmentmagazine.org/Archives/Back%20Issues/March-April%202009/Nisbet-full.html.

Nisbet, M. & Mooney, C. (2007). Framing science. *Science* 316(5821), 56.

Nordhaus, T. & Shellenberger, M. (2007a). *Break through: From the death of environmentalism to the politics of possibility*. Boston, MA: Houghton Mifflin Co.

Nordhaus, T. & Shellenberger, M. (2007b). Second life: A manifesto for a new environmentalism. *The New Republic*, September 24, 30–33.

Nordhaus, T. & Shellenberger, M. (2009). Apocalypse fatigue: Losing the public on climate change. *Yale Environment 360*. Retrieved November 16, 2009: http://e360.yale.edu/feature/apocalypse_fatigue_losing_the_public_on_climate_change/2210.

Nordhaus, T. & Shellenberger, M. (2011). The long death of environmentalism. The Breakthrough Institute. Retrieved March 7, 2011: http://thebreakthrough.org/blog/2011/02/the_long_death_of_environmenta.shtml.

O'Neill, S. & Nicholson-Cole, S. (2009). 'Fear won't do it': Promoting positive engagement with climate change through visual and iconic representations. *Science Communication*, 30(3), 355–379.

Pew Research Center for the People and the Press. (2013). *Deficit reduction rises on public's agenda for Obama's second term: Public's policy priorities: 1996–2013*. Pew Research Center for the People & The Press. Retrieved January 31, 2013: http://www.people-press.org/2013/01/24/deficit-reduction-rises-on-publics-agenda-for-obamas-second-term.

Potsdam Institute for Climate Impact Research and Climate Analysis. (2012). *Turn down the heat: Why a 4°C warmer world must be avoided*. Washington DC: World Bank. Retrieved April 5, 2013: http://issuu.com/world.bank.publications/docs/turn_down_the_heat.

PricewaterhouseCoopers. (2012). *Too late for two degrees? PwC low carbon economy index 2012*. PricewaterhouseCoopers. Retrieved April 5, 2013: http://www.pwc.com/gx/en/sustainability/publications/low-carbon-economy-index/index.jhtml.

Revkin, A. (2006). Yelling 'fire' on a hot planet. *The New York Times*. Retrieved March 16, 2011: http://www.nytimes.com/2006/04/23/weekinreview/23revkin.html?pagewanted=all.

Revkin, A. (2007). Are words worthless in the climate fight? *Dot Earth, NYTimes.com*. Retrieved March 7, 2010: http://dotearth.blogs.nytimes.com/2007/12/03/are-words-worthless-in-the-climate-fight.

Rosa, E. A., York, R., & Dietz, T. (2004). Tracking the anthropogenic drivers of ecological impacts. *Ambio*, 33(8), 509–512.

Schmidt, G., Mann, M., Ammann, C., Benestad, R., Bradley, R., Rahmstorf, S., Steig, E., Archer D., Pierrehumbert, R., de Garidel, T., & Bouldin, J. (2009). RealClimate: Hit the brakes hard. Retrieved March 18, 2013: http://www.realclimate.org/index.php/archives/2009/04/hit-the-brakes-hard.

Schor, J. B. (2010). *Plenitude: The new economics of true wealth*. New York: The Penguin Press.

Shellenberger, M. & Nordhaus, T. (2004). The death of environmentalism: Global warming politics in a post-environmental world. The Breakthrough Institute. Retrieved March 1, 2013: http://thebreakthrough.org/archive/the_death_of_environmentalism.

Spence, A. & Pidgeon, N. (2010). Framing and communicating climate change: The effects of distance and outcome frame manipulations. *Global Environmental Change*, 20(4), 656–667.

Van Zomeren, M., Spears, R. & Leach, C. (2010). Experimental evidence for a dual pathway model analysis of coping with the climate crisis. *Journal of Environmental Psychology*, 30(4), 339–346.

Vanderheiden, S. (2010). Living green and living well: Climate change and the low-carbon imaginary. Annual Meeting of the Western Political Science Association (pp. 1–23). San Francisco, CA.

Witte, K. & Allen, M. (2000). A meta-analysis of fear appeals: Implications for effective public health campaigns. *Health Education & Behavior*, 27(5), 591–615.

York, R., Rosa, E. A., & Dietz, T. (2003). Footprints on the Earth: The environmental consequences of modernity. *American Sociological Review*, 68(2), 279–300.

2

POLAR BEARS, INUIT NAMES, AND CLIMATE CITIZENSHIP

Understanding climate change visual culture through green consumerism, environmental philanthropy, and indigeneity

Doreen E. Martinez

Modernity and coloniality in climate citizenship

In response to climate change outcomes, the US visual culture focuses on purchasing citizenship, and green consumption while, at the same time climate change philanthropy efforts focus on saving the polar bear. These two climate change response models comprise what I refer to as climate citizenship. Both models situate Western/Euro-nationalistic values with higher and more desirable citizenship practices than tangible climate change reduction and rectification efforts. These models achieve what Goodman refers to as a political ecological framework (Goodman, 2004) and Luke explains is "the American state's rationalized harmonization of political economy with global ecology as a form of green geopolitics" (Luke, 1999, p. 124). In my work here, US political economy embeds green consumption and global ecology is reflected in environmental philanthropy, while green geopolitics mirrors climate citizenship.

Although, Goodman focuses on fair trade/foods, he offers foundational insights I will apply to the commoditization of American nationalism through green consumption and environmental philanthropy via nationalistic ethics of care (e.g., save the environment for the polar bear, save the polar bear). As he offers, "the key to the creation of this 'ethics of care' is precisely the commoditization of these ... [images] that presents their meaningful nature to Northern consumers" (Goodman, 2004, p. 895). The Northern consumers' (the northern or first-world citizen) heart strings are pulled and exploited at the plight of the polar bear. In such, climate change devastations on Indigenous lifeways are nullified, hidden, and erased.

My thesis is that climate citizenship operates under the precepts of green consumption and environmental philanthropy operates under and sustains nationalistic privilege of Western ideologies.

"As it is discursively constructed by contemporary technoscience, the art of government now finds 'the principles of rationality' and 'the specific reality of the state' (Foucault, 1991, p. 97), like the policy programmes of sustainable development, balanced growth or ecological harmony" (Luke, 1999, p. 122) that are defined by privileged normative/defaulted Western beliefs and practices. Rationally, we must save the polar bear by changing our consumption modes instead of decreasing consumption patterns. And, buying green is situated as a reality of our progressive and humanitarian state.

Further, Mingolo's work on the relationship between modernity and coloniality offers a theoretical basis to my claim and demonstrates how even when other beliefs and values are present, privileged values silence those discourses. He states,

> subalternization of knowledge is being radically transformed by new forms of knowledge in which what has been subalternized and considered interesting only as object of study becomes articulated as new loci of enunciation.
>
> (Mingolo, 2000, p. 13)

Knowledges of preservation and sustainability, especially from Indigenous cultures and marginalized populations, were subalternized. The beliefs and values were negated previously through demands of progress and materialism that sought to promote and achieve American nationalism. Today, under the same ever-pressing nationalistic needs, consumption patterns are being heralded via pseudo-green values and philanthropy enunciated through practices of extinction prevention (aka morality). Moreover,

> Consumption is not merely the terminus for the productive capabilities of food and commodity networks; rather, the processes of consumption are the (often class-based) ability to work and re-work one's identity through the overtly meaningful acts of consumption and engagement with commodities.
>
> (Goodman, 2004, p. 894)

Meaningful acts and engagements are defined and achieved through nationalistic ethics of care that produce and meet climate citizenship identities. Commoditization is "the cultural economic processes by which fair trade's bid for a moral economy is made both material and meaning-full and the dialectical relationships that inform these processes" (Goodman, 2004, p. 894). Polar bears provide that dialectical cultural relationship of meaningful climate citizenship, or American nationalism.

And as Mingolo illustrates, knowledge suggested within climate citizenship achieves "modern reason" and therefore, privilege and muzzling effects.

> by looking at the emergence of new loci of enunciation, by describing them as "border gnosis" and by arguing that "border gnosis" is the subaltern reason

striving to bring to the foreground the force and creativity of knowledges subalternized during a long process of colonization of the planet, which was at the same time the process in which modernity and the modern reason were constructed.

(Mingolo, 2000, p. 13)

The new loci of climate citizenship enunciation are presented in green consumerism versus a materialistic consumerism. It is green consumerism that seeks to nullify, or at least abate, the colonization of the planet that occurred through previous consumption patterns (which were seen as progressive and modern). Similarly, environmental philanthropy serves as a tool to illustrate moral reason achieving the marriage of American nationalism and the border gnosis of modernity. The humanitarian efforts to save a beloved species are highlighted in creative and forceful imagery, through frequency of polar bear images and story-lines, which reinforces concepts of modernity – preservation over extinction. Knowledges surrounding impacts of climate change (the colonization of communities and cultures) are then subalternized, "Colonial difference, the classification of the planet in the modern/colonial imaginary, by enacting coloniality of power, an energy and a machinery to transform differences into values" (Mingolo, 2000, p. 13). Climate citizenship values embed green consumerism as a form of active, good, and valued capitalism and environmental philanthropy as moral and continually progressive American nationalism. Conceptually and in the project analysis, I focus on the naming and identifying of these practices as forms of climate citizenship that promotes neo-colonial understandings and actions that explicitly and implicitly challenge sovereignty and citizenship of Indigenous communities.

Even when voices of Indigenous issues exist, green consumption and environmental philanthropy are deemed and defined as the voices and actions of change, and primarily worthy of attention, pursuit, and display. As Foucault (1982) indicates,

systems of thought and knowledge ('epistemes' or 'discursive formations') are governed by rules (beyond those of grammar and logic) which operate in the consciousness of individual subjects and define a system of conceptual possibilities that determines the boundaries of thought.

Thus, expectations and performances of climate citizenship are defined and viewed as patriotic and innate. The governing rules of a first world democratic society are subsumed into the consciousness of consumers and humanitarianism, while ultimately distorting and negating the disproportionate impact of climate change on Indigenous cultures. Significantly, these nationalistic discursive foundations often go unchecked, become normalized, and even become celebrated. This climate citizenship system and repetitions of nationalistic representation becomes a "stable cultural convention that is taught and learned by members of a society" (Kates & Shaw-Garlock, 1999, p. 34). This project focuses on US culture that dwells in the visual conventions of commercials and brand imaging including the visual codes and images of philanthropy.

Additionally, my project builds upon Noel Sturgeon's work on environmentalism in popular culture (see Sturgeon, 2008) with particular analysis on the "frontier myth." Sturgeon's work discusses the naturalization of violence and conquest, and the naturalization of the white, suburban, nuclear family in environmentalism. Her vital theorizing demonstrates "the maintenance of these kinds of beliefs [of violence, conquest, and nuclear family that] satisfies the human need for psychological equilibrium and order, finding support and reinforcement in ideology" that Merskin notes (2001, p. 161). It is the naturalization of ideological messages that people live; and the American frontier myth and values of capitalism and humanitarianism that the polar bear reiterates; paralleling Sturgeon's film and entertainment analysis of penguins that represent family values, heterosexuality, and overcoming obstacles through amazing persistence (Sturgeon, 2008, pp. 120–146). My theorizing and analysis connects the contemporary messages of green consumption and environmental philanthropy to a naturalization of climate citizenship. The achievement of these naturalizations on a primary level is green consumerism and environmental philanthropy as necessary and moral. The secondary achievement is on-going imperialism and neo-colonial decisions that disproportionately and distinctively harm, kill, and damage Indigenous communities. It is a cadence of destruction that Indigenous peoples are confronting.

Methods

While Sturgeon has analyzed the visual use of nature, gender, and race (including Indigenous peoples) and Merskin directly confronts the branding of Indigenous cultures, my work investigates how these practices are reproduced and reemphasized in the Nissan Leaf polar bear commercial and the Environmental Defense Fund use of Inuit names to achieve climate citizenship, thus, negating or subalternizing knowledge of Indigeneity, which is witnessed, discussed, and evidenced in climate colonialism and food sovereignty issues. I will focus on this latter part of my claim after I provide examples of US climate citizenship visual culture.

The power of images and the visual culture moves beyond an image or 'picture.' US visual culture extends past monetary gain to reflect and speak for values, ideologies, and beliefs. All brands, advertisements, and logos seek to embody meaning that transcends words, yet, speaks to us. As Merskin in her discussion of brands, advertisements, and images and the stereotyping of Indigenous cultures emphasizes,

> To every ad they see or hear, people bring a shared set of beliefs that serve as frames of reference for understanding the world around them. Beyond

its obvious selling function, advertising images are about making meaning. Ads must 'take into account not only the inherent qualities and attributes of the products they are trying to sell, but also the way in which they can make those properties mean something to us.'

(Merskin, 2001, p. 161)

Green consumerism and environmental philanthropy count on an American nationalistic meaning of enlightened material worth and heroic savior of animals and, at times, land.

As Sturgeon and Merskin's bodies of work have demonstrated, environmentalism's branding of visual culture is a paramount site of analysis. The data in this project focus on the highly acclaimed Nissan Leaf commercial and a few environmental advocacy organization mailers. My work explores a larger theoretical framework versus covering and engaging in broad empirical data collection. This theoretical framework utilizes and builds upon Connell's work with dirty theory. She states that a cornerstone of dirty theory is to, "use the spirit of the narratives, the local kin terminology and other materials from local culture to picture local society and establish its relationship … to translate the local symbolism" (Connell, 2007, p. 220). I merge this precept with numerous works within public sociology that seek to transcend academia and more directly align to Indigenous methodologies. In doing such,

Our interest as researchers is to maximize the wealth of materials that are drawn into the analysis and explanation. It is also our interest to multiply, rather than slim down, the theoretical ideas that we have to work with. … that includes multiplying the local sources of our thinking.

(Connell, 2007)

The data I focus on are seen and received on televisions and computers and in e-mail boxes by millions of citizens. The cultural symbolism of the polar bear has turned into an iconic image of hope, freedom, and American values.

As Connell states, dirty theory emphasizes,

The power of social science generalisations is multiplied if they can be linked to the characteristic of the context *within* which they apply. This suggests an argument against pure general theory, in favour of what we might call dirty theory – that is, theorizing that is mixed up with specific situations. The goal of dirty theory is not to subsume, but to clarify; not to classify from outside, but to illuminate a situation in its concreteness.

(2007, p. 53)

Specifically, to demonstrate green consumerism, I utilize the nationally acclaimed and highly touted Nissan Leaf commercial. During the National Football League (NFL) opening game between the Minnesota Vikings and the

New Orleans Saints that drew a 28 percent share equaling 17.7 million viewers, the Nissan Leaf commercial was aired (Florio, 2010). This game had the highest NFL opening night rating ever. Early the next morning, one headline from the website Climate Progress stated: "Wow! Watch the Nissan Leaf's provocative, irreverent polar bear ad, which markets global warming ... and makes the anti-science disinformers go nuts" (Romm, 2010). Also, from the Green Skeptic, "How many of you caught this Nissan LEAF polar bear commercial during last night's Saints-Vikings game? I know some environmentalists will hate this, but I think it's very clever" (Anderson, 2010).

I also utilize the Environmental Defense Fund (EDF) e-mailers to demonstrate how their philanthropy focus serves to achieve climate citizenship. The EDF received a four out of four star rating from Charity Navigator and had a total revenue of $96,358,261 (Charity Navigator, 2011). Furthermore, "The Environmental Defense Fund ... has become a thought leader in the climate change community. They are exceptionally knowledgeable on cap and trade, and have made huge policy gains around this and other strategies" (Philanthropedia, 2012). They use Inuit names for a polar bear family as part of a campaign that helped them to achieve this ranking.

My work clarifies how climate citizenship is guised in green consumerism and environmental philanthropy, which promotes the "metabolism of man and nature" that Marx discusses. Building upon Sturgeon's analysis, I seek to "move beyond individual modifications of ways of living [purchasing a Nissan Leaf or donating to EDF] to address the systematic, institutionalized structures that maintain inequality and promote environmental devastation" (Sturgeon, 2008, p. 182). And in such, I illustrate how, within this climate citizenship context, Indigenous cultures and sovereignty are challenged, disrupted, and maligned.

Green consumption: the Nissan leaf and polar bears

> Because of its wide impact, U.S. popular culture is an important arena for oppositional activists to enter in order to convince, persuade, and mobilize others to their cause.
>
> (Sturgeon, 2008, p. 6)

In the United States during the fall of 2010, to great fanfare and high acclaim, Nissan released its new commercial for their electric car graciously called *The Leaf* (Nissan USA, 2010). As it reached nearly 18 million viewers during its initial airing, it spawned a host of media and environmental praise. Fred Meier from USA Today's, Drive On series noted,

> The company got its marketing money's worth out of this one: The ad engages the viewer, then hammers home the message: Save the planet one Leaf at a time.

It's also generating pop-culture and online buzz well beyond e-car crowd. It's even prompted earnest warnings from animal savvy folks not to try this at home: Polar bears are not that cuddly, or even friendly, and mostly hungry.

(Meier, 2010)

As Goodman notes, "the mounting campaign of fair trade is a distinct focus on raising the niceness of capitalist development" (Goodman, 2004, p. 891). We save the planet and create buzz by buying one Leaf at a time.

The commercial starts with a close-up of water dripping from a chunk of ice. As a piano evocatively invites the viewer in, the camera pulls back to show an iceberg and pans to a polar bear spread across a small ice pad floating in a large sea, looking rather longingly and sad. The scene pulls back. The polar bear, desolate in the vast waters, is then shown swimming. It reaches a shore – land, absent of snow or ice. The piano continues – quickens – as the polar bear walks a wooden trail and rests in a large roadside culvert as rain falls and a vehicle quickly passes overhead.

Next, the polar bear continues down a railroad track, stands and looks in wonder at a butterfly circling it. As the scene shifts to the polar bear walking on the side of a road, an 18-wheeler passes it and it raises its head slightly and roars. Then we see it sitting, the bear's back to the viewer, in the distance a large city landscape of buildings, sky-scrapers, and lights fills the screen. Next, as the piano softens, the polar bear walks along a city bridge: buildings, parking meters, traffic lights, and cars taking up all the space around it. It crosses, walks into an alley, drinks from a large puddle as a raccoon scurries near it and looks at the bear somewhat in puzzlement and gives a slight chatter. The bear looks up as water drips from its mouth: the sound of lips smacking is slightly offered. A garbage truck passes over the screen.

The polar bear is now walking down a suburban road: uniform looking houses, manicured lawns to it. The polar bear growls slightly at the garbage truck. The view shifts to a middle-aged suit-wearing (minus the tie) man walking out of his suburban house towards his car – parked in the driveway. The house and surroundings are a muted green, brown, and white. The car is soft blue. As he leans over and reaches for the car door, out of the corner of his eye coming around the back of the car is the polar bear. He drops his briefcase. The man stands and turns toward the bear. The bear approaches, speaks, and stands on its back two legs. Then the bear places its two front paws on the shoulders of the man – embracing him. The man wraps his arms around the bear. The piano has picked up its tempo to an enchanting tone. A voice-over states, "The 100 percent electric Nissan Leaf. Innovation for the planet. Innovation for all." The Nissan logo on a black screen appears. The commercial ends.

There is no mention, no word, no acknowledgment of the Indigenous peoples dealing with land loss, rising sea levels, direct challenges to sustainable lifeways, and cultural performativity. Anthony Watts, a commentator, on Romm's Think Progressive posting, offered one of the rare critiques. Watts stated, "The ad agency that serves Nissan (as does Nissan management) deserves a smack upside the head for promoting the idea that you can hug a polar bear. Some people are actually stupid enough to try it" (Romm, 2010). However, the praise and accolades continued. MLuu for Visual Inquiry – a discussion forum for visual studies at the Annenberg School for Communication proclaimed,

> The Nissan LEAF Polar Bear Commercial integrates CGI and live action shots to create an emotional and compelling commercial for the all-electric car with zero tailpipe emissions. ... The variety of scenes keeps the viewer interested and invested as they, too, follow her on this journey. It ends by her hugging a man who is helping the environment by driving an electric car. ... The emotional hug scene was an associational montage that encourages the audience to associate driving the Nissan LEAF with helping the environment. The commercial ends on an optimistic note because the Nissan LEAF offers a potential solution to the global warming crisis. This commercial is very memorable because it tugs at the heartstrings.
>
> (MLuu, 2012)

The Nissan Leaf commercial speaks volumes regarding nationalistic rhetoric, value, and importance that are being sold to the American public as citizenship. Vizenor discusses, "that aural sense of presence is the premise of a distinctive aesthetics" (Vizenor, 2009, p. 1). The aural visuals employed in the commercial evoke an identity through a sense of space, the wide open lands of America, the cityscape, the playful butterfly, and even a raccoon in the streets of an urban city, all speak to a nationalistic presence (the frontier). They are the postcards of our journeys: the American pastime – road trips. The distinctive aesthetics and presence is reinforced as it is softly keyed throughout the piece by the piano. The facade of American ideologies is embedded in the gratefulness of the polar bear's extensive travels, through and over various terrains to reach the hero – the conscious green consumer, who is a white male.

Again, there were few minor critiques of the ad. In the posting "Nissan Leaf's Strangely Moving Polar Bear Ad" in the Huffington Post, poignantly, the headline actually suggests the ad is about the polar bear. They offered BrandChannel's note that stated,

> It's interesting, too, that for the ad, Nissan positioned Leaf in a driveway, untethered – not in a garage where it's actually likely to be found each morning, connected by a cord to an electrical outlet, when an owner leaves the house to get into the vehicle for the commute.
>
> (Huffington Post, 2010)

Also, as stated and reiterated in the article, "The ad has already earned some raves from eco-minded bloggers. *Good* says the ad's 'irreverence is perfectly tuned.' Ecorazzi notes that it ends in an 'Awwwww'." *Good* promotes itself as a "community for people who give a damn" (Price, 2010). While *Ecorazzi's* tagline is "good gossip" (Destries, 2010). The coverage supports innovative and 'heart pulling' green consumerism that serve as visual images of modernity.

The continuance of American capitalism that is central to the excessive amounts of gas emissions and the literal destruction of the polar bear's homelands is ignored and veiled by the telling of the polar bear's plight and US consumer's commitment to the environment. Yes, the vehicle is a Nissan; however, this commercial was specifically created for the US market. The Nissan Leaf's main achievement is the promotion of American nationalism through green consumption. Nissan USA created a commercial promoting the purchase of a new vehicle (that supposedly at least pays attention to climate change issues) as an act of civility and morality deeming grace and thanks.

Environmental philanthropy: polar bears and Inuit names

During this same time period, fervent efforts were being made to save the polar bear.

> Indeed, as humanity faced 'the limits of growth', and heard 'the population boom' ticking away, ecologies and environments became more than something to be judged morally; they became things the state must administer. Ecology, then, has evolved into 'a public potential'.
>
> (Luke, 1999, p. 124)

Thus, the Environmental Defense Fund, the World Wildlife Federation, the National Wildlife Federation, Defenders of Wildlife, Natural Resources Defense Council, and Greenpeace all have various campaigns to save the polar bear. The Center of Biological Diversity even has "endangered species condoms" (Endangered Species Condoms, 2010). The Center points out that it has been engaged in efforts to save the polar bear since 2005. As part of this campaign you can get a free polar bear ringtone. They also promote condom use through "Wrap with Care ... Save the Polar Bear" as well as several other animal reference puns (Endangered Species Condoms, 2010).

The expert review of EDF heralded its efforts. They wrote that,

> Their [EDF] advocacy work includes influencing the EPA's emission standards for power plants and petroleum refineries, legal victories related to the Clean Air Act, and more. Their organizational strategies of engaging a range of stakeholders, focusing on environmental stewardship, and establishing themselves as independent from many other organizations, have proved effective in many ways. Their work on developing market-driven climate change strategies has had a huge impact in shifting priorities within businesses.
>
> (Philanthropedia, 2012)

Here is a glimpse into the Environmental Defense Fund's personal solicitation for my involvement. The request, which I have received in the mail and via email, comes complete with photographs of a polar bear family, a mother and two cubs – one of which is standing on its back legs eagerly looking ahead; the mother is reaching with her glance towards it. A snow field surrounds them. EDF states:

A Polar Bear Family Begins Its Journey!
Wednesday, March 31, 2010 12:32 PM

Dear Doreen,
Today we introduce you to a fictional polar bear family – Aakaga and her three-month old cubs Qannik and Siku –as they make their perilous journey in a melting Arctic world. – Find out what happens.

EDF's crusade for the polar bear is just one example and this particular story is only part one of the journey. More powerfully, it is an example of how privileged ignorance operates and allows a lack of knowledge and commitment to social issues that particularly challenge and confront American practices (e.g., mass consumption and high carbon emissions). Saving the polar bear reinforces good, humanitarian, moral, and just work that is guised and wrapped up in 'extinction' and/or 'endangered species.' We, as Americans, will be the saviors and the icon of progress; we will save what others so willingly kill off. The privileged ignorance lies in stark contrast for the polar bear family members are all given names – Inuit names we will learn.

The preponderance of materials to save the polar bear shout and prioritize the national ethos that we, conscientious citizens, must respond to. Thus, it allows a blinding or ignorance that is privileged on these values, ideologies, and rhetoric of nationalism. Simply put, what information is deemed worthy (by nationalism) and valuable to share or promote allows the public to ignore the rest. It is privileged in that the confronting realities of Indigenous peoples and communities are well known. However, to acknowledge the realities of various communities devastated by climate change would require reciprocal change of those complicit. Further, the ability to donate money to save the polar bear additionally refuses to acknowledge or name the responsibility and root cause of the environmental loss – the very American ideals it truly seeks to reinforce. The EDF plea for my donation continues:

- Icy, windy, freezing – it might not look like spring to a human. But to a polar bear like Aakaga (whose name means "my mother" in Inuit), today, March 31, is the end of a dark, harsh winter.
- Today is the day she'll lead her tiny, three-month-old cubs, Qannik (her name is Inuit for "Snowflake") and Siku (his name is Inuit for "Ice"), on an Arctic trek to find pack ice – the frozen, floating sea ice where polar bears spend most of their lives.

- Aakaga is nervous.
- Her cubs need a few more days to acclimate to the broad, big world. Since they first poked out their shiny, black eyes from the comforting darkness of their maternity den, Qannik and Siku have spent the last eight days tumbling and playing in the fluffy, crystal powder snow outside the entrance.
- But today, Aakaga's sharp nose has caught a scent of a wolf pack, upwind and hunting.

In this passage, the creators anthropomorphize the polar bear family adding to the permission and ease of focusing attention to the animals rather than the people of the region. The process, anthropomorphizing, also reinforces the nobility of certain animals – even populations – that we (read American ideologies) deem worthy because of an iconic stature to *save*.

The devastating impact of climate change on the Inuit and Alaska Native cultures is about extinction and/or forced cultural change. Cultures are constantly adapting and changing, rarely static. "Yet we have fallen into the trap of codifying certain cultures, and those deemed 'indigenous' have been particularly prone to such reductionism" (Plaice, 2006, p. 23). Therefore, the polar bear family members can be given Inuit names – most likely by non-Inuit peoples. Yet, the strife, catastrophic loss, and cultural damage maintain a location of possible sorrow. But, more often, it is reduced to making sense since progressive citizens would live in modern geographic spaces. As a testament to this phenomenon, a common retort at COP15 was the need to *put a human face* on climate change consequences. The polar bear is there.

Consequences of climate citizenship: climate change and indigenous sovereignty

The polar bear serves climate citizenship emblematically as the new tool, the welcome visual, safe, and humanitarian disguise of US nationalism, built upon ideologies of privilege and entitlement. As a parallel, the United States was defined as a place of discovery, exploration, freedom, progress, and expansion. It has been through deliberate naming and shift in ideological analysis that we have evidenced and concluded the colonial policies, actions, and behaviors of US discovery and progress. Similarly, we have seen a shift in the naming and recognition of modernity regarding climate impacts. We have gone from global warming to climate change, to climate colonialism. The colonialistic practice and outcome of US climate citizenship must be named and understood in the depth, breadth, and severity of the outcomes it produces.

Foucault argues that, "'discourses' emerge and transform not according to a developing series of unarticulated, common worldviews, but according to a vast and complex set of discursive and institutional relationships, which are defined as much by breaks and ruptures as by unified themes" (Foucault, 1982, p. 34). The shift from climate change discourse to naming and recognizing climate colonialism is just one necessary tool of decoloniality. In this decolonial process, first, a "re-embodiment and relocation of thought in order to unmask the limited situation of modern knowledge and their link to coloniality" occurs (Mingolo, 2007). In part, this limited situation is evidenced when there is a shift from global warming to climate change. More significantly, and what I argue is jointly foundational to Indigeneity, is to name climate change, climate colonialism. To refer to it as only climate change limits modern knowledge to colonial goals and proposed achievements. Climate colonialism forces a re-embodiment and relocation of how, why, and whom is responsible. The climate is failing to merely change. It is being colonized and forced to alter, modify and (as the catastrophes possibly indicate) rebel, and resist this forced assimilation.

To focus on saving the polar bear is a focus on saving US colonialistic practices. This (re)naming process subsequently centrally reframes and repositions cultures and ideologies that are silenced, negated, and fatally impacted by climate change citizenship. Although identifying consequences of climate citizenship has been done by Indigenous peoples and communities, it is paramount to see the devastation of climate colonialism on all entities – humans, land, water, animals, futures.

The voices of climate colonialism include: internationally, rising seas are affecting the Pankhali region in Bangladesh and the island nations of the Maldives and Tuvalu so dramatically that their respective governments are now considering wholesale migration as a matter of public safety (Carbon Capture Report, 2010). Because of similar threats, 3,000 residents of the Carteret Islands in the South Pacific are evacuating to Papua New Guinea (Carteret Islands Project, 2011). As Huhndorf explains, "Concentrating on the connections that tie indigenous communities together rather than on the boundaries that separate them allows me to raise questions about gender, imperialism, class and the worldwide circulation of culture which have garnered little sustained attention" (Huhndorf, 2009, p. 2). Rather than seeing each crisis, complication, or climate change issue in relation to region, type of catastrophe, or even Indigenous nation issue, we must view the totality – separately and jointly – as paramount challenges and conflicts to Indigenous sovereignty.

Indigenous daily lifeways are directly altered and, at times, devastated by climate change, from the loss of habitable Arctic land-bases, to glacial melt that is washing away centuries of sustainable lifeways. The impact of devastations is experienced within and beyond food, habitat, and shelter. For, as Eva Garroute explains, "culture is not something people merely 'practice' or 'preserve' but something within which they properly *dwell*" (Garroute, 2003, p. 150). As sea levels rise and wash away homes and droughts overtake lands, destroy crops, and in places eliminate basic drinking water needs, culture and the intellectual, spiritual, emotional, and ancestral spaces where we dwell are being assaulted.

Significantly, "The numbers of people affected by disasters have risen sharply over the past decade with an average 211 million people directly affected each year, nearly five times the number affected by armed conflict in the same period" (United Nations, 2008). Even amidst wars in Afghanistan, Iraq, Somalia, the

Democratic Republic of Congo, and conflicts in Turkey, Malawi, and others, the number of people impacted by climate change is higher than the victims of these hostile campaigns. All over the world, Indigenous cultures suffer from inconsistent and unequally high rates of poverty, health problems, crime, and human rights abuses (United Nations, 2009, p. 7). More specifically, Indigenous peoples' lives bear the exponeniated reality of climate change consequences and fear of such consequences. Climate change realities such as the loss of habitat, loss of water, or excess water impact the quality and capacity of life. These are our dwelling spaces.

Indigeneity names the coloniality of modernity

Indigeneity is a tool of Native nation citizenship. As Niezen states, "challenging state notions of citizenship, national culture, and individual rights ..." is fundamental to Indigeneity (Niezen, 2003, p. xv). It is Indigeneity, Indigenous advocacy, agency, voice, and representation, that is enhanced and proclaimed in the claiming and naming of the true-life realities of climate colonialism, instead of climate citizenship. Critical to this decolonial process is creating, developing, and implementing a new epistemic frame (Mingolo, 2006) and challenging state citizenship notions. This shift in knowledge and understanding of climate change is reflected in the naming and claiming of climate colonialism that identifies disparities, destruction, and death. In such, the epistemic shift reflects a decoloniality that demands a type of other-thinking that calls for plurality and intercultural dialogue (Mingolo, 2006). Indigeneity presents an intercultural dialogue of sovereignty that is erased through climate citizenship, while plurality breaks open the multiple locations of knowledge and value of earth's resources, limitations, responsiveness, and imperviousness. It introduces stewardship and responsibility versus consumption and colonial citizenship.

Strikingly, in Alaska, "The irony here is that we are trying to avert a disaster," Mike Black muses as he hikes up the hillside at the site of Newtok's proposed new village. Mike Black is the deputy commissioner of the Department of Commerce for Community and Economic Development and is one of the most senior officials promoting Newtok's relocation. "If you wait for a disaster like Katrina, at least you have a mandate and funding" (York, 2010). There are concrete climate change vulnerabilities that are impacting Indigenous peoples globally that must be recognized as colonialistic and an affront to sovereignty.

Moreover, re-embodying how agriculture is being utilized within climate change colonialism has created new and pressing questions regarding food sovereignty. Again, the very act of shifting the location and situation of food to food sovereignty realigns the imperial coloniality (food at all costs,) to food accessibility for all. Skyrocketing food prices sparked riots in more than 40 countries and grabbed headlines in the first half of 2008 (Walt, 2008). Pictures of people fighting over cups of rice or access to water pipes spanned international media sources; the causes of those shortages were absent. Subsequently, about 75 percent of the world's poorest people live in rural areas and depend on agriculture for their livelihoods (2008). Fundamental issues regarding land-use have erupted because of flooding, aridity, and loss of land. With ever-increasing land loss, water access, and rights, food sovereignty stakes are also raised. Food sovereignty is further illustrated by rising sea levels that have devastated staple food supplies. Glacier melts in Bolivia have permanently altered, if not eliminated, historic agricultural lands. United Nations Intergovernmental Panel on Climate Change (IPCC) projections indicate that for some countries in Africa, yields from rain-fed agriculture could fall by up to 50 percent by 2020, threatening the survival of large populations dependent on semi-subsistence farming.

In August of 2010, the news source ClimateWire's headline asked, "If a country sinks beneath the sea, is it still a country?" (Friedman, 2010). For, as it states further on: "theoretical questions become real." In 2007, the IPCC estimated that by 2100, sea levels could rise by anywhere between 7 and 23 inches. Tuvalu, Marshall Island, Carteret Island, and Cook Island residents have been dealing with relocation needs for nearly two decades already. Initial relocation occurred inland – away from histories and cultural artifacts. Some residents are seeking relocation in Australia, New Zealand, and Britain (those countries which have agreed to accept them). As one Cook Island Indigenous person mentioned at COP15: "we must go anywhere they will take us." As a follow-up, she was asked if this was occurring in a way that community could be retained. She said, "No. We must go where we can have a home."

Significantly, what occurs through the (re)naming process is a positioning and advocacy of communities disproportionately and gravely impacted by climate change rather than existing as objects or material artifacts of the colonial acts. Ultimately, I argue for the recognition of Indigenous citizenship and sovereign existence to take precedence over climate citizenship.

References

Anderson, S. (2010). *Nissan leaf polar bear commercial*. Green Skeptic. Retrieved February 1, 2012: http://www.thegreenskeptic.com/2010/09/nissan-leaf-polar-bear-commercial.html.

Carbon Capture Report. (2010). *Daily report: Geographic focus*. Carbon Capture Report. Retrieved March 16, 2010: http://www.carboncapturereport.org.

Carteret Islands Project. (2011). *Issues related to relocation*. The Carteret Islands Project. Retrieved Ocotber 8, 2011: http://resourceventures.wordpress.com.

Charity Navigator. (2011). *Environmental Defense Fund*. Charity Navigator: Your Guide to Intelligent Giving. Retrieved January 28, 2012: http://www.charitynavigator.org /index.cfm?bay=search.summary&orgid=3671.

Connell, R. (2007). *Southern theory*. Oxford: Polity Press.

Destries, M. (2010). *Nissan polar bear commerical ends with an awwwww ...* Ecorazzi. Retrieved March 10, 2012: http://www.ecorazzi.com/2010/09/10/nissan-leaf-polar-bear-commercial-ends-with-an-awwwww.

Endangered Species Condoms. (2010). Endangered species condoms. Retrieved October 2, 2010 from the Center for Biological Diversity: http://www.endangeredspeciescondoms.com.

Florio, M. (2010). Vikings-Saints drew NFL's highest opening night rating ever. *NBC Sports*, September 10, Retrieved October 11, 2010: http://profootballtalk.nbcsports. com/2010/09/10/vikings-saints-drew-nfls-highest-opening-night-rating-ever.

Foucault, M. (1982). *The archeology of knowledge*. London: Vintage Press/Random House.

Foucault, M. (1991). Governmentality. In G. Burchell and C. Gordon (Eds.), *The Foucault effect: Studies in governmentality* (pp. 87–104). Chicago, IL: The University of Chicago Press.

Friedman, L. (2010). Nations: If a country sinks beneath the sea, is it still a country? *ClimeWire*. Retrieved August 23, 2010: http://www.eenews.net/climatewire.

Garroutte, E. (2003). *Real Indians: Identity and the survival of Native America*. London: University of California Press.

Goodman, M. K. (2004). Reading fair trade: Political ecological imaginary and the moral economy of fair trade foods. *Political Geography*, 23, 891–895.

Huffington Post. (2010). Nissan leaf's strangely moving polar bear ad. *Huffington Post*, September 10. Retrieved February 2, 2012: http://www.huffingtonpost.com/2010/09/10/ nissan-leaf-polar-bear-ad_n_712714.html.

Huhndorf, S. V. (2009). *Mapping the Americas: The transnational politics of contemporary native culture*. New York: Cornell University Press.

Kates, S. M. & Shaw-Garlock, G. (1999). The ever-entangling web: A study of ideologies and discourses in advertising to women. *Journal of Advertising*, 28(2), 34.

Luke, T. (1999). Environmentality as governmentality. In E. Darier (Ed.), *Discourses of environment* (pp. 121–151). Oxford: Blackwell.

Meier, F. (2010). How they made the Nissan polar bear ad. *USAToday*, Drive On, Setpember 14. Retrieved February 1, 2012: http://content.usatoday.com/communities/driveon/ post/2010/09/how-they-made-that-nissan-leaf-polar-bear-ad/1#.Ugkt2rx1E8g.

Merskin, D. (2001). Winnebagos, Cherokees, Apaches, and Dakotas: The persistence of stereotyping of American Indians in American advertising brands. *The Howard Journal of Communication*, 12(3), 159–169.

Mingolo, W. (2000). *Local histories/global designs*. Princeton, NJ: Princeton University Press.

Mignolo, W. (2006). As discussed by P. Cheah, *The Limits of Thinking in Decolonial Strategies*. Retrieved January 8, 2012: http://townsendcenter.berkeley.edu/article10.shtml.

Mingolo, W. (2007). *Delinking: The rhetoric of modernity, the logic of coloniality and the grammar of de-coloniality*. Retrieved November 16, 2011 from Townsend Center University of California Berkeley: http://townsendcenter.berkeley.edu /sites/default/files/ wysiwyg/De-linking_Mignolo.pdf.

MLuu. (2012). *Nissan leaf polar bear commercial with CGI*. Visual Inquiry: A discussion forum for visual studies. Retrieved February 1, 2013 from the Annenberg School of Communication, University of Pennsylvania: http://www.visualinquiry.org/blog/?p=1116.

Niezen, R. (2003). *The origins of indigenism: Human rights and the politics of identity*. Berkeley, CA: University of California Press.

Nissan USA. (2010). Nissan leaf polar bear commercial. YouTube. Retrieved September 12, 2010: http://youtu.be/eG7ueitiW-w.

Philanthropedia. (2012). Come together. Give better 2012. *Environmental Defense Fund*. Retrieved February 21, 2012: https://www.myphilanthropedia.org/top-nonprofits / national/climate-change/2012/environmental-defense-fund.

Plaice, E. (2006). The concept of indigeneity. *Social Anthropology*, 14, 1, 22–24.

Price, A. (2010). The Nissan leaf polar bear ad is pretty great. *Good: A Community for People Who Give a Damn*. Retrieved March 10, 2012: http://www.good.is/posts/the-nissan-leaf-polar-bear-ad-is-pretty-great.

Romm, J. (2010). Wow! Watch the Nissan leaf's provocative, irreverent polar bear ad, which markets global warming. *Think Progress*, September 11. Retrieved January 28, 2012: http://thinkprogress.org/climate/2010/09/11/206702/nissan-leaf-polar-bear-ad-global-warming.

Sturgeon, N. (2008). *Environmentalism in popular culture: Gender, race, sexuality, and the politics of the natural.* Tucson, AZ: University of Arizona Press.

United Nations. (2008). *Ten stories the world should hear more about.* The United Nations 2008. Retrieved October 5, 2011: http://www.un.org/en/events/tenstories/08/climatechange.shtml.

United Nations. (2009). *State of the world's indigenous peoples.* United Nations Economic & Social Affairs. Retrieved October 10, 2011:http://www.un.org/esa/socdev/unpfii / documents/SOWIP_web.pdf.

Vizenor, G. (2009). *Native liberty: Natural reason and cultural survivance.* Lincoln, NE: University of Nebraska Press.

Walt, V. (2008). The Worlds Growing Food-Price Crisis. *Time Magazine*, February 27. Retrieved February 27, 2011: http://www.time.com/time/world/article/0,8599,1717572,00.html 2008.

Williamson, J. (1978). *Decoding advertisements: Ideology and meaning in advertising.* New York: Marion Boyars.

York, A. (2010). *Alaskan village stands on leading edge of climate change.* Retrieved October 5, 2010 from The University of North Carolina Chapel Hill, Powering a Nation: http://unc.news21.com/index.php/stories/alaska.html.

COMMENTARY ON PART I

Beyond climate, beyond change

Mike Hulme

I am writing this commentary on Thursday 9 May 2013, the day on which the daily-average measured atmospheric concentration of carbon dioxide at the Mauna Loa Observatory in Hawaii exceeded 400 parts per million (ppm) for the first time. This signature measurement drew a fair amount of attention amongst the world's media, with headlines such as "carbon dioxide passes symbolic mark," "CO_2 crosses dreaded 400 ppm milestone," "NOAA debunks 400 ppm CO_2 panic." The concentration of carbon dioxide in the atmosphere has never before in human evolutionary history exceeded this amount. But what does 400 ppm symbolize? Why might it cause dread and panic? Or why is this notice any more significant than, say, the eradication of smallpox in 1979, total column ozone falling below 200 Dobson Units in October 1985, the human population reaching 7 billion in 2011, or the number of Facebook users reaching 1 billion in 2012? "The world changes; get over it." Not even the most committed climate contrarian would challenge the veracity of this measurement of 400 ppm and only a few would deny that human burning of fossil fuels and land use changes have something to do with it. And not that many more would deny that elevating the concentration of carbon dioxide in the atmosphere will have at least *some* repercussion for the climate system and the consequent patterns of local weather. So how do we extract meaning from the brute fact of 400 ppm? Of what exactly is 400 ppm symbolic? Or to connect with the two preceding chapters in this book, how does 400 ppm relate to Cheryl Hall's conclusion that we need to explore our values, identify where they conflict and consider how and why they might be prioritized differently? And how does 400 ppm relate to Doreen Martinez's advocacy for "the recognition of Indigenous citizenship and sovereign existence to take precedence over climate citizenship" (p. 52)? Since both Hall and Martinez frame their analysis explicitly in terms of climate change, and since 400 ppm is important to arguments about climate change, there must be some credible connection between 400 ppm and the conclusions they reach. In this brief commentary I explore why and how such connections are made.

Over the last 25 years the idea of 'climate change' has entered into nearly all human cultures, driven the creation of new social movements, inspired new artistic enterprises and re-shaped the politics of energy, poverty, and development. This is not just about scientific discovery, experimentation, and prediction. Climate change is not just another environmental problem seeking a solution. The phenomenon of climate change is fundamentally different from, for example, the depletion of stratospheric ozone in the late 1980s. The idea of the ozone hole, or indeed acid rain before it, did not accomplish any of the things I've just mentioned. Nor is it these older ideas that Hall enlisted to call for the re-thinking of human values or Martinez to defend the rights of Indigenous peoples. It is not just some invisible stratum of the distant sky that humans are altering, nor merely the localized chemical composition of raindrops. There is clearly something more powerful, more unsettling, about the idea that human actions are persistently altering the momentary weather which all of us experience intimately on a daily basis.

There is a bewildering array of human practices which are implicated in the idea of anthropogenic climate change – cultivating, eating, traveling, heating, cooling, building, manufacturing, recreating, even procreating. When combined with the familiarity of our weather experience, it is not surprising that climate change has taken on a much wider cultural significance than earlier, more circumscribed, environmental perturbations. And as I remarked a few years ago, "The emergent phenomenon of climate change – understood … simultaneously as physical transformation and cultural object, as a mutating hybrid entity in which the strained lines between the natural and the cultural are dissolving – … needs a new examination" (Hulme, 2008, p. 5).

And we have here two examples of such an examination, from Cheryl Hall and Doreen Martinez. In "Beyond 'gloom and doom' or 'hope and possibility,'" Hall issues a call for positive visioning in the communication of climate change, the development of an inspirational narrative of change. But she argues that change will also always be sacrificial in the sense that certain human technologies, practices, or habits will be displaced. She favors radical sacrificial change in human social practice over mere reform, but realizes it won't be easy. Her problem comes when she contemplates how these two different responses to climate change can be reconciled in pluralist societies through democratic processes.

In "Polar bears, Inuit names, and climate citizenship," Martinez draws attention to how the polar bear is used to promote a certain expression of American (environmental) citizenship. Using a visual studies approach, she deconstructs two recent climate change advertising campaigns in the United States, the Nissan Leaf polar bear commercial promoting a new electric car and an Environmental Defense Fund campaign to raise public funds to "save the polar bear." In the name of climate change both adverts, she claims, subvert the cultural symbolism of the polar bear "into an iconic image of hope, freedom, and American values" (p. 43), whilst being blind to the deep cultural and material significance of the polar bear for the Inuit people.

These two chapters therefore provide excellent examples of how the idea of climate change is made to perform different types of cultural work. For Hall, climate change becomes a site for political argument about what sort of world we are creating, what sort of future is desired, and the difficulty of working constructively with plural and divergent values. Climate change therefore becomes "precisely the issue of democracy itself: whether and how citizens in communities … can collectively decide what is to be done" (p. 34). Martinez on the other hand, laments how climate change becomes a way of exoticizing and then appropriating "the other," in her case Indigenous cultures. In this sense she follows an analytical tradition reaching back to Edward Said's classic exploration of orientalism: how for Westerners the East became 'othered' and made exotic (Said, 1978). Martinez argues that climate change seen as environmental philanthropy allows the polar bear to be co-opted by neo-colonial projects of challenging, disrupting and maligning Indigenous cultures. (Yet I sense there is a danger that by essentializing such cultures Martinez too ends up 'exoticizing' the Indigenous; cf. Cameron, 2012; Hastrup, 2013).

What both these examples show is just how deep into our cultural, ethical and political discourse the idea of climate change has penetrated. The conclusions that Hall and Martinez reach are a long way from the measurements of carbon dioxide concentrations at the Mauna Loa Observatory. Yet they implicitly assume their conclusions *are* connected in some way to 400 ppm through the elaborate chains of reference which we use to construct the idea of climate change. The theories, instruments, measurements, analyses, simulations, communications, interests, values, and interpretations that support this referential chain are long and intricate and embrace what Latour calls radically different "modes of existence" (Latour, 2013): science, law, religion, economics, politics, art and so on.

A powerful example of how such a construction has been made to function in social life is Bill McKibbin's campaigning social movement: *350.org*. McKibbin combines the scientific measurement of atmospheric carbon dioxide with a normative judgment as to what concentration is desirable, namely 350 ppm. The campaigning goal of a world freed from its reliance on fossil fuels is thus reified in a number, appropriating science for a political cause. 350 ppm becomes the device which anchors the campaign to the authority of science. The goal is overtly political, but it is a goal warranted, apparently, on the basis of science, not values. And one can see how 400 ppm then becomes a signal event for the movement. As its website today proclaims: "Passing 400 is a sober reminder that we have much work to do. The only good news is that we're doing it" (350.org, 2013).

Another example of such anchoring is the 100-month campaign launched by the *new economics foundation* in the UK in August 2008 (onehundredmonths. org, 2013). In this case, its call for a radical restructuring of global society and energy systems is tethered to the scientific narrative of two degrees. If the global temperature of two degrees warming is not to be exceeded then global emissions of carbon dioxide must start falling no later than 100 months after August 2008. The clock is ticking and global restructuring is called for.

Hall and Martinez are by no means as explicit as *350.org* or *onehundredmonths.org* in the chains of reference they employ, but employ them they do. Hall argues that the "urgent need for significant transformation" arises from the need to prevent further climate change: "... the longer we wait to act, the worse the situation gets [i.e., the higher carbon dioxide concentrations will rise above 400 ppm] and the bigger the changes required" (p. 26). For Martinez the referential chain is more opaque. She observes that responsible climate citizenship seems to be equated with changing consumption modes (consumers thus taking responsibility for their part in causing climate change; i.e., for elevating carbon dioxide concentrations to 400 ppm and beyond). But she then criticizes such environmental philanthropy as it promotes "neo-colonial understandings and actions" which undermine the rights of Indigenous communities.

As we can see, both authors indirectly draw upon the narrative of 400 ppm being a significant event for humankind, but then to develop their argument they need to engage with other forms of non-scientific reasoning. In the case of Hall it is whatever imaginative resources are needed to "help people re-imagine what it might mean to be free, powerful and happy" (p. 31). It is not clear exactly what these are, but the fact of 400 ppm alone is clearly insufficient. For Martinez it is her moral philosophy which privileges the rights and sovereignty of Indigenous peoples above the "good, humanitarian, moral and just work that is guised and wrapped up in 'extinction' and/or 'endangered species'" (p. 48).

This brings me to the subtitle of this volume, "how information shapes our common future." For both the contributions considered here, information (and in this commentary I have used 400 ppm to stand-in for information) is clearly insufficient to justify the conclusions they reach about what climate change signifies and for how it acquires cultural meaning. The futures they advocate, futures beyond climate change we might say, are inspired by particular sets of values – about what it means to be free and happy, about what it means to respect the rights and cultures of others. This is mobilizing more than information.

I am reminded of the claim made by the Alliance of Religions and Conservations in their 2007 statement on climate change (ARC, 2007):

> the climate change 'activist' world ... has all too often sought refuge in random use of apocalyptic imagery without seeking to harness the power of narrative. The emphasis on consumption, economics and policy [and science I can add] usually fails to engage people at any deep level because it does not address the narrative, the mythological, the metaphorical or the existence of memories of past disasters and the way out. Without narrative, few people are ever moved to change or adapt. The faiths have been masters of this for centuries.

Information is inescapable and, it seems today, increasingly unlimited. But information can only be held together meaningfully through constructed narratives which convey truth, engage the imagination, and inspire virtuous human acts. It is these which we are most in need of today.

References

350.org. (2013). 350.org. Retrieved May 9, 2013: http://350.org.

ARC. (2007). *UN and ARC launch programme with faiths on climate change*. Alliance of Religions and Conservation/UNDP Programme Statement on Climate Change, December 7. Retrieved May 9, 2013: http://www.arcworld.org/news.asp?pageID=207.

Cameron, E. S. (2012). Securing indigenous politics: A critique of the vulnerability and adaptation approach to the human dimensions of climate change in the Canadian Arctic. *Global Environmental Change*, 22(1), 103–114.

Hastrup, K. (2013). Anthropological contributions to the study of climate: past, present, future *WIREs Climate Change*, 4(4), 269–281.

Hulme, M. (2008). Geographical work at the boundaries of climate change. *Transactions of the Institute of British Geographers*, 33(1), 5–11.

Latour, B. (2013). *An inquiry into modes of existence: An anthropology of the moderns*. Cambridge, MA: Harvard University Press.

Onehundredmonths.org. (2013). Onehundredmonths.org. Retrieved May 9, 2013: http://onehundredmonths.org.

Said, E. W. (1978). *Orientalism*. London: Vintage Books.

PART II

Media as actors and contributors to climate politics and policy

3

#CLIMATENEWS

Summit journalism and digital networks

Matthew Tegelberg, Dmitry Yagodin and
Adrienne Russell

Introduction

The issue of climate change in general and United Nations climate summits in particular offers a rich case to study the changing media landscape and the new actors, tools, and practices that increasingly shape associated coverage. At climate summits, geo-political realities collide with the politics of the climate justice movement, creating opportunities to examine the ways media activists doing journalism-related work and professional journalists influence one another in terms of practice and content. Elisabeth Eide and Risto Kunelius have suggested that climate summits provide unique moments to investigate these networks of communication flows since they "enable and force global and national civil society actors to interact with representatives of states and international political bodies" (Eide, Kunelius & Kumpu, 2010, p. 12). This chapter examines what role emerging digital media platforms play in facilitating exchanges between the diverse cross section of actors that come together at UN climate summits. It also considers how and to what extent these actors compete or collaborate in the complex networks of communication which emerge during these events.

During the UN climate summits in Copenhagen (COP15) and Durban (COP17), independent and commercial media outlets, activists, and NGOs introduced an array of innovative online platforms, content, and collaborations. This chapter tracks, analyzes, and compares some of these trends in news coverage of the 2009 and 2011 climate summits in Canada, the United States, and Russia. It combines content analysis, interviews, and web mapping to locate and visualize issue networks, placing emphasis on how the networked news environment around climate change has evolved since 2009.[1] Three national cases were selected in order to identify similarities and differences in the connections between organizations, actors, and issues, as well as the differing levels of activist and social media integration in these particular climate news networks. The choice of these nations also corresponds with our broader efforts to understand how and to what extent digital climate news travels across differing linguistic and cultural news systems (see Russell et al., 2012). By comparing two North American cases, where climate news moves fluidly between highly developed online and offline English-language news networks, with the Russian case, where online news is expanding rapidly while the national media space remains relatively isolated and exclusive, we aim to expand the scope of our research beyond the limits of English-language centered digital news networks. The case studies provide evidence of two significant changes in online climate news practices and products: a heightened level of integration between activist and social media news content and the increasingly widespread adoption of Twitter and other digital tools by professional journalists working in all three national contexts. The chapter concludes with a discussion of future directions for research on media and climate change.

Digital climate news landscapes from Copenhagen to Durban

It is widely acknowledged that traditional journalism, or journalism produced by professionals and distributed primarily via mass media, is declining in many areas of the world, with business models failing and public trust waning (Pew Research Center, 2010; Schudson & Downie, 2009). Some fear this is leading to a decline in accountability journalism (McChesney & Nichols, 2010), while others celebrate the new forms of horizontal watchdog journalism that are emerging, which include everyday voices, eschew the appearance of objectivity, and treat journalism as a collaborative endeavor rather than one based on competition between journalists and among media outlets (Benson, 2010; Shirky, 2009). A growing number of scholars have argued that this mass entry of so-called amateurs introduces a new variable into the mediascape – and into journalism in particular (Benkler, 2006; Benson, 2010; Jenkins, 2006; Papacharissi & Oliveira, 2012). According to Zizi Papacharissi and Maria de Fátima Oliveira (2012), a blend of subjective experience, opinion, and emotion is increasingly making its way into the global news media landscape. The authors refer to this blending process as an *affective news stream*, where distinctive news products are collaboratively constructed by an array of professional and non-professional news makers (2012, pp. 279–280). Questions remain among journalists and journalism scholars, however, about how the amateur variable is influencing the field and to what end. This chapter examines how this mingling of professional and alternative journalism and the shifting journalistic norms and practices that accompany it is reflected in news coverage of UN climate summits.

The UN climate summit in Copenhagen (COP 15) created an unprecedented stir among civic activists and media organizations, which also acted as a catalyst for the emergence of a complex model of networked news coverage in the context of climate journalism. While traditional national print and broadcast journalists worked in cordoned off sections of the Bella Centre, the news of the summit that unfolded was more significantly shaped by those on the other side of the ropes. The raw material – audio, visual, and textual documentation of the event – generated by activists, NGO representatives, institutional and independent journalists, politicians, and delegates at COP15 later became the content for news stories, reports, and feeds. These different streams of media were brought together on Web platforms like Climate Pulse, created by the Italian online platform development company eVectors, which monitored and aggregated blog posts, news websites, Twitter, and a range of other online sources. Climate Pulse widgets made content available on third-party sites and user feedback, ratings, and comments on the widgets was fed back into the general flow of Climate Pulse's coverage of the summit.

Official and unofficial partnerships were also established between journalists and activist groups. Copenhagen News Collaborative, for example, was created by *Mother Jones* and *The Nation*, politically liberal investigative magazines, and TreeHugger, an online environmental advocacy outlet, to run an alternative news wire of about 40 reporters, editors, and commentators. The participatory media hub The Uptake, which trains "citizen journalists" to use innovative methods of low-cost information gathering and reporting, such as live broadcasting from cell phone camera feeds, shared resources at COP15 with members of the Copenhagen News Collaborative. The hub offered tech support and reporting resources, while simultaneously posting footage and reports on their site.

Climate Pulse and Copenhagen News Collaborative each combined rich media from a variety of genres including advocacy journalism, analysis, straight reports, and dispatches from the scene, with a range of sources including professional journalists, activists, NGOs, scientists, and politicians. Mainstream news outlets also pooled resources and attempted to connect with the public and generate user content. One example was Climate Pool, a Facebook page, created by AP and 10 other international news agencies including France's AFP, Portugal's LUSA, and Russia's RIA Novosti, to facilitate communication between journalists and the public during COP15. Professional journalists, in turn, used Twitter to provide dispatches from the action. Re-tweets of amateur material taken from personal feeds became part of the reporting. Zizi Papacharissi and Maria Oliveira suggest "the use of Twitter by journalists, news organizations, and individual users creates a complex and networked system of social awareness. These patterns introduce hybridity into the news system by further blurring boundaries between information, news, and entertainment" (Papacharissi & Oliveira, 2012, p. 3). And it is precisely this sort of complex network that we observed in the online networks of climate communication that emerged during the COP summits.

In 2011, news interest in the UN climate summit in Durban, South Africa diminished significantly in many parts of the world (Eide and Kunelius, 2012b). This lack of interest is explained, in part, by a significant decline in overall news coverage of climate change (Boykoff, 2011; Brainard, 2013). However, coverage of COP17 continued to reflect the growing complexity of online news products and practices, with journalists and media activists often using the same tools and platforms that were rolled out in Copenhagen. These different streams of media were brought together in online platforms like Oneclimate.net, a social networking space dedicated to sharing ideas and encouraging action on climate change. OneClimate editor Adam Groves was self-reflexive about how to build a new, participatory news environment:

> When we debrief in a few weeks we'll be talking about the emphasis on live and interactive versus 10 minutes ago. The more you commit yourself to live the more you are constrained in some ways – you are tied to one spot, you are subject to the chaos of what's going on around you.
>
> (Personal Correspondence, 2011)

OneClimate's live-streaming was set in the context of a larger narrative by combining it with round-the-clock news, analysis, and audio/video interactions.

These examples attest to the emergence of a dynamic field of communication that can serve as a resource for traditional reporting or as an alternative to mainstream news outlets, depending on the context. More specifically, they highlight the influence Internet users can exert on the engineering and architecture of the global news environment. The reconfiguration of technological tools and networks and the remediation of content, seen in coverage of climate summits, are becoming essential to the process by which institutional and participatory media engage with one another. These new modes of organization facilitate what Bennett and Segerberg call connective action (2012). Their work on social action proposes that the underlying social and political dynamics of protest have changed significantly due to the ways in which politics, social institutions, and identity formation have been altered by economic globalization. Bennett and Segerberg suggest that ideology, party loyalties, and elections are being replaced with issue networks that offer more personalized, activist-oriented solutions for problems. These new configurations of activism also suggest that powerful new spaces of public discourse with the capacity to transcend national borders are emerging.

The case of summit journalism resonates with this broader transformation and draws attention to the possibilities it opens for new actors to contribute to a media landscape where the lines between traditional and emergent journalisms are becoming thin and elastic. Scholars have focused attention on the liberating potential of these shifts, as well as the repressive potential of technologies, especially in the context of authoritarian governments. There is little research, however, that addresses social media's influence on how news varies in different national and political contexts. Hence, this chapter aims to provide a more nuanced understanding of the various fields of journalistic production by examining online news coverage of two climate summits in three national contexts.

#method: mapping and tracking online climate news

Our methodological approach combines content analysis and detailed description with the use of IssueCrawler to map and analyze the overlap between traditional and emergent forms of journalism in three national contexts. Combining these methods enables us to provide quantitative observations on each of the summits (number of articles, tweets, blog entries, presence of journalists and bloggers, etc.) and qualitative observations on how journalists and activists use online media tools (LiveJournal, blogs, and Twitter) to collaborate and exchange information in the process of communicating climate news.

The content analysis is based on two previous studies that focused on coverage of COP15 and COP17 in two major newspapers from each national context (Eide, Kunelius, & Kumpu, 2010; Eide and Kunelius, 2012a). Stories with the keywords 'climate,' 'Copenhagen,' and 'Durban' were collected over a three-week period from December 1 to December 22 in 2009 and from November 23 to December 14 in 2011. The sample was then analyzed to determine what extent content initially produced for online social media was referred to in newspaper coverage of both summits. Our next step was to map online coverage of COP15 and COP17 from the same period in Canada, the United States, and Russia. In each national context, a relevant selection of social media content published during the summits was run through IssueCrawler in order to identify connections between different sources of online climate news.

IssueCrawler is a web-mapping tool that maps connections among sites in order to visualize issue networks. The 'crawl' begins with a list of URLs that serve as starting points or seeds in a search to define the issue to be mapped. The crawler then identifies links present in the seeds, searches the pages these links point to, and repeats the process of finding and gathering links up to three times, depending on the crawl depth set by the researcher. To narrow results to a core network, IssueCrawler performs an analysis to find 'co-link' identifying sites linked to and from at least two of the starting points. The starting points for each national map consisted of five links representing relevant and active hubs of information and/or opinion on COP15 and COP17 – the news blog of one mainstream media outlet, two NGO blogs, and two other blogs (scientist, activist, etc.). Google is then used to identify the top-trafficked sites and choose starting points based on our own judgments concerning the relevance of these various sites to the summits. On the issue maps, each circle represents a site on the web. The circle size is determined by the number of links a site receives from other sites. The larger the circle, the more links and 'authority' a site is considered to have. The distance among circles is determined by the strength of the links between sites. The sites positioned at the center of the map are considered the 'core' and are central to the actual issue network. The final step in our analysis is to interpret these issue maps, observing differences and similarities in networked news coverage of COP15 and COP17.

Climate news in Canada, the United States, and Russia

In Canada and the United States, mainstream press coverage of climate change has been on the decline. In 2007, the release of the IPCC's Fourth Assessment Report and Al Gore's *An Inconvenient Truth* generated considerable public interest and engagement around the issue in both countries. However, since then, coverage has steadily diminished due, in part, to aggressive efforts to discredit climate science. *Toronto Star* columnist Antonia Zerbisias notes that while traditional media interest in climate change has waned, the Internet has kept the issue on the radar (Zerbisias, 2012). In *Who Speaks for the Climate? Making Sense of Media Reporting on Climate Change*, Maxwell Boykoff confirms this assessment arguing that online news coverage has been rising (Boykoff, 2011). In 2011, nearly eight out of 10 households in Canada (79.2 percent) and the U.S (78.1 percent) had access to the Internet (Internet World Statistics, 2011). Statistics Canada reported that half of all connected households use more than one type of device to go online and that over a third accessed the Internet from home using a wireless handheld device (Statistics Canada, 2011). The pervasiveness and widespread influence of mobile communications devices, combined with limited news budgets, help explain the decline in offline climate news and a corresponding rise in online coverage.

By contrast, less than half of Russia's population (44.3 percent) has access to the Internet. The majority of users prefer national versions of social networking sites and only 3.8 percent of Russians use Facebook (Internet World Statistics 2011). These numbers reflect the country's relatively low integration with global digital networks. The blogging platform LiveJournal.com, however, is widely used in Russia with more than 2.5 million users (LiveJournal Stats, 2012), making it a central node for online news. Interest groups use LiveJournal to build community networks and prominent bloggers can attract audiences that are comparable in size to a national daily newspaper. Despite a growth in the use of other online tools, such as Twitter and Facebook, LiveJournal remains the most popular platform for lengthy multimedia publications. LiveJournal's widespread popularity has led many Russian opinion leaders to engage in blogging subculture to expand their webs of influence, including national political elites encouraged by the example of former President Dmitry Medvedev (Yagodin, 2012). Naturally, civil society actors concerned about issues that are ignored in traditional media turn to LiveJournal as a means of engaging broader audiences. Past research on global climate news has shown Russian newspapers to be among the least interested in climate change of the 19 countries examined (Yagodin, 2010). The marginal status of climate news in traditional mass media may account for the higher level of attention the issue has received in the Russian blogosphere.

The following case studies demonstrate how traditional and emergent forms of journalism began to commingle in online and offline coverage of COP15 and COP17. In Canada and the US, this overlap moved in multiple directions with professional journalists using digital tools to broaden the scope of their coverage while grassroots actors worked with the same tools to attract the attention of mainstream news outlets. In both cases, online content became the focal point for climate news that appeared in the national mainstream press, attesting to a heightened blurring of the lines between professional and online climate news coverage. In the Russian context, however, there is a relatively weak integration of traditional and social media. In coverage of climate summits there remains a division between low mainstream interest in climate news and exposure to the issues at the same time as there is persistent coverage in the Russian blogosphere.

Canada

The Copenhagen summit (COP15) generated significant interest across a range of offline and online news sources in Canada. During COP15, Canada's two most widely circulated newspapers, *Toronto Star* and *Globe & Mail*, featured over 263 items with the keywords 'climate' and/or 'Copenhagen.' Each newspaper sent a reporter to Copenhagen, with their stories accounting for 17.2 percent of the total summit coverage (Tegelberg, 2010). In both newspapers, offline summit coverage often featured references to digital source material drawn from Facebook, blogs, and other digital tools and networks; a practice which, in turn, generated exposure to the perspectives of grassroots actors and groups in mainstream summit journalism.

In some instances, online source even became the focal point for a climate story during COP15, blurring the lines between professional, activist, and social news categories. This was exemplified by a *Toronto Star* feature article on Stephen McIntyre, a retired mining analyst and active blogger. Climate Audit is a personal blog McIntyre created in 2004, without any funding or formal expertise, to test the math behind climate research and share his findings. The article describes the significant impact McIntyre's fact-checking work has had on the scientific research community. According to the author, a 2006 report he produced, which questions the data used to construct the widely influential 'hockey stick' graph, resulted in a US National Academy of Sciences investigation and US congressional hearings. His subsequent research allegedly forced NASA to take back a mistaken claim that 1998 was the warmest year on record in the United States. This highly trafficked blog also helped McIntyre generate considerable mainstream media exposure during COP15. He was the subject of interviews with several major media outlets including CNN, *The Wall Street Journal*, and CTV news in Canada. The example demonstrates how journalists began looking to online social media as a source of content during COP15. Moreover, the positioning of a prominent citizen blogger as the focal point of a climate story attests to the role a diverse group of news producers can play in the journalistic field. In this case, McIntyre has effectively used digital tools to engage with international scientific and media channels; a clear instance of the heightened levels of integration between professional journalism and social networked news content in Canada.

Canadian environmental reporter Tyler Hamilton offered more evidence of the dynamic field of communication that emerged in the context of climate news at COP15. During the summit, Hamilton wrote stories for the *Toronto Star* that followed traditional journalistic norms and included standard reports on environmental policy, energy issues, sustainability, and the emerging clean technology environment. On his blog, cleanbreak.ca, Hamilton was more opinionated, distinguishing the blogger voice from his institutional voice at the

Toronto Star. Commenting on a public opinion survey released during COP15, he wrote, "The position of most Canadians couldn't be farther apart than the position of their federal government" (Hamilton, 2009). The title of a post from a few days later reads "Bipartisan U.S. climate bill is weak, but it still beats Canada." Hamilton's political rhetoric and advocacy stance contrasts with the standard tone of his reporting for the *Toronto Star*. The practice attests to a wider trend among professional journalists of using digital tools and platforms to voice opinions and link to relevant contextual information that is not always possible in institutional settings where they are constrained by form, space, and tradition.

In 2011, the Durban summit generated far less attention in print and online news sources in Canada. The two Canadian newspapers cited above published only 73 relevant news items within the same timeframe (Tegelberg & Roosvall, 2012). Geoffrey York, an African correspondent for the *Globe & Mail*, was the only Canadian reporter in Durban to cover the summit. York filed eight stories for the *Globe* during the summit. He also tweeted over 200 times, regularly updating followers on the proceedings. Several tweets included hyperlinks to York's reports for the *Globe*, as well as international press coverage of Canada's performance at the talks.

York often used social media to integrate alternative voices into his coverage, frequently drawing attention to the media strategies and content produced by Canadian activists. York was on location as six members of the Canadian Youth Delegation (CYD) turned their backs on Environment Minister Peter Kent during a speech. As the event unfolded, he tweeted that the protesters "were very Canadian: very polite and obedient as guards whisked them away" (York, 2011). Later York re-tweeted the reaction of a CYD activist after her colleagues were evicted from the summit: "viewpoint of Canadian youth: @amarapossian UNFCCC secretariat should be revoking Canadian gov't badges for disrupting progress, not ours." The next morning York's report for the *Globe* featured a large image depicting the Canadian activists with their backs to Kent. However, none of the CYD members were cited in the print article. This example demonstrates, once again, how online and offline news coverage from the same Canadian reporter took on different characteristics. The coverage of the event originated on Twitter and eventually made its way into print with the voices of different actors amplified in each context.

The CYD was also one of the more active groups in the Canadian blogosphere during COP17. Members of the CYD posted several times daily. These posts consisted of updates on the latest developments at COP17, poignant criticism of Canada's official stance at the climate talks, and provocative images of the group in action. These stimulating visuals generated exposure in offline press, as in the example above. Mainstream Canadian news blogs offered limited coverage of COP17. The CBC news blog 'Your Community' had seven posts on the climate talks and considerable discussion on comments pages. Large NGOs such as Pembina Institute and Equiterre also had a presence in the Canadian blogosphere. However, overlap between the activity on these blogs and offline media was less explicit. One noteworthy exception was an Op-Ed column in the *Globe & Mail* by Matt Horne, Director of Climate Change at Pembina Institute. The article included a link to Pembina's website where staff bloggers made several relevant posts during the summit.

The examples suggest that, in spite of a significant decline in the coverage of COP17, there continued to be overlap between professional journalism and emerging online media platforms in Canada. The case also reveals how Twitter and other social media platforms are changing Canadian news products by facilitating conversations and collaborations between professional journalists, grassroots actors, and media activists during COP summits.

The Canadian issue maps show Twitter as the largest node, positioned close to the center of a highly concentrated core of interconnected sites. The networks are fairly evenly distributed with links to a variety of science, NGO, activist, news, and government sites. Both maps show connections between the websites

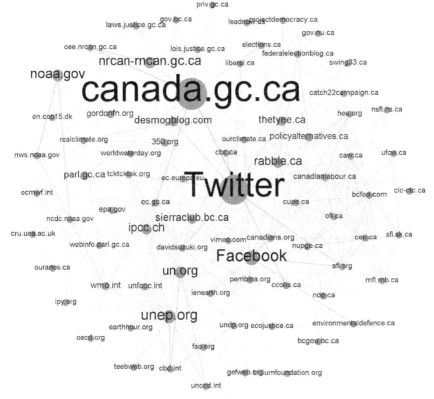

FIGURE 3.1   Issue Map for Canadian Digital Networks: COP 15. Data for this map was collected using IssueCrawler (www.issuecrawler.net) and visualized with the interactive platform Gephi (Bastian et al., 2009). A modified version of this issue map originally appeared in *Media Meets Climate: The Global Challenge for Journalism* (Eide and Kunelius, 2012).

of mainstream news outlets (CBC.ca, thetyee.ca, theglobeandmail.ca, gazette. ca), NGOs, and activist media sites (rabble.ca, sierraclub.ca, davidsuzuki.org, etc.) providing further evidence of the collaborations and exchanges between professional journalists, media activists, and other grassroots actors that took place during COP15 and COP17.

The Canadian issue maps show several connections to US blogs and government websites (350.org, desmogblog.com, noaa.gov, epa.gov), pointing to the ties between Canadian summit journalists, activists, and advocacy groups and the coverage produced by their counterparts in the United States. This differs from the US case where no Canadian links appear on either of the issue network maps (see Figures 3.3 and 3.4). The discrepancy suggests that the communication between professional journalists and advocacy groups in these two nations only flowed in one direction, from the United States to Canada. The Canadian maps highlight a strong presence of national institutions and labor unions (Environment Canada,

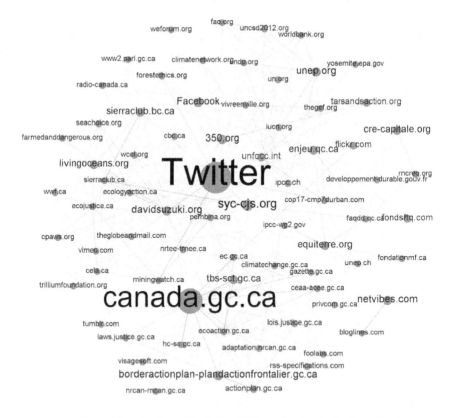

FIGURE 3.2 Issue Map for Canadian Digital Networks: COP 17. Data for this map was collected using IssueCrawler (www.issuecrawler.net) and visualized with the interactive platform Gephi (Bastian et al., 2009). A modified version of this issue map originally appeared in *Media Meets Climate: The Global Challenge for Journalism* (Eide and Kunelius, 2012).

Natural Resources Canada, Canadian Auto Workers' Union, and Canadian Labour Congress), attesting to the influential role governmental and non-governmental organizations continued to play in online issue networks. There are also nodes representing the French-language websites of several environmental organizations, based in the province of Quebec (fondsftq.com, tcktcktck.org, equiterre.org), that each maintained an active media presence during both summits.

United States

A 2012 report issued by Pew Research Center for People and the Press describes a US news media landscape in which more and more Americans are getting their news online than from radios or newspapers, and in which television is increasingly vulnerable to declining audiences as relatively inexpensive and mobile devices become ubiquitous. Nineteen percent of Americans say they got news from social networking sites in the 2012 survey, up from 9 percent in 2010. Moreover, Americans under 30 are now just as likely to get their news from social media as television or print (Pew Research Center, 2012).

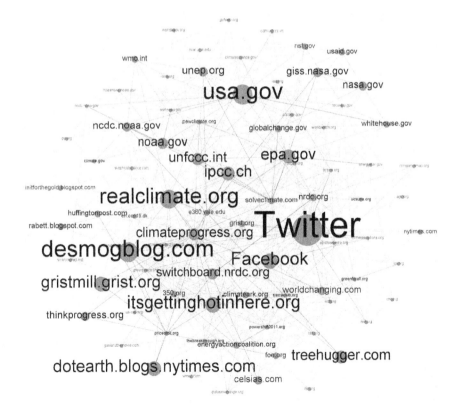

FIGURE 3.3 Issue Map for United States Digital Networks: COP 15

This shift from mass to networked production and distribution has come with significant shifts in journalism norms and practices; as well as in the character of the news landscape, which is no longer exclusively or even primarily dominated by traditional professional news outlets (Benkler, 2006; Benson, 2010; Rosen, 2006; Russell et al., 2008). Consequently, it makes sense to not only examine coverage by traditional news outlets but also material produced for online media platforms that Americans are increasingly accessing and relying on as a source of climate news. Several studies have documented the decline in the amount of climate coverage by traditional US news outlets since 2009, at the same time as there has been an upward trend in online networked climate news (Boykoff, 2011; Brulle et al., 2012). These broader trends between 2009 and 2011 are each reflected in coverage of COP15 and COP17. *The New York Times* and *USA Today* ran 102 stories during COP15 and, while this is sparse compared to coverage in the newspapers of other countries, it far exceeded the amount of relevant climate news (30 stories) that were published in these newspapers during COP17 (Russell, 2010).

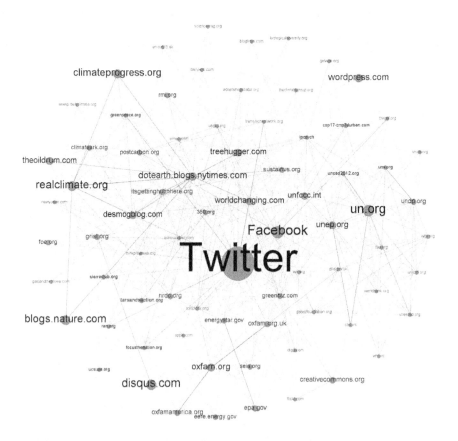

FIGURE 3.4   Issue Map for United States Digital Networks: COP 17

New York Times reporter and blogger Andrew Revkin walked a sometimes contentious line between what he referred to as "front page and homepage reporting." Just before COP15, the Times came under fire for their treatment of coverage of the hacked emails of several prominent climate scientists who were accused of being involved in a conspiracy to overstate the human influence on global warming. Revkin was accused by Steve Milloy, author of junkscience.com, among other so-called climate deniers of having "a conflict of interest" because he wrote or was mentioned in some of the emails that the University of East Anglia claimed were stolen. Others wondered why *The New York Times* did not make the email available on its website, and scoffed at a blog post where Revkin explained that the emails contained "private information and statements that were never intended for the public eye." Others accused *The New York Times* of playing down a story with global implications.[2] The attention *The New York Times* paid to the accusations of a community of skeptical bloggers attests to the influential role content from social media platforms began to play in mainstream journalistic coverage of COP15.

New media platforms also gave voice to climate justice activists. The US-based activist group the Yes Men became part of the COP15 news cycle by orchestrating a mock press release to announce that Canada would make an ambitious 40 percent cut in its emissions by 2020. ClimatePool arranged a real time web question and answer session with the pranksters. People asked questions via Facebook and Twitter about the group's aims and tactics, deepening coverage of the prank and engaging networked publics in the story. This online interactive forum broke the standard mold of protest coverage, providing the Yes Men with a platform to communicate their view of the issues at COP15 to a wider audience and therefore expanding the sphere of legitimate debate (Hallin, 1986). In the mass media era, traditional news media largely defined the sphere of legitimate debate because the public was connected to the media but not to one another. Today it is much cheaper and easier for user-participants to find each other and exchange opinions and information. In doing so they often realize that the official news-generated sphere of debate doesn't reflect their own (Rosen, 2006).

New York Times coverage of COP17 was also clearly informed by activist media networks at work trying to influence the actual events and media framings of the summit. John Broder, the *New York Times* reporter in Durban, filed a story on December 8th that highlighted voices critical of the US role in negotiations, including activist Abigail Borah, a 21-year-old college student thrown out of the summit for criticizing US tactics. The story also described US negotiator Todd Stern's language as "convoluted" and his endorsement of the EU plan as "ambiguous." Broder tweeted twice from Durban, one read "I think I got my point across" and linked to the story from December 8th. The tweet refers to a statement by Abigail Borah, but also seems to reinforce Broder's critical assessment of the US delegation. Andrew Revkin tweeted frequently during the summit, even though he was not in attendance. He acknowledged that news flows from activist and social media outlets were far more robust than legacy journalism, encouraging readers to use Twitter for "the best way to track the finale and afterthoughts" (Revkin, 2011). The climate justice movement and its media activists used sophisticated tools and platforms to create alternative news content to counter this faux balance and challenge the status quo; with some of these efforts generating varying degrees of mainstream interest and exposure.

The United States issue map shows Facebook and Twitter at the center of a dense core made up of NGOs, including 350.org, Sierra Club, and SustainUS; online blogs and magazines such as Worldchanging, Treehugger, Desmogblog, and New York Times' Dotearth blog; and the United Nations Framework Convention on Climate Change site. Main climate blogs, Dotearth and Desmogblog, generated many links to diverse sources, including governmental sites and UN institutions. Another large node, 350.org, also generated many links, the majority of which are to other NGOs and activist sites. The role of UN institutions (upper right sector of the map) is more visible than the role of US government (lower left side).

The maps of the US issue network also show strong connections between various blogs, governmental websites (epa.gov), ecological movements (350.org), and other non-profit organizations (grist.org). However, the role of mainstream media blogs (Huffingtonpost.com) appears to be relatively weak. In fact, the maps in Figures 3.3 and 3.4 suggest that the online climate debate in the US mostly focused on national grassroots movements, specialized state agencies, and well-developed collective blogs.

Russia

In Russia, COP15 and COP17 were marginal events on the public agenda not unlike the issue of climate change in general. During both summits, digital networks were mostly a site of content sharing and a means of delivery rather than a platform for innovative news-making or a powerful channel for grassroots voices. COP15 generated more media attention and involved extended coverage of President Medvedev's participation in the summit. More Russian journalists reported from the scene than ever before and environmental organizations used blogs and other digital tools to disseminate information and perspectives on the event. In total, 36 journalists represented Russia in Copenhagen (Painter, 2010, p. 29) while only three went to Durban. During COP15, digital networks served as a tool for concerted action, unifying the efforts of international environmental groups, political institutions, and global media which, in turn, mobilized eco-activists to produce local accounts. The efforts created a powerful external discourse that the media and political establishment inside Russia could not disregard. By contrast, COP17 went largely unnoticed by the mainstream media and had a rather limited presence in digital networks (Russell et al., 2012, p. 204).

There are two contrasting examples of the overlap between traditional and emerging forms of journalism in Russian climate news. First, in the LiveJournal blog of Vladimir Chuprov from Greenpeace Russia (diary_cop15.livejournal. com) we can observe bottom-up attempts to report climate news from the scene

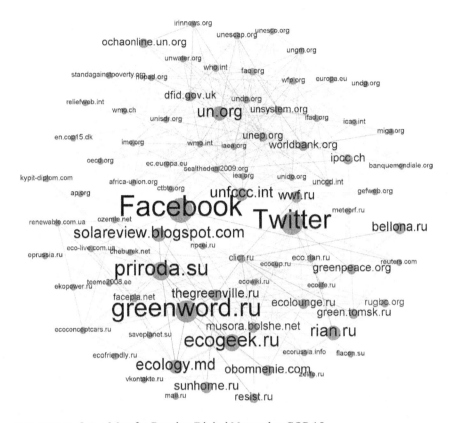

FIGURE 3.5 Issue Map for Russian Digital Networks: COP 15

at COP15. His contribution included 22 blog entries based on original textual and visual content, which were cross-posted and occasionally cited on other blogs. Chuprov's first-hand accounts of events in Copenhagen were not directly used in the news media. However, several journalists interviewed Chuprov, as an environmental expert: he was one of the main voices in several *RBKdaily* articles (Liul'chak, 2009; Leonov & Liul'chak, 2009) and *Slon.ru* included a link to his LiveJournal page (Chapkovsky, 2009). Ten of Chuprov's publications appeared in the news section of the Russian Greenpeace website. Given the generally low coverage of COP15 in Russian media, such an output by a single activist is remarkable.

In another example, Olga Dobrovidova reported on COP17 for the Russian news agency *RIA Novosti* and supplemented her work by using Twitter and LiveJournal. Her attempt to integrate online tools into the traditional routine of news-making was hampered by lack of time and weak ties within digital climate networks. Dobrovidova registered her Twitter (@thegreendrafts) and LiveJournal (o-dobrovidova.livejournal.com) accounts shortly before the trip to Durban but did not have enough followers or connections with other climate bloggers and journalists to make full use of these digital networks. Consequently, Dobrovidova

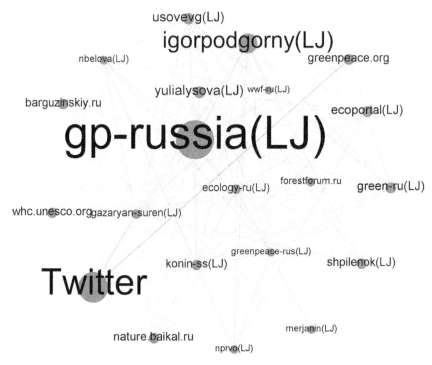

FIGURE 3.6 Issue Map for Russian Digital Networks: COP 17

mainly used Twitter to stay informed by following relevant news sources and the work of prominent English-speaking climate journalists at *BBCEarth, NYTimes Science,* and *Reuters Science News.* These two examples demonstrate potential advantages and difficulties with the widespread integration and adoption of new media tools by traditional journalism, on one hand, and emerging grassroots voices on the other. Broadened opportunities for media participation allow activists like Chuprov to fill in the gap of climate news in mainstream journalism. At the same time, the example of Dobrovidova illustrates that effective communication through social media needs established networks of followers or subscribers, just as traditional media outlets need an audience.

Correspondingly, issue maps representing the dominant news nodes in Russian online space during COP15 and COP17 point to a limited extension in the scope of these networks (see Figures 3.5 and 3.6). The Copenhagen issue map shows a strong linkage between international NGOs, UN institutions, and local environmental sites. However, there are almost no connections to mainstream journalistic sites. The Durban issue map had news media and NGO sites among the starting points for the issue crawl but these sites eventually dropped out of the network due to limited or missing connections with the other nodes. The results suggest the low profile of COP17 left the Russian climate news network confined to LiveJournal, environmental blogs, and other digital platforms, with Twitter occasionally playing a complementary role.

Conclusion

The Russian case study exemplifies a relatively weak exchange of information between professional journalists and social media activists. In coverage of both climate summits, there is a clear divide between low mainstream interest and exposure and persistent coverage in the Russian blogosphere. Journalists are beginning to use new media tools and platforms to connect with online networks. However, the role of social networks and micro-blogs is limited to a small number of websites and active environmental bloggers. In Canada and the United States, high levels of Internet access, coupled with a wider variety of social media platforms and content produced more dynamic exchanges between professional journalists, activists, and other grassroots actors in mainstream and emergent forms of summit journalism. This was evidenced by the rising influence of blogs and social networks like Twitter and Facebook. The popularity of these social media platforms facilitated collaborations and dialogue between actors from diverse spheres of influence. This was reflected by networked news environments in both national contexts with greater signs of commingling between activism and journalism. This differed from the less liberal context of networked climate news in Russia where coverage remained characterized by the separation between institutional media forms and a civic culture of densely concentrated blog networks.

This chapter used basic tools of network analysis to visualize digital networks that emerged during online coverage of two UN climate summits. The method is useful for measuring the scale and outreach of digital networks in different national contexts. However, because this type of network analysis demands a great deal of interpretation, future research on networked climate news must design more sophisticated methods of mapping, tracking, and analyzing online news coverage. This chapter takes steps in that direction by demonstrating how content analysis, thick description, and mapping tools from network analysis can be combined to identify key trends in the networked news coverage that emerges around a climate event. It also draws attention to the necessity for broader comparative research that describes and interprets networked climate news coverage in diverse national and international contexts. The three cases examined here begin to provide evidence of how differing cultural and political factors shape and influence the dynamics of the digital news networks that form around the issue of climate change.

Notes

1 The scope of the chapter is limited to material from COP15 and COP17 and does not include coverage of COP16 in Cancún or material from the most recent UN climate summit in Doha (COP18). However, the material examined in the chapter is sufficient to offer a preliminary picture of the networked news landscape which emerges in different cultural and political contexts during COP summits.
2 See ombudsman Clark Hoyt's opinion piece addressing these accusations (Hoyt, 2009).

References

Bastian, M., Heymann S., & Jacomy, M. (2009). *Gephi: An open source software for exploring and manipulating networks.* International AAAI Conference on Weblogs and Social Media.

Benkler, Y. (2006). *The wealth of networks: How social production transforms markets and freedom.* New Haven, CT: Yale University Press.

Bennett, W. L. & Segerberg, A. (2012). The logic of connective action. *Information, Communication & Society,* 15(5), 739–768.

Benson, R. (2010). Futures of the news: International considerations and further reflections. In N. Fenton (Ed.), *New media, old news: Journalism and democracy in the digital age,* (pp. 187–200). London: Sage Publications.

Boykoff, M.T. (2011). *Who speaks for the climate? Making sense of media reporting on climate change.* Cambridge: Cambridge University Press.

Brainard, C. (2013). Climate coverage rebound? Maybe, but the press has a long way to go, *Columbia Journalism Review,* January 7. Retrieved February 16, 2013: http://www.cjr.org/the_observatory/climate_change_global_warming.php.

Brulle, R. J., Carmichael, J., & Jenkins, J. C. (2012). Shifting public opinion on climate change: An empirical assessment of factors influencing concern over climate change in the US, 2002–2010. *Climatic Change,* 114(2), 169–188.

Chapkovsky, P. (2009). Rossiia mozhet obrushit' uglerodnie rynki. *Slon.ru,* December 8. Retrieved November 25, 2012: http://slon.ru/world/rossiya_mozhet_obrushit_uglerodnye_rynki-206991.xhtml.

Eide, E. & Kunelius, R. (2012a). Moment of hope, mode of realism: On the dynamics of a transnational journalistic field during UN climate change summits. *International Journal of Communication,* 6, 266–285.

Eide, E. & Kunelius, R. (Eds.). (2012b). *Media meets climate: The global challenge for journalism.* Sweden: Nordicom.

Eide, E., Kunelius, R., & Kumpu, V. (Eds.). (2010). *Global climate, local journalisms: A transnational study of how media make sense of climate summits.* Freiburg: Projekt Verlag.

Hallin, D. (1986). *The uncensored war: The media and Vietnam.* New York: Oxford University Press.

Hamilton, T. (2009). Copenhagen brain squeeze: Day 2. *Clean Break,* December 8. Retrieved December 25, 2012: http://www.cleanbreak.ca/2009/12/08/copenhagen-brain-squeeze-day-2.

Hoyt, C. (2009). Stolen e-mail, stoking the climate debate. *New York Times,* December 6. Retrieved February 21, 2013: http://www.nytimes.com/2009/12/06/opinion/06pubed.html?_r=1&.

Internet World Statistics, 2011. *Internet usage and population in North America.* Internetworldstats.com. Retrieved February 10, 2012: http://www.internetworldstats.com/stats14.htm.

Issue Crawler. (2012). Retrieved December, 2012: https://www.issuecrawler.net/.

Jenkins, H. (2006). *Convergence culture: Where old and new media collide.* New York: NYU Press.

Leonov, V. and Liul'chak, E. (2009). Holodnoe poteplenie, *RBCdaily,* December 18. Retrieved November 25, 2012: http://www.rbcdaily.ru/2009/12/18/focus/562949978994735.

Liul'chak, E. (2009). Kopengagenu ne do klimata. *RBCdaily,* December 17. Retrieved November 25, 2012: http://www.rbcdaily.ru/2009/12/17/focus/562949978994867.

Livejournal Stats. (2012). Livejournal.com. Retrieved December 6, 2012: http://www.livejournal.com/stats.bml.

McChesney, R. & Nichols, J. (2010). *The life and death of great American journalism.* New York: Nation Books.

Painter, J. (2010). *Summoned by science: Reporting climate change at Copenhagen and beyond.* London: Reuters Institute for the Study of Journalism.

Papacharissi, Z. & Oliveira, M. (2012). Affective news and networked publics: The rhythms of news storytelling on #Egypt. *Journal of Communication,* 62(2), 266–282.

Personal Correspondence. 2011. Interview with A. Groves, editor at One Climate, December 5. Interview by Adrienne Russell [recorded]. UN Climate Change Conference, Durban, South Africa.

Pew Research Center. (2010). The state of the news media: An annual report on American journalism. *Pew Project for Excellence in Journalism.* Retrieved March 5, 2010: http://stateofthemedia.org/2010/overview-3/key-findings.

Pew Research Center. (2012). In changing news landscape, even television is vulnerable. *Trends in News Consumption,* September 27. Retrieved February 10, 2013: http://www.people-press.org/2012/09/27/in-changing-news-landscape-even-television-is-vulnerable.

Revkin, A. (2011). Young voices reverberate at indeterminate climate talks. *New York Times, DotEarth,* December 10. Retrieved March 10, 2012: http://dotearth.blogs.nytimes.com/2011/12/10/young-voices-at-deadlocked-durban-climate-talks.

Rosen, J. (2006). The people formerly known as the audience. *Pressthink,* June 27. Retrieved April 10, 2012: http://archive.pressthink.org/2006/06/27/ppl_frmr.html.

Russell, A. (2010). The United States: Old media, new journalism – the changing landscape of climate news. In E. Eide, R. Kunelius, & V. Kumpu (Eds.), *Global climate, local journalisms: A transnational study of how media make sense of climate summits* (pp. 325–339). Freiburg: Projekt Verlag.

Russell, A., Ito, M., Richmond, T., & Tuters, M. (2008). Culture: Media convergence and networked participation. In K. Varnelis (Ed.), *Networked Publics* (pp. 43–76). Cambridge, MA: MIT Press.

Russell, A., Tegelberg, M., Yagodin, D., Kumpu, V., & Rhaman, M. (2012). Digital networks and shifting climate news agendas and practices. In E. Eide & R. Kunelius (Eds.), *Media meets climate: The global challenge for journalism* (pp. 195–217). Sweden: Nordicom.

Schudson, M. & Downie, L. (2009). The reconstruction of American journalism. *Columbia Journalism Review,* October 19. Retrieved January 5, 2012: http://www.cjr.org/reconstruction/the_reconstruction_of_american.php.

Shirky, C. (2009). Newspapers and thinking the unthinkable. *Shirky.com,* March 13. Retrieved January 5, 2012: http://www.shirky.com/weblog/2009/03/newspapers-and-thinking-the-unthinkable.

Statistics Canada. (2011). Canadian internet use survey. Retrieved February 10, 2012: http://www.statcan.gc.ca/daily-quotidien/110525/dq110525b-eng.htm.

Tegelberg, M. (2010). Canada: The dirty old man of climate politics? In E. Eide, R. Kunelius, & V. Kumpu (Eds.), *Global climate, local journalisms: A transnational study of how media make sense of climate summits* (pp. 97–114). Freiburg: Projekt Verlag.

Tegelberg, M. & Roosvall, A. (2012). Misframing the messenger: Scales of justice, traditional ecological knowledge and media coverage of Arctic indigenous peoples and climate change. In E. Eide & R. Kunelius (Eds.), *Media meets climate: The global challenge for journalism* (pp. 297–312). Sweden: Nordicom.

Yagodin, D. (2010). Russia: Listening to the wind – clientism and climate change. In E. Eide, R. Kunelius, & V. Kumpu (Eds.), *Global climate, local journalisms: A transnational study of how media make sense of climate summits* (pp. 275–290). Freiburg: Projekt Verlag.

Yagodin, D. (2012). Blog medvedev: Aiming for public consent. *Europe-Asia Studies*, 64(8), 1415–1434.

York, G. (2011). Viewpoint of Canadian youth. *Twitter*, December 7. Retrieved January 28, 2012: https://twitter.com/geoffreyyork.

Zerbisias, A. (2012). Climate change coverage by the media diminishing as Earth continues to heat up. *Toronto Star*, December 10. Retrieved April 7, 2012: http://www.thestar.com/news/insight/2012/01/13/climate_change_coverage_by_the_media_diminishing_as_earth_continues_to_heat_up.html.

4

TV WEATHERCASTERS AND CLIMATE EDUCATION IN THE SHADOW OF CLIMATE CHANGE CONFLICT

Vanessa Schweizer, Sara Cobb, William Schroeder, Grace Chau and Edward Maibach

Introduction

Public opinion remains strongly divided in the United States on various issues related to climate change such as whether it is happening, whether human activities are to blame, and how to respond (e.g., Leiserowitz et al., 2010). Nevertheless, across the spectrum of American public opinion, television broadcast meteorologists (hereafter called 'weathercasters') are consistently rated as trustworthy sources of information on global warming (Leiserowitz et al., 2010). Additionally, weather reports are one of the most reliable draws to news in the US in general (Silcock et al., 2007; Smith, 2007). Because weathercasters play unique roles in news reporting – that is, they are regular fixtures in the daily news, and their topic area (weather) is recognized by the public as related to climate – they could potentially serve as informal science educators[1] on climate change (Wilson, 2008).

However, in contrast to the consensus on human-caused climate change existing in the scientific community (Anderegg et al., 2010; Doran & Zimmerman, 2009), weathercasters' views on climate change are diverse. Recent surveys of American weathercasters (Maibach et al., 2010; Maibach et al., 2011a) reveal that significant numbers of weathercasters remain unconvinced that human activities are the principal cause of a changing climate. In line with scholarship on the moderating effects of political orientation on climate change attitudes among members of the general public (e.g., McCright, 2011), some have concluded that the climate change views of weathercasters can also be explained primarily by their political views (Maibach et al., 2011b; Wilson, 2012). In contrast to those studies, this work examines weathercaster views through the lens of conflict analysis. This study does more than simply examine weathercaster views in a new light; we contend that interpretive conflict analysis introduces an additional technique for investigating data typically overlooked or treated anecdotally in survey studies.

In this chapter, we discuss insights obtained through an interpretive conflict analysis of the climate change views of TV weathercasters. Our analytical approach restores the personalism of the climate change conflict, and, hopefully, provides new meaning and helpful strategies for moving past unproductive conflict. Differences between weathercaster views, and the motivations for those views, may bear implications for actively enlisting weathercasters as informal climate change educators. In this chapter, we explore these issues in four parts, where we first provide brief essential background to the approach of our study. Second, we describe our analytical methods, which are rooted in scholarship on conflict resolution. Third, we describe our main findings on three types of barriers perceived by weathercasters to actively delivering informal climate education (occupational, interpersonal, and cultural). Fourth, we discuss how these barriers exert constraints on weathercasters in different ways, which may also bear implications for their orientations toward climate education.

Background

A recent survey (Maibach et al., 2011a) of American weathercasters (n = 430) found five distinct views on climate change. These views, and their prevalence among weathercasters, are: (1) global warming is happening, and it is due primarily to human activities (19 percent); (2) global warming is happening, and it is due about equally to human activities and natural causes (35 percent); (3) global warming is happening, and it is due primarily to natural causes (29 percent); (4) undecided whether global warming is happening (8 percent); and (5) global warming is not happening (9 percent).[2] This diversity of views among weathercasters, and the fact that most of these views diverge from the scientific consensus (81 percent of weathercasters, segments 2–5), suggests that much could be learned from further study of weathercasters' views.

It is important to note, however, that framing weathercasters who do not hold the scientific consensus view as climate change "skeptics" does little to illuminate the complexity of their views. Research on "skeptic discourses" (e.g., Hobson & Niemeyer, 2012) reveals the presence of multiple and distinct discourses, each with its own world view, belief structures, and associated scenarios. Hobson and Niemeyer (2012) identified and labeled five distinct examples of skeptic discourses, which shows that those who do not agree with the scientific consensus have diverse and at times competing views. This generates opportunity for conflict within and across the skeptic categories, as well as open conflict with those that espouse the scientific consensus. Even talking about climate change in a public setting can invoke the conflict between these discursive groups, as Hobson and Niemeyer (2012) found while they studied the evolution of these discourses over the course of a public deliberation.[3] For this reason, the analytical tools employed for conflict resolution may offer a foundation for both understanding differences between groups as well as for supporting engagement across these groups. This chapter is an example of continued scholarship on the diversity of discourses around climate change and possible opportunities for moving past unproductive conflict.

Methods

In this study, conflict is defined as a dynamic in which two or more descriptions about reality compete for legitimacy. In settings characterized by conflict, parties cast their own viewpoints as legitimate and the viewpoints of others as illegitimate. Under these circumstances, the likelihood of communication and learning across parties diminishes; in other words, communication itself falls victim to polarization (Deutsch et al., 2006). However, analyzing the drivers and structure of conflict can uncover strategies that could defuse it. In this chapter, we inspect different understandings of climate change conflict across five weathercaster segments (Maibach et al., 2011a) through narrative and positioning analysis.

Our dataset consists of recorded conversations about climate change with 75 weathercasters at a professional meeting hosted by the American Meteorological Society, or AMS (Schweizer et al., 2011). These conversations took place in the context of (1) semi-structured in-depth interviews (n = 48; interviews were audio recorded and transcribed) or (2) a problem-solving workshop (n = 27; plenary discussions were audio recorded and transcribed; small-group discussions were not audio recorded but recorded with hand-written notes). Problem-solving workshops are an approach for conflict analysis and resolution that creates a space for participants to (a) express emotion, (b) reflect on the history of the conflict, and (c) engage in mutual learning about shared suffering (Rouhana & Kelman, 1994). The objectives of problem-solving workshops are to create an environment that enables conflicting parties to transform their relationships with each other and to challenge existing beliefs and storylines that are the root of the conflict (Kelman & Ezekiel, 1970). We accomplished this through a facilitated exercise elaborated in the next paragraph.

The problem-solving workshop began with weathercasters reflecting on the climate change conflict collectively. After a plenary and dyad discussion, weathercasters were asked to self-select into breakout affinity groups[4] corresponding to each of the five segments. Within the affinity groups, weathercasters reflected on which of the other groups had the greatest differences from their own, what those differences were, and considered additional questions contrasting the essential assumptions of their affinity group to the group most different from themselves. After the breakout, weathercasters returned to plenary to report on their discussions and revisit their perceptions of the climate change conflict as a large group.

In our overall conflict analysis, responses to questions from the interviews and discussions from the workshop were analyzed separately in their own contexts and then compared to identify storylines operant by weathercaster segment. To enable a segmented analysis of weathercasters' statements, interviews began with asking weathercasters to classify their climate change views into one of the five segments (Yes-Human, Yes-Human & Natural, Yes-Natural, Don't Know, No). Interviewees were then invited to elaborate on why that segment best represented their views as well as to explain their understandings of why some scientists think the climate is changing primarily due to human activities. Similarly, in the problem-solving workshop setting, the breakout affinity group session provided weathercaster statements by segment.

Our narrative analysis of weathercasters' statements drew on Hajer and Versteeg's (2005) notion of "storyline" and its relation to environmental conflict. Narrative analysis (Labov and Waletzky, 1967) began with transcripts from the interviews, where special attention was paid to scientific claims made by weathercasters (related either to scientific facts or practices) to justify their climate change views. We then identified features of each storyline (Chatman, 1980) relative to Freytag's (2008) five-part plot structure (i.e., exposition, rising action, climax, falling action, and resolution). Analysis of storyline plot structure reveals, in the speaker's view, protagonists and antagonists, as well as other storyline qualities such as how the conflict is framed. For each interview classified to each segment, we examined how each individual described his/her perspective on climate change as well as his/her understanding of the perspective of scientists who have concluded that global warming is happening and is primarily due to human activities. From the interviews, we could identify statements that were repeated across speakers classified to a segment as well as new statements voiced by only one or a few weathercasters. We then considered the isolated weathercaster statements as a set across all speakers in the segment and looked for the structure of a narrative consisting of protagonists, antagonists, exposition, rising action, climax, etc. The narrative structures identified by our analysis of the interviews were then compared to the narrative structures recorded in the problem-solving workshop. The workshop narratives were unadulterated in comparison to the narrative analysis of the interviews and thus served primarily as observational data for narrative structures 'in the field' of active conflict.

Our discourse position analysis drew on positioning theory (Harré & Slocum, 2003) to examine how speakers telling the aforementioned storylines constructed positive and negative positions in the discourse as well as what parties were afforded positive or negative positions. For the Self (and for those who view the conflict as the Self does; such parties could be thought of as sympathizers or allies), it was expected that positive positions would be constructed, while negative positions were expected to be constructed for respective Others (those with whom the Self would disagree; such parties could be thought of as opponents or detractors). Positioning analysis was performed on the interview transcripts only.

Findings

From transcripts and recorded notes of weathercaster statements collected during the interviews and workshop, we noted common assertions, themes, and narrative structures and grouped them by segment. We also considered barriers to climate change reporting that arose in weathercaster conversations and discuss them according to three types: occupational, interpersonal, and cultural barriers.

Throughout the interviews and workshop discussions, regardless of weathercasters' climate change views, two common perceived barriers emerged to discussing climate change on-air. First, weathercasters work in competitive markets, so there is strong incentive to avoid any public statements that could possibly alienate viewers. Since climate change is perceived as a political issue, many weathercasters stated that they are loath to address it. Second, in response to questions about educating their viewers on climate change, weathercasters often appealed to one of their journalistic norms, which is balance (Boykoff, 2011). They often noted the need to present climate change in such a way that viewers could 'make up their own minds' on the issue. We consider these perceived barriers to be occupational.

Despite these occupational constraints, most weathercasters did have their own conclusions about climate change. From a positioning analysis perspective, when talking about their own views, all segments generally described themselves as apolitical, impartial, knowledgeable, responsible, and willing to engage others with whom they disagree. Similarly, all segments generally described their Others as political, ignorant, irresponsible, or unwilling to listen. For example, a weathercaster identifying with the Yes-Human & Natural segment said,

> I do want to at least leave open the possibility that maybe we don't have a full understanding of the scales of natural variability, but we talk on television about weather records, "Oh, this is unprecedented." Well, it goes back to 1880 or something like that, and when you compare that to the existence of the Earth, it's a drop in the bucket. … I know that we look at the ice cores and so forth and try to draw some information from that, but I guess I'm still not completely sure that we have a perfect handle on what's natural and what isn't, and I just want to leave that open. But I also want to be very open to the possibility that man is principally responsible for what's happening. … I get frustrated sometimes when a major weather event occurs and then I see the band wagon starting to roll down the hill faster and faster, "Well this is proof that the climate is changing and that this has something to do with it," because I don't think that you can attribute individual weather events and say categorically that this is proof that that's happening. I think … and I'm as guilty as anybody, I think, in general, and this is politically, scientifically, in all areas of life, we all want easy answers. We want things that we don't have to think a lot about, and it's much easier to say, "Oh yeah, that Katrina is proof that we're messing things up." Well, what if it isn't proof? I mean, what if you have to dig a little bit deeper than that? … Are any of us willing to dig deeper to really find out and formulate a responsible opinion on what's really going on here?

In this first example, the weathercaster has constructed a positive position for him-/herself as open-minded, skeptical, questioning, and responsible. A negative position has been constructed for the Other who is overly certain and not sufficiently diligent ('we all want easy answers'). It is also implied that the Other may be irresponsible. Meanwhile, a weathercaster identifying with the No segment said,

> I just want to bring [to my viewing audiences] the whole other world of views and opinions from truly credentialed scientists who refute that which is being espoused by the IPCC and being promulgated on national media. …[T]he last place I would go [for information on climate change] would be the UN … because I believe it's a political organization … that is so overwhelmingly political that I would not go there.

In the second example, the weathercaster has constructed a positive position for him-/herself as impartial ("the whole other world of views … from truly credentialed scientists"), while a trusted source for the Other – the UN IPCC (Intergovernmental Panel on Climate Change) – is described as "overwhelmingly political."

An important difference between segments was that the Yes-Human group saw the scientific consensus as undisputed evidence supporting their view, while all alternative segments viewed doubt – including doubting whether there really is scientific consensus – as healthy skepticism. The prior statement by the Yes-Human & Natural weathercaster also serves as an example of this position.

Narrative analysis of the in-depth-interviews provides further context. Table 4.1 summarizes general versions of climate change conflict narratives by weathercaster segment. It should be noted that each segment describes the climate change conflict in distinctly different ways – at times, describing it with completely different protagonists and antagonists. These differences may bear implications for weathercaster attitudes not only toward the topic of climate change but also for their approaches toward delivering informal climate education.

For the Yes-Human segment, the science is settled and there is a clear scientific consensus. For instance, one weathercaster said,

> [M]y point of view is strictly based on the science that I have personally read and the seminars that I have attended … [T]he leading scientists in this field across the planet are all in agreement. I say all – and you're going to see some outliers, no matter what you're studying or looking at – but the most respected scientists in the field who are a whole lot smarter than me, who spend their career, like I spend my career in broadcast television telling people about the weather, spend their career studying this very topic. They tell me this is what they've found, and it's black and white, in my opinion. You just sat in the same session I did, I think, an hour ago, the professor from Rutgers. Where is their possible disagreement in that data? I mean, the science is the science, and how politics has come to play such a role is mindboggling to me, but science is science in my opinion, and I believe it.

For all other segments unconvinced of this view, the science is far from settled, and "scientific consensus" sounds suspiciously like an oxymoron. Representative comments from weathercasters identifying with other segments are below.

Yes-Human & Natural weathercaster: I disagree with the degree of certainty that both extremes [i.e. Yes-Human and No segments] have, where one extreme will say we know that without a doubt, this is due to this. Actually, they both say that, but I can't accept either of the extremes.

Yes-Natural weathercaster: Why don't you investigate how many dollars the NSF has spent trying to disprove [anthropogenic] global warming? The answer is virtually zero. ...[W]e have these universities who are spending tax dollars to go out and build these multi-disciplinary climate study institutes, which means there's no institutional incentive to disprove global warming. None. And, as President Eisenhower said in his Farewell Address, this is to be quote, "gravely regarded," unquote – the government intervention in science.

No weathercaster: ...[D]on't tell me that it's climate versus weather. ... [Y]ou still can't predict the climate 50 years from now... by half a degree or a degree. [The climate system is] a very complex mechanism. We don't understand half the things going on.

Some weathercasters referred to an assortment of scientific claims that have been used to challenge the veracity of anthropogenic enhancement of Earth's greenhouse effect (e.g., the siting of temperature gauges, Milankovitch cycles, sun cycles); however, such claims were often window dressing in the conflict narrative.[5] This is because the things that give narrative structure are protagonists, antagonists, rising action, climax, etc. In Table 4.1, the summary column 'conflict framing' succinctly describes differences in narrative structure with reference to identifiable protagonists and antagonists. Structurally, the conflict narratives of the Yes-Human and No segments mirror each other, where affinity groups corresponding to each segment (in the case of the Yes-Human, climate researchers; in the case of the No, researchers who challenge the reality of global warming) are in direct conflict with each other. However, the narrative structures of other segments describing the climate change conflict, and their attendant concerns, are quite different. In this regard, it should be noted that the Yes-Human & Natural and Yes-Natural segments (segments 2 and 3, or 64 percent of weathercasters) describe a conflict that has less to do with the struggle of contending scientific claims and more with concern over the condition of the scientific profession itself ('Science vs. politics' in Table 4.1). We investigate a possible meaning of these different descriptions of the climate change conflict in the next section and consider how these differences may be indicative of a second potential barrier to weathercasters for discussing climate change. This barrier could be considered philosophical, as it is rooted in different views of science; however, we have labeled it cultural, as philosophical differences may be related to particular on-the-job experiences shared by weathercasters.

TABLE 4.1 Summary of climate change narratives by weathercaster segment. Numbers in parentheses pertain to the number of weathercasters interviewed, while percentages pertain to the size of the weathercaster segment according to survey responses (Maibach et al., 2011a).

Segment	Narrative	Conflict framing (protagonist vs. antagonist)
1. Yes-Human (n = 15) 19% of weathercasters	Others who oppose our view accuse us of political motivation, but we simply present theoretical and empirical evidence. Multiple climate models accounting only for the natural causes of global warming were unable to produce the observed recent warming trend. Only after anthropogenic factors were included could the current rate of warming be simulated.* Because of the weight of much evidence, the consensus is that anthropogenic global warming is happening; there are countless climate experts and organizations supporting this viewpoint.	Affinity group (e.g. climate change researchers) vs. opponents
2. Yes-Human & Natural (n = 19) 35% of weathercasters	Evidence shows that human and natural processes play roles in global warming, but data is insufficient to conclude the relative importance of each one. On each end of the spectrum of views on climate change, people express absolute certainty, which is unacceptable in science. We cannot say that we know everything about what influences climate; science is an open investigation, and theories evolve with new information. We also draw conclusions from data that is incomplete or requires adjustment. This increases uncertainty for how much influence each variable has on climate. Politics has given rise to the different views on climate change. Therefore, we need to question the science behind climate studies because of political influences.	Science vs. politics
3. Yes-Natural (n = 8) 29% of weathercasters	Historically, many natural processes influenced global warming. Proponents of anthropogenic global warming overemphasize the significance of carbon dioxide and fail to properly account for natural processes actually causing present warming. This error persists because it frames climate change as a human-caused problem, so humans need to find solutions. This opens the door for political interests to advocate their agendas.	Science vs. politics

4. Don't Know (n = 4) 8% of weathercasters	We don't question that the earth has been warming over the last 150 years. We question how to determine the degree to which humans or natural processes have influenced warming because attribution is difficult. Nevertheless, if we don't agree with views at either end of the spectrum, pressure is put on us to join one side or the other, otherwise we're branded as sheep for the opposing side. We get tired of being inundated with alternative views. We just disengage because of the pressure.	Self vs. Others
5. No (n = 2) 9% of weathercasters	The scientific community cannot yet conclude that mechanisms influencing Earth's climate are completely understood. Statistical studies, datasets, and climate models embody many subjective assumptions. Proponents of anthropogenic global warming put too much stock in climate models, which we know have the same limitations as weather forecasting models. Our views are not frequently cited in scientific journals. This is because peer reviewers are a social network that is biased to publish articles with similar conclusions; it's much harder to get published with different views.	Affinity group (those unconvinced climate is changing) vs. climate change researchers

* This study was prominently featured in the most recent Assessment Report of the Intergovernmental Panel on Climate Change (IPCC). See IPCC (2007, p. 40).

The Yes-Human & Natural and the Don't Know segments (segments 2 and 4, or 43 percent of weathercasters) expressed storylines that were more personal, voicing frustration with the certainty asserted by the Yes-Human, Yes-Natural, and No segments. For example, a weathercaster in the Don't Know segment lamented,

> I'll be perfectly honest. Part of the reason I probably do not know [what to attribute global warming to] yet is because of I've kind of disengaged myself from even pursuing [it].[6] Because it's difficult to – whether intentional or not, the AMS and other organizations have allowed this perception to develop that they are intentionally trying to – because there is consensus, … it may be a genuine goodhearted attempt to say, "Okay, since there's a consensus, we're only going to focus on this science here," and I can understand elimination of the flat-earthers. But we do have Fellows that have some legitimate questions about AGW [anthropogenic global warming]. That those viewpoints seem increasingly – AMS has been increasingly hostile to the point of exclusion. And so suddenly you're thinking, "You know what? My position here, I can't even make it known," because you get the feeling that if you're not the "yes, and it's caused mostly by human activity" [segment] you're immediately dismissed as part of the problem and not part of the solutions. So at that point, you just back off [from the topic of climate change].

These narratives were also observed in the problem-solving workshop. We consider these perceived barriers, which have to do with pressure or frustration experienced in the context of other social actors who are more confident of their views, to be interpersonal.

Anecdotally, another potentially important finding emerged briefly in conversation during the problem-solving workshop. Weathercasters may be more willing to actively discuss climate change when the topic is tied to changes in the frequency of extreme weather events (e.g., hurricanes). Stepping away from questions of the causality for climate change, the vast majority of weathercasters (segments 1–3, or 83 percent) agreed in the workshop setting that they have a professional responsibility to warn their communities of changes in the frequency of extreme weather if it is happening.

Finally, the number of interviews conducted for each segment appears to replicate the experience of Hobson and Niemeyer (2012), where weathercasters with views that differ most substantially from the scientific consensus (e.g., the Yes-Natural segment) chose not to engage in our investigation as readily as weathercasters from other segments.[7] We find this to be a likely explanation, since the size of the Yes-Natural segment in particular is comparable in size to segments that did engage with us most readily (the Yes-Human and Yes-Human & Natural segments).[8]

Discussion

The statements that we collected and analyzed from weathercasters provide a more nuanced picture of the barriers they perceive to discussing climate change with their viewing audiences. Perceived barriers are multi-faceted and involve three main categories: *occupational* constraints, such as the competitive market for viewers and journalistic norms for balance; *interpersonal* strife when engaging the polarizing topic of climate change; and different philosophical viewpoints on the proper division between science and politics, which could have a *cultural* basis among weathercasters. Below, we discuss the influence of each of these perceived barriers on weathercaster behavior. Additionally, findings from the narrative and positioning analyses provide clues for styles of science communication weathercasters from different segments are likely to embrace should they be expected to intentionally act as informal climate change educators.

Weathercasters in the Yes-Human and Yes-Human & Natural segments, which correspond to a majority of weathercasters (54 percent), accept that human influences on the climate are significant. This could be taken as a positive sign that the majority of weathercasters may eventually decide to actively deliver informal climate change education that explains the reality of anthropogenic climate change to viewers.

However, it is important to bear in mind how larger political conflicts over climate change intersect with weathercasters' perceived barriers to climate change news reporting. Starting with perceived occupational barriers, in their competitive market setting, weathercasters' concerns for alienating viewers are strong. Thus weathercaster statements reflect a prevailing strategy to 'stay out of the political fray' on climate change. This results in two practices: (1) avoid reporting on climate change, or (2) when climate change news is reported, do so in a balanced way so that viewers can 'make up their own minds.'[9] These practices are tractable for at least three reasons. First, by following these practices, the weathercaster guards against alienating her/his viewing audience. This is important to weathercasters, as they aim to be perceived by viewers as approachable, trustworthy sources of news. Second, the weathercaster appears to be a good journalist by upholding the norm of balance. Third, as revealed by the positioning analysis of weathercaster statements, the weathercaster also avoids the personal discomfort of conflict with Others who are perceived as political, ignorant, irresponsible, or unwilling to listen. This latter benefit dovetails with perceived interpersonal barriers to reporting on climate change.

Interestingly, the narrative analysis reveals a third potential reason to adhere to the two dominant reporting practices noted above, which we have referred to as culturally influenced differences in philosophical views of science. This particular barrier is more subtle and complex but can be understood in two parts. First, we discuss the philosophical differences towards science across weathercaster segments. Second, we discuss how these philosophical differences may be influenced by on-the-job experiences shared by weathercasters – in effect, how dominant philosophical views may be a product of weathercaster 'culture.' Regarding philosophical differences toward science, two findings from the positioning and narrative analysis discussed above are notable. While weathercasters in the Yes-Human segment (19 percent) have concluded that the scientific consensus is undisputed evidence supporting their view, weathercasters in the Yes-Human & Natural and Yes-Natural segments (segments 2 and 3, or 64 percent of weathercasters) have concluded (1) consensus is not customary in science, i.e., skepticism is the norm, and (2) climate change has become such a political topic that the veracity of scientific claims can no longer be assumed. Arguably, weathercasters completely unconvinced that climate is changing (the No segment, an additional 9 percent of weathercasters) also share these views. The concern that politics have infiltrated science is particularly important, as weathercasters in these segments repeatedly criticized the involvement of non-scientific actors (e.g., governments, corporations) in scientific research and science communication. To interpret what these differences in weathercaster views on the scientific consensus and science communication mean, we draw from a concise framework for conceptualizing different idealized roles for science in society presented in Pielke (2007).

Pielke described four idealized roles for science and scientists in society, which are distinguished by two attributes: views of democracy and views of science. In this analysis, alternative views of science are relevant. One view of science is the 'linear model,' which Pielke described as "emphasiz[ing] the importance of basic research and freedom for scientists from political accountability" (2007, p. 12). In contrast, the "stakeholder model" envisions a highly interactive process between scientists and non-scientists, where knowledge is co-produced. In the latter case, scientists become politically involved by aiming to provide policy-relevant advice.

In effect, weathercasters insisting on a bright line between science and politics reject the stakeholder model view. Pielke's descriptions of the two idealized roles rejecting the stakeholder model make this more apparent. These idealized roles correspond to the 'Pure Scientist' and the 'Science Arbiter.' Pielke described the Pure Scientist as follows,

> Research results [from the work of the Pure Scientist] … are placed into a reservoir of knowledge where they will be available to all decision-makers. Those from various factions in society have access to the reservoir from which they can draw the knowledge that they need to clarify and argue their interests. In principle, … *the scientist remains removed from the messiness of policy and politics* [emphasis added].

(2007, p. 15)

Of the Science Arbiter, Pielke wrote,

> The Science Arbiter seeks to stay removed from explicit considerations of policy and politics like the Pure Scientist, but recognizes that decision-

makers may have specific questions that require the judgments of experts, so unlike the Pure Scientist ... [s/he] has direct interactions with decision-makers. ... A key characteristic of the Science Arbiter is a focus on *positive* questions that can ... be resolved through scientific inquiry. In principle, *the Science Arbiter avoids normative questions and thus seeks to remain above the political fray* [emphasis added]...

(2007, p. 16)

In contrast, Pielke's other two idealized roles, the 'Issue Advocate' and the 'Honest Broker of Policy Alternatives,' describe the conduct of scientists who choose to engage in the fray of policy and politics in accord with the stakeholder model of science.

Why would 73 percent of weathercasters hold views on science consistent with the linear model? A possible explanation is the lived experience, or culture, of weathercasters. Already we have discussed the occupational and interpersonal norms that encourage them to remain removed from the messiness of political topics. Providing further context for this disposition are the findings of Wilson (2009), where one of the common questions weathercasters receive about climate change is, "If you can't get the five-day forecast right, why should I believe anything you say about long-term climate predictions?" (2009, p. 1462). Wilson (2009) pointed out that this question is especially immediate for weathercasters, since they often receive negative feedback from audiences if their weather forecasts are inaccurate. Essentially, by developing weather forecasts daily and reporting them to their viewers, weathercasters already behave as Science Arbiters.

Recognizing these different views on the proper roles of scientists may bear implications for weathercaster attitudes toward learning more about climate change and for actively serving as informal climate change educators. First, regarding attitudes toward learning more about climate change, the narrative analyses of Yes-Human & Natural and Yes-Natural weathercasters already suggest that differences over the linear and stakeholder model views of science serve as a barrier to accepting the findings of the scientific consensus. This may be because the authoritative scientific body assessing the state of climate science – the UN IPCC – is a hybrid scientific and governmental organization. It clearly conducts itself according to the stakeholder model view of science, as the bright line between science and policy (assuming such a boundary exists) is breached by design.[10] This insight potentially explains why the IPCC came in last or second-to-last place as a somewhat or strongly trusted scientific source for information about climate change among weathercasters in a recent survey (Maibach et al., 2010).[11]

Second, different views on science may also bear implications for the conduct of weathercasters themselves when doing climate news reporting. The AMS has an initiative to bill weathercasters as 'station scientists,' since weathercasters are often the only staff in television newsrooms with formal science training (AMS, 2011; Wilson, 2008). Although this initiative encourages weathercasters to act as informal science educators, for climate change, it may not necessarily mean that weathercasters would embrace informal climate change education in the manner that climate scientists have. To contrast the scientific norms and orientations of the two communities, climate scientists, such as those whose work is assessed by the IPCC, focus on communicating what is understood about the linkages between climate change and extreme weather as well as what is understood about the enhancement of the greenhouse effect despite remaining scientific uncertainties. In contrast, 'station scientists' acting in accordance with the linear model of science may emulate a different science communication style, where they dodge political discussions of climate change mitigation by focusing instead on scientific uncertainties for impacts from a changing climate, human attribution, or simply continue to avoid climate change as a news topic.

In spite of the occupational, interpersonal, and cultural barriers to climate change reporting discussed in this section, weathercasters see themselves as responsible for issuing alerts about extreme weather. In this regard, climate change information connected to changes in the frequency of extreme weather events is of great interest to weathercasters. This suggests that weathercasters are primed to fulfill a particular niche in informal climate education, where the focus is disaster preparedness and possibly the communication of impacts from climate change. This niche is different from the role of an informal climate change educator who attempts to concisely explain to viewing audiences what climate change is and why scientists have concluded that it is primarily human caused. Admittedly, some weathercasters (the Yes-Human segment, or 19 percent) may already be motivated to serve as such informal climate change educators, and some already do so (e.g., Satterfield, 2012). However, many more weathercasters (the Yes-Human & Natural and Yes-Natural segments, or 64 percent) have reservations with assuming this type of informal climate change education role. Instead, developing the professional capacity of weathercasters to discern and discuss noteworthy changes in the pattern of local weather events and climate (e.g., with partnerships with local climatologists, continuing education, and tools such as story templates) would be more consistent with weathercasters' professional charge. Such a shift in focus may motivate substantially more weathercasters to actively deliver informal climate education.

Conclusion

Weathercasters are perceived as trustworthy sources of information on climate change by the general American public and could potentially serve as informal climate change educators. Through a conflict analysis of transcripts collected from interviews and a problem-solving workshop, however, we identified multiple challenges – perceived occupational, interpersonal, and cultural barriers – to active pursuit of this role. Occupational constraints, such as working in competitive markets, make weathercasters cautious about issuing any public statements that could alienate members of their viewing audiences. Because climate change has become so politicized, many weathercasters are reluctant to discuss it. Related to this concern are journalistic norms of balance. In the case of weathercasters, balanced reporting of climate change news (so that audiences can 'make up their own minds') is a strategy to hedge against alienating viewers. Furthermore, it may also be a strategy for avoiding the interpersonal barrier of conflict, since all segments of weathercasters referred to their own views on climate change as apolitical, impartial, and knowledgeable, while the views of others with whom they would disagree were characterized as political or ignorant. We also found that the statements of a vast majority of weathercasters (corresponding to 73 percent) reflect a suspicion of political influences in climate science. We suggest that this is evidence of a particular cultural view of science among the weathercaster community, the linear model view, which contrasts with the stakeholder model view of science embodied by institutions like the IPCC. These differing cultural views of science may further inhibit weathercasters from delivering informal climate change education in a manner similar to climate change researchers, where such researchers focus on communicating what is understood about the changing climate, human influences, and potential climate change impacts despite remaining scientific uncertainties.

However, expecting weathercasters to educate their viewers about climate science per se may be misguided. We found anecdotal evidence that most weathercasters (64 percent) may prefer to act as informal climate educators in the context of disaster preparedness, as this is more consistent with their professional charge. Developing professional partnerships (e.g., with state climatologists) or resources (e.g., continuing education, story templates) that develop the capacities of weathercasters to discern and discuss noteworthy changes in the pattern of local weather events and relate these patterns to climate is a largely untapped opportunity. If weathercasters focus their climate education efforts on the connections between frequencies of extreme weather events and climate change, it may not necessarily improve viewer understanding of global warming's human causes or mitigation implications. Nevertheless, framing the "weathercaster as climate educator" role in this way could potentially motivate a substantially larger number of weathercasters to productively engage with climate change in their professional capacities.

These recommendations are based on findings derived from an analytical approach that aims to understand the concerns and motivations of weathercasters when they are asked to discuss climate change. By going beyond primarily statistical investigations of weathercaster views, we found that a majority of weathercasters (the Yes-Human & Natural and Yes-Natural segments, 64 percent) expressed concern for the vitality of the scientific enterprise itself. We discussed that this may be indicative of cultural differences between weathercasters and professional scientists studying climate, as the former are highly sensitive to the limits of prediction and believe good science should be entirely separate from political actors (e.g., governments, corporations), while the latter focus on isolating meaningful signals from a noisy climate system and believe good science should be policy relevant. Passing these differences off as ignorance on the part of weathercasters (e.g., Homans, 2010) or overwhelmingly political motivations (e.g., Wilson, 2012) does little to resolve polarization around climate change. In our view, a future need and improvement in studies on climate change communication should be to analyze conflict directly, that is, to investigate how parties describe the conflict itself and what the differences between these descriptions are. Such detailed interrogations may more usefully provide guideposts for new directions to move past unproductive conflict.

Acknowledgments

This research was supported by a National Science Foundation Climate Change Education Partnership award to George Mason University (# DUE-1043235). For useful discussions and logistical support of research activities, the authors thank Keith Seitter, Steve Harned, Gene Bierly, Julie Robinson, Carole Mandryk, and Bob Henson. The authors would also like to thank anonymous reviewers for constructive feedback. The National Center for Atmospheric Research is funded by the National Science Foundation and managed by the University Corporation for Atmospheric Research.

Notes

1 *Informal science education* is a term that was originally coined by the National Science Foundation but is now generally understood to refer to all forms of science education outside classroom or tutorial settings, which are formal science education venues (Alpert, 2010).

2 It should be noted that a similar previous survey (Maibach et al., 2010, n = 571) considered only three segments of weathercasters, where (1) global warming is happening and caused mostly by human activities (31 percent), (2) global warming is happening and caused mostly by natural changes in the environment (63 percent), or (3) global warming isn't happening (6 percent).

3 Hobson and Niemeyer (2012) found not only that the discourses resisted change but also that Emphatic Deniers walked out of the process itself, as they were convinced that other participants in the study did not take their views seriously.

4 In the context of this study, the term "affinity group" refers to some segment that the weathercaster either currently identifies with or is sufficiently familiar with that s/he could convincingly appear to belong to or sympathize with it.

5 Some weathercasters spoke at length about these topics, which suggests that they put great stock into the scientific arguments or found them relevant to discuss during the interview. However, such claims often were not essential to the structure of the conflict narrative that they also articulated.

6 This weathercaster chose the Don't Know segment because s/he did not identify with the four other segments. This interviewee agreed that climate was changing but did not know if it was primarily human caused, primarily naturally caused, or could be attributed about equally to human and natural causes.

7 To clarify, the number of weathercasters interviewed for the Yes-Human and Yes-Natural segments is disproportionate. Yes-Human weathercasters are overrepresented (19 percent of n = 49 is 9; we interviewed 15), while Yes-Natural weathercasters are underrepresented (29 percent of n is 14; we interviewed 8). This means that the

findings from our narrative and positioning analyses for underrepresented or small segments (i.e., Yes-Natural, Don't Know, No) may be incomplete compared to other segments. Additionally, in the problem-solving workshop, no weathercasters willingly volunteered to represent the No segment. We had to encourage weathercasters who were familiar with the views of the No segment to 'stand in' during the breakout portion of the workshop. We take the lack of adequate representation of the Yes-Natural and No segments in the interview and workshop settings to be a reflection of the silencing atmosphere caused by conflict around climate change rather than a reflection of inherent limitations to our research approach.

8 Another likely explanation is that weathercasters modified their reported segment affinity when interviewed. It is possible that some weathercasters who labeled themselves as Yes-Human & Natural in our study would have labeled themselves as Yes-Natural under different circumstances. For example, one could imagine that when in the company of other Yes-Natural weathercasters, a Yes-Human & Natural weathercaster might choose to emphasize aspects of his climate change views that most closely resemble Yes-Natural views.

9 When discussing climate change reporting, weathercasters frequently made appeals to the journalistic norm of balance. However, when further inspected, this appeal is suspect. Weathercasters would hardly agree to do their weather reports this way. Instead, they see themselves as experts on weather who inform and educate their audiences.

10 We acknowledge that Pielke (2007) criticizes the IPCC for behaving as an Issue Advocate rather than an Honest Broker. In either case, Issue Advocates and Honest Brokers adopt the stakeholder model of science, as they actively cross the boundary between science and policy (assuming such a boundary exists). We leave it to other scholars to determine if Pielke is correct in his assessment of the IPCC.

11 Other scientific sources of information that outranked the IPCC in terms of trustworthiness were (in order of presentation; see Maibach et al., 2010) climate scientists, peer-reviewed science journals, AMS conferences/proceedings, NWA conferences/proceedings, NOAA/NWS, state climatologists, and other weathercasters (outranked IPCC as a somewhat trusted source).

References

Alpert C. L. (2010). *RISE partner guide*, glossary. Retrieved February 21, 2013: http://risepartnerguide.org/?page_id=28.

AMS (American Meteorological Society). (2011). *Station scientist*. Retrieved August 31, 2012: http://www.ametsoc.org/stationscientist/index.html.

Anderegg, W. R. L., Prall, J. W., Harold, J., & Schneider, S. H. (2010). Expert credibility in climate change. *Proceedings of the National Academy of Sciences*, 107(27), 12107–12109.

Boykoff, M. T. (2011). *Who speaks for the climate? Making sense of media reporting on climate change*. New York: Cambridge University Press.

Chatman, S. B. (1980). *Story and discourse: Narrative structure in fiction and film*. Ithaca, NY: Cornell University Press.

Deutsch, M., Coleman, P. T., & Marcus, E. C. (Eds.). (2006). *The handbook of conflict resolution: Theory and practice* (2nd ed.). San Francisco, CA: Jossey-Bass.

Doran, P. & Zimmerman, M. (2009). Examining the scientific consensus on climate change. *Eos*, 90, 21–22.

Freytag, G. (2008). *Freytag's technique of the drama: An exposition of dramatic composition and art*. Trans. E. J. MacEwan, Charleston: BilbioBazaar, LLC.

Hajer, M. & Versteeg, W. (2005). A decade of discourse analysis of environmental politics: Achievements, challenges, perspectives. *Journal of Environmental Policy & Planning*, 7(3), 175.

Harré, R. & Slocum, N. (2003). Disputes as complex events – on the uses of positioning theory. *Common Knowledge*, 9(1), 100–118.

Hobson, K. & Niemeyer, S. (2012). 'What sceptics believe': The effects of information and deliberation on climate change skepticism. *Public Understanding of Science*, 22(4), 396–412.

Homans C. (2010). Hot air: Why don't TV weathermen believe in climate change? *Columbia Journalism Review*, January 7. Retrieved February 26, 2013: http://www.cjr.org/cover_story/hot_air.php?page=all.

IPCC (Intergovernmental Panel on Climate Change). (2007). *Climate change 2007: Synthesis report. Contribution of Working Groups I, II and III to the Fourth Assessment Report of the Intergovernmental Panel on Climate Change*. Core Writing Team, R. K. Pachauri & A. Reisinger (Eds.), Geneva: IPCC.

Kelman, H. C. & Ezekiel, R. S. (1970). *Cross-national encounters*. San Francisco, CA: Jossey-Bass.

Labov, W. & Waletzky, J. (1967). *Narrative analysis: Oral versions of personal experience*. Seattle, WA: University of Washington Press.

Leiserowitz, A., Maibach, E., Roser-Renouf, C., & Smith, N. (2010). *Global warming's six Americas*, June 2010. Retrieved August 24, 2010 from Yale University and George Mason University, Yale Project on Climate Change: http://environment.yale.edu/climate/files/SixAmericasJune2010.pdf.

Maibach, E., Wilson, K., & Witte, J. (2010). *A national survey of television meteorologists about climate change: Preliminary findings*. Retrieved February 28, 2013 from George Mason University, Center for Climate Change Communication: http://www.climatechangecommunication.org/images/files/TV_Meteorologists_Survey_Findings_%28March_2010%29.pdf.

Maibach, E., Cobb, S., Leiserowitz, T., Peters, E., Schweizer, V., Mandryk, C., Witte, J., Clark, L., & Thaker, J. (2011a). *A national survey of television meteorologists about climate change: Education*. Retrieved August 29, 2012 from George Mason University, Center for Climate Change Communication: http://www.climatechangecommunication.org/images/files/2011_Mason_AMS_NWA_Weathercaster_Survey_Report_NA_doc_pdf%281%29.pdf.

Maibach, E., Witte, J., & Wilson, K. (2011b). 'Climategate' undermined belief in global warming among many American TV meteorologists. *Bulletin of the American Meteorological Association*, 92(1), 31–37.

McCright, A. M. (2011). Political orientation moderates Americans' beliefs and concern about climate change. *Climatic Change*, 104, 243–253.

Pielke, Jr., R. A. (2007). *The honest broker: Making sense of science in policy and politics*. New York: Cambridge University Press.

Rouhana, N. N. & Kelman, H. C. (1994). Promoting joint thinking in international conflicts: An Israeli-Palestinian continuing workshop. *Journal of Social Issues*, 50(1), 157–157.

Satterfield, D. (2012). Taking the heat: A weathercaster's view. *AtmosNews*, February 6. Retrieved March 5, 2013: https://www2.ucar.edu/atmosnews/attribution/features/6395/taking-heat-weathercaster-s-view.

Schweizer, V., Cobb, S., Schroeder, W., Chau, G., Maibach, E., Henson, R., Mandryk, C., & Witte, J. (2011). Reframing the (discursive) environment in the climate change conflict for American weathercasters. Politecnico di Milano, Milan: Mediation in Environmental Conflicts Management: New Frontiers workshop, November 28–29, 2011.

Silcock, B., Heider, D., & Rogus, M. (2007). *Managing television news: A handbook for ethical and effective producing*. Mahwah, NJ: Lawrence Erlbaum Associates, Inc.

Smith, D. (2007). *Power producer: A practical guide to TV news producing*. Fredericksburg, VA: Radio Television and Digital News Association.

Wilson, K. (2008). Television weathercasters as science communicators. *Public Understanding of Science*, 17, 73–87.

Wilson, K. (2009). Opportunities and obstacles for television weathercasters to report on climate change. *Bulletin of the American Meteorological Society*, 90(10), 1457–1465.

Wilson, K. W. (2012). Ideology trumps meteorology: Why many television weathercasters remain unconvinced of human-caused global warming. *Electronic News*, 6(4), 208–228.

5

RE-EXAMINING THE MEDIA–POLICY LINK

Climate change and government elites in Peru

Bruno Takahashi and Mark S. Meisner

Introduction

Despite the overwhelming and unprecedented scientific consensus on climate change, the intricacy of the issue at the policy and political levels has prevented a rapid and consensual response, especially at the national and international levels (Selin & VanDeveer, 2009). This is especially true in developed countries that are mandated by the Kyoto Protocol to reduce their emissions. On the other hand, within the global climate change governance regime, most developing countries do not have such mandates, but have to deal with their limited ability to adapt to the climatic changes and related impacts. Peru is one such country.

Peru is highly vulnerable to climate change (Brooks et al., 2004; Cosa Seria Este Clima, 2007). This is already resulting in the loss of tropical glaciers and diminishing water availability, more intense weather events such as El Niño, a decline in fisheries, and the reduction of forests, among other impacts (see Vuille et al., 2008). Within this context, climate change is not a politically divisive issue in Peru; government, private, and educational sectors mostly support taking mitigation and adaptation actions (Lanegra, 2008).

Peru is also strongly positioned to take advantage of international adaptation funds via the United Nations' REDD (Reducing Emissions from Deforestation and forest Degradation) program because of its large rainforest (70 million ha.) (Chatterjee, 2009; Hajek et al., 2011). The Peruvian government has taken various policy steps within the international arena, and at the national level. These include the signing of the United Nations Framework Convention on Climate Change (UNFCCC) in 1992, and the ratification of the Kyoto Protocol in 2002. The government also created the National Committee of Climate Change in 1993. However, the committee failed to accomplish any meaningful policy outcome. In 2003, the committee was reactivated and restructured, and the country officially adopted a National Strategy of Climate Change. More recently, in 2008, the government created the Ministry of the Environment (see Takahashi & Meisner, 2012), which has taken the lead on climate change. In late 2010, the Ministry developed the Mitigation and Adaptation Action Plan against Climate Change.

Despite these efforts, relatively little is known about how climate change policy decisions are made in Peru and other developing countries. We also do not know much about how different sources of information, especially the mass media, influence political and public perceptions of climate-related issues. In this chapter we analyze and discuss the links between climate change policymaking and mass media coverage, hence expanding the limited scholarship in this area. We also contribute to this area of research by extending our geographic focus to a developing country. The study applies theories of information processing, framing effects, and agenda setting, to data from media coverage, a survey, and interviews in order to present a detailed case study of a single issue, climate change, in the Peruvian Congress. We hope to better understand the individual-level dynamics (Wood & Vedlitz, 2007) that explain the broader effects found in previous studies, and to build on and overcome the methodological limitations of past efforts (Walgrave, 2008). In this study we are guided by the following research question: In what ways, and under what circumstances, does information from the media influence the understanding of climate change and the policy behaviors of legislators in Peru?

Climate change, the mass media, and political elites

The study of media and policymaking has received limited attention (Koch-Baumgarten & Voltmer, 2010; Van Aelst et al., 2008). Some scholars have argued for the need to study media effects on political elites because of the impact these individuals can have on the general population and the environment through their policy decisions (Kepplinger, 2007). Yanovitzky (2002, p. 425) explains that "the effect of media coverage of issues on policy making is likely to be manifested in two forms: the timing of intensive issue-related policy making and the type of policy choices pursued by policy makers." This is particularly important in the context of Peru and other developing nations, especially when it refers to the implementation of mitigation and adaptation initiatives.

Scholars in this area have traditionally followed an agenda-setting perspective. These studies have considered the parallels between media and congressional agendas, mostly in the US (Baumgartner et al., 1997), and the effects of indicators, focusing events, and feedback (Kingdon, 2003; Liu et al., 2011). Most of these studies point to a reciprocal relationship where the media can play an important role in setting governments' agendas under certain conditions, such as the political mood and the state of public opinion. However, few studies have utilized an individual level perspective to determine specific media influence. This individual level refers to decisions by specific policy makers involved with climate change policy proposals. Similarly, very few studies have been conducted outside the United States (Walgrave et al., 2008), and fewer studies are found in developing nations. Recently, some researchers have made important theoretical and empirical contributions (e.g., Elmelund-Præstekær et al., 2011; Helms, 2008; Kepplinger, 2007; Vliegenthart & Walgrave, 2011; Walgrave, 2008). Following this work, we suggest that more attention be given to the media–policy link and that this research be extended to other cultural and political contexts.

The interests of politicians in particular issues discussed in the media will play a determining role in the level of media effects (Green-Pedersen & Stubager, 2010). Entman (1989) suggested that attention to new information depends on its salience, and on its engagement with individuals' interests. For example, in Belgium, opposition parties appear to be more inspired by media coverage than government parties because of their greater need to attract attention (Walgrave & Lefevere, 2010). Similarly, more knowledge and firsthand experience of an issue creates more interest in media coverage, but also makes individuals more reliant on their own judgments and political predispositions over the media's information (Newton, 2006; Yanovitzky, 2002). For politicians "there is a very low likelihood that this coverage will alter their beliefs and attitudes regarding issues they believe to be important, unless they are challenged by cogent contrary information ..." (Yanovitzky, 2002, p. 425).

Domestic scientific information about climate change is sparse in Peru (Takahashi, 2010), and knowledge about the issue in Congress is low (Takahashi & Meisner, 2011). Most information about the issue that makes it into the national policy-making context of developing nations originates outside those nations (Lahsen, 2007). On the other hand, policy makers are "likely to follow media prescriptions of responsibility and solutions to problems if they already fit into their own belief structure and if they present an opportunity for political gain" (Yanovitzky, 2002, p. 426). Thus, beliefs and attitudes are an important area of inquiry since they serve as mediators of framing effects (Chong & Druckman, 2007; Reeher, 1996; Reeher, 2006). In other words, the recognition and characterization of a condition as a social problem, as well as the choice of alternatives, are partially a function of personal traits and perceptions.

Some conditions, such as issue attributes, have also been found to regulate the level of media effects (Bartels, 1996). Walgrave (2008, p. 446) argued that "(t)he media seem to affect symbolic political agendas considerably more than substantial political agendas." In the case of climate change, extensive research on media coverage of the issue across nations shows its symbolic nature (Boykoff, 2009; Sonnett, 2010). Additionally, Robinson (2001) suggested that the media have a stronger level of influence when there is elite dissensus and policy uncertainty. If there is no policy in place, elites might feel pressured to respond to critical media coverage in order to avoid criticism. In summary, as Newton (2006, p. 226) explained, media effects "may be stronger on matters that are new, complex and unrelated to existing cleavages and values," which, as we will soon discuss, appears to be the case for climate change in the Peruvian context.

However, information from the media does not exist in isolation and the study of information processing in government must be systematic (Workman et al., 2009). Significant factors for legislators include media use (Bybee & Comadena, 1984), the mediating role of staff members (Lewis & Ellefson, 1996), and the use of new information technologies (Mayo & Perlmutter, 1998). Unlike in the US, in most developing countries there is an under supply of information, especially concerning issues with highly technical matters (see Jones & Baumgartner, 2005). This includes the lack of a strong environmental non-governmental movement that could influence both environmental discourses and policy making (Takahashi & Meisner, 2012).

With this in mind, this case study analyzes how these dynamics operate in the Peruvian Congress. Congress's awareness and interest in climate change increased in the legislative period from 2006 to 2011. In 2007, the Special Committee on Climate Change and Biodiversity was formed, but it also failed to produce any meaningful work and was deactivated soon after. It was reactivated in late 2010. Other initiatives include the development of at least six bills related to climate change. Of those, only one was approved by the Committee on Andean, Amazonian, and Afro-Peruvian Populations, Environment, and Ecology for debate on the floor. In addition to dealing with national policies, Congress is also responsible for ratifying international agreements (Lanegra, 2008). Therefore, any post-Kyoto treaty will have to be debated in Congress. Based on the current stage of environmental governance in the country, and the expectations of an upcoming international climate regime, it can be expected that Congress will eventually deal with several pieces of legislation related to climate change.

Methods

Green-Pedersen and Stubager (2010, p. 667) have stated that "One of the reasons why relatively few studies of mass media influence on macro-politics exist is the data challenge." In this respect, quantitative longitudinal studies generally find a symbiotic relationship between media attention and policy making (e.g., Jones & Wolfe, 2010; Trumbo, 1996), but provide limited evidence of the processes and circumstances that are involved (Howarth 2010). On the other hand, qualitative case studies are critiqued for using anecdotal evidence that cannot be used in the formulation of theories and models.

This study relies on a mixed methods approach to overcome these methodological limitations. We triangulate data from interviews, a survey, and newspaper articles, to understand media influence at the individual level. This reflects Jones and McBeth's (2010) argument that there are few studies on narrative political tactics of interest groups, the media, and elites, and how those actually influence decision makers' behaviors and opinions (see also Shanahan et al., 2008). Additionally, Pump (2011) argued in favor of a focus on venues to help provide a ground for richer descriptions, and to understand the ways in which information processing by political institutions influence policy formulation. Therefore, the focus here is on the Peruvian Congress during the 2006–2011 legislative period, with special attention on the Committee of Andean, Amazonian, and Afro-Peruvian Populations, Environment, and Ecology and the special Sub-committee of Climate Change and Biodiversity.

Survey

A survey of legislators asked for a ranking of major policy issues, including environmental issues (see Table 5.1). The survey also included questions about media consumption, trust in media, sources of information, and perceptions about climate change. A self-administered paper-based survey was delivered to every congressional office (n=120), and follow-up calls and visits were conducted, resulting in a 42 percent response rate (n=50). The response rate is not representative of the population, so results are interpreted with that in mind. Frequencies are presented to generally describe the ways in which the media and other sources of policy information are used by legislators.

In-depth interviews

Seventeen in-depth interviews with a purposive sample of legislators, top advisers, and other staff members involved in climate change and environmental initiatives were conducted. Interviewees were selected for their involvement in climate change legislation initiatives. They centered on perceptions and policy actions about climate change, and the channels used to get information about climate change and other related policy issues. In a few instances the interviewer asked directly about perceptions of the media, but for the most part, mentions of it were unprompted. This approach attempted to overcome the limitations of studies that directly ask about media, since elites may be hesitant to admit the media's influence on their policy practices (Walgrave, 2008; Yanovitzky, 2002). Thematic coding was used to identify common themes within and between interviews.

Content analysis of newspaper coverage

Previous studies have found that newspapers have a stronger influence than television on politicians (Walgrave et al., 2008; Walgrave & Van Aelst, 2006), and that they have the strongest influence on political agenda setting. Additionally, Shoemaker and Reese (1996) stated that most media effects studies have focused on the social-psychological processes at the individual and societal levels, but often neglect the content of the media as well as the factors that shape it. With these considerations in mind, this study focuses on newspaper coverage of climate change. A content analysis of media coverage of climate change was conducted from 2000 to 2010 in the main Peruvian newspapers (ten national newspapers). The leading Peruvian newspaper, *El Comercio*, maintains a database containing articles from these newspapers. We searched it using the keywords "climate

TABLE 5.1   Issue priority and expertise on policy issues

Issue	Issue priority	Capacity
Drug issues	20.0%	0.0%
Education	70.0%	21.7%
Government reform	32.0%	28.3%
Environment	20.0%	15.2%
Unemployment	28.0%	2.2%
Salaries	6.0%	4.3%
Economic crisis	20.0%	6.5%
Other	–	21.7%

change," "global warming," "greenhouse effect," and "greenhouse gases" (in Spanish: "cambio climático," "calentamiento global," and "gases de efecto invernadero") in the header and sub-headers. A total of 459 articles were collected for analysis. Following previous work (Boykoff, 2008; McComas & Shanahan, 1999; Takahashi, 2011), we coded for main frames (effects, politics, science, society, and opportunities), sources, authorship, and geographic focus.

Results

Newspaper coverage of climate change in Peru

Media coverage of climate change in the Peruvian press has been characterized by limited attention, with predictable peaks during key events, similar to the cyclical coverage reported in other countries (Brossard et al., 2004; McComas & Shanahan, 1999; Trumbo, 1996). Figure 5.1 shows the frequency of the coverage by year from 2000 to 2010. The 2007 and 2008 peaks can be attributed to several events, including the release of *An Inconvenient Truth*, and the subsequent Nobel Prize presented to both Al Gore and the IPCC in 2007. The IPCC had released reports in the first half of 2007 that presented evidence about the significant role played by human activities in current global climate change. In 2008, Peru hosted the Latin America, the Caribbean, and European Union Summit, which focused on climate change as a main topic (see Takahashi, 2011). Additionally, Peru created the Ministry of the Environment in 2008. In 2009 climate change received less attention than the previous two years, despite the widespread coverage that the COP16 meeting in Copenhagen garnered worldwide. This might be a function of the data collection approach, since Copenhagen-related articles not including the search keywords might not have been captured. The coverage during the study period (2006–2011) represents the highest since the issue started to receive serious attention from the media and the government, leveling off in 2010. It is expected that the salience of the issue in the media during 2007–2009 is a necessary circumstance or condition for media effects to occur.

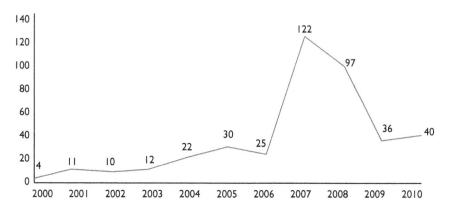

FIGURE 5.1 Media coverage of climate change 2000–2010

Media coverage was mostly characterized by the use of an effects and vulnerability frame. This included discussions about ecological, human, and economic effects. The analysis did not reveal any skepticism about climate change and its effects. A dominant theme in this frame is the melting of tropical glaciers in the Andes. Headlines such as "CONAM's president mentioned that 22 percent of the glaciers have been lost during the last 25 years, which represents the equivalent to the water consumed in the city of Lima during ten years," exemplify the recognition of the inevitability of these impacts and the country's sense of helplessness.

The second most prominent frame was 'politics.' Most of the articles using this frame focused on the international negotiations for a climate change agreement. The conferences of the parties (COP) meetings in Bali (2007), Poznan (2008), Copenhagen (2009), and Cancún (2010) received some or considerable coverage. On the other hand, policy discussions received less attention, with even less focus on Peruvian national, regional, or local policy discussions.

Approximately one-third of all articles were from a wire service, and more than half of all sources were foreign. Moreover, while Peruvian national government sources were dominant, there were few local and regional sources, as well as few local scientists. During an interview, one consultant who worked on a climate change bill and was knowledgeable on the issue, emphasized that the information coming from expert sources was too complex and therefore too hard to communicate by the media, which would explain the focus on 'easy' themes such as the effects and the misconceptions sometimes presented in the coverage (see Ungar, 2000). Knowledge about climate change among environmental journalists in the US has been found to be relatively low (Wilson, 2000). It is reasonable to expect that similar or lower levels would be found in other countries such as Peru because of the lack of professionalization in environmental journalism. This would also help explain the heavy reliance on wire service stories. The limited number of expert local sources can also serve as an explanation. This is discussed in more detail in the next section.

Finally, media coverage discusses climate change as a serious issue, without presenting conflicting positions, unlike in the US (Boykoff, 2007; Boykoff & Boykoff, 2004; Boykoff & Boykoff, 2007). There is also a lack of discussion of issues at the regional and local level within the country, and a significant presence of discourses that originate abroad. Additionally, the coverage of mitigation actions outweighs that of adaptation, which is consistent with previous studies (e.g., Olausson, 2009). The coverage overwhelmingly portrayed climate change as a negative issue. The issue and the fate of its effects were accepted as a fact, and few articles discussed basic scientific concepts or adaptation measures relevant to the country (see Takahashi & Meisner, 2013).

Climate change and the competition with other policy issues

Before discussing the circumstances that allow for media effects, this section discusses the salience of environmental issues and climate change in Congress. In the survey, respondents were asked: "What are the two most important current policy issues for you?"[1] Table 5.1 shows that education is considered one of the two most important policy issues (70 percent), while the environment ranks relatively low at 20 percent. Similarly, legislators were asked: "In what policy area do you consider you have the greatest capacity?" In this respect, 15.2 percent identified the environment as the policy area where they believe they perform best. Despite some notorious environmental issues, especially those related to social-environmental conflicts (Laplante & Phenicie, 2009), most legislators perceive the environment as a lower policy priority than education, government reform, and unemployment.

Notwithstanding this apparent low salience of environmental issues, climate change has become the main environmental issue for legislators and for the Peruvian population (Estado de la Opinión Pública, 2009). Table 5.2 shows the results from the question: "What are the two most important environmental issues in the country?"

The high awareness of the issue was confirmed when the legislators were asked: "Recently, climate change has become a significant issue that receives

TABLE 5.2 Main environmental issues in Peru

Issue	%
Air pollution	14.0
Water pollution	38.0
Deforestation of the Amazon	46.0
Climate change	56.0
Loss of biodiversity	6.0
Solid waste	2.0
Water scarcity	40.0

considerable attention within governments, the public, and the media. How much have you heard or read about climate change?" Most legislators have either heard or read quite a bit (62 percent), or a lot (20 percent), while only 18 percent have heard or read little about it. Similarly, 52 percent of the sample said that climate change has been established as a serious issue, 38 percent said that there is enough evidence that climate change is taking place, and 10 percent said that we don't know enough about climate change and more research is necessary. Legislators have no doubt that climate change has already started (97.9 percent agree with this affirmation). Of this group, 64.6 percent attribute climate change to human actions, 4.2 percent to only natural causes, and 31.3 percent to both. Finally, 95.8 percent think the effects will be somewhat or very serious, while only one respondent thinks that the effects will not be serious. In summary, this set of questions paints a picture in which climate change is an issue that legislators think about, with broad agreement about its causes and effects.

Sources of policy information

The study also looked into the sources of policy information in order to determine the role of the media in comparison to other sources. Important differences between sources of information used in climate change, and those used in other policy issues were expected based on the specific issue attributes of climate change (complexity, perceived uncertainty, and long-term and distant effects). Table 5.3 reveals such differences, where the media appear to play an important role generally.

Legislators and advisers were receiving most of their information on the topic from the media, with very limited input from experts. Table 5.4 shows that 70 percent of respondents received climate change information from newspapers several times a month or more frequently. Seventy-four percent used the Internet that frequently. Legislators and advisers reported much lower exposures to experts. Sixty-six percent of the respondents received information from experts less than once a month, and 14 percent said they never receive such information. Moreover, in the interviews, policy makers rarely mentioned scientists or other experts as relevant sources of information. Despite the importance of these results, it is necessary to consider that frequency alone might not be the most valid measure of reliance on information sources.

TABLE 5.3 Where would you go for policy information about ...?

Policy source	Any policy issue	Climate change
Experts, scientists, and/or scientific publications	32.0%	73.5%
Family and/or friends	0.0%	0.0%
Government institutions	8.0%	4.1%
The media	26.0%	14.3%
Peers, co-workers, and/or staff at my institution	34.0%	6.1%
Other	0.0%	2.0%

TABLE 5.4 Frequency of use of sources of climate change policy information

Sources of climate change information	Never	Less than once a month	Several times a month	Several times a week	Every day or almost every day
Experts, scientists, and/or scientific publications	14.0%	66.0%	18.0%	2.0%	0%
Family and/or friends	28.0%	52.0%	16.0%	2.0%	2.0%
Internet	2.0%	24.0%	48.0%	20.0%	6.0%
Magazines	4.0%	50.0%	40.0%	4.0%	2.0%
Newspapers	6.0%	24.0%	54.0%	12.0%	4.0%
Peers, co-workers, and/or staff at my institution	16.0%	44.0%	28.0%	10.0%	2.0%
Radio	14.0%	34.0%	40.0%	8.0%	4.0%
Schools and/or universities	20.0%	50.0%	30.0%	0%	0%
Television	8.0%	28.0%	46.0%	14.0%	4.0%

Media use

Tagina (2009) reported that in 2006, 73 percent of Peruvian legislators stated that the media did not have a major influence on their own decision making. A similar question in the present study yielded a similar result of 77 percent agreeing with this position. We also asked: "To what extent do the media influence the decision making of your colleagues in Congress?" Results were reversed, with 75 percent suggesting that the media have a lot or a complete influence on their colleagues. This could be attributed to the third-person effect theory. The use of interviews is useful in this respect to dispel the apparent contradictions. Most interviewees believe that the media generally play an important role in setting the agenda and prioritizing issues in Congress. Therefore, it would be reasonable to expect that unique contextual features and internal rules of institutions (Walgrave & Van Aelst, 2006) could moderate the levels of influence, and the perceptions of such influence.

The Peruvian Congress has been a highly questioned institution in most governments of the new democratic era (especially after the 1970s military governments), which included a dissolution by President Fujimori in 1992 (see Conaghan, 2005). Congressional approval ratings have remained low, with 79 percent of the public stating that they had little to no trust in Congress towards the end of the 2006–2011 period (Estado de la Opinión Pública, 2011). It is therefore no surprise that there is a high level of public scrutiny of the actions of legislators, and therefore close attention to their performances by the media. Kepplinger (2007) refers to this as reciprocal effects. More specifically, the political nature of the institution makes legislators feel a sense of commitment to try and resolve those problems discussed in the media that they feel reflect public opinion. Moreover, legislators worry about the feedback from the media and the effect that such coverage might have on their political careers. One legislator described these institutional constraints in these terms:

TABLE 5.5 Media consumption per week (%) and trust (mean)

Media	0–1 hour	1–10 hours	10–20 hours	20–30 hours	More than 30 hours	Mean trust (1–5)
TV	6.3%	47.9%	29.2%	12.5%	4.2%	3.1
Newspapers	6.3%	45.8%	33.3%	6.3%	8.3%	3.2
Magazines	20.8%	62.5%	8.3%	8.3%	0.0%	3.3
Internet	10.4%	45.8%	29.2%	8.3%	6.3%	3.3
Radio	6.3%	54.2%	27.1%	10.4%	2.1%	3.5

Because of the weakness in the organization of political parties, and faced with the existence of a dispersion of small groups in Congress, which is part of the fragility and weakness of the parties, sometimes the media are the ones that end up dictating the agenda, even national. Many times legislators choose and respond to issues because of social pressure. Therefore, here comes into play the political savviness of the legislator to see how to hook up with an issue that is also of national interest. For example, the five themes of the committee [of environment] are of national and world agendas. Therefore, there was not much difficulty in hooking up with the media. The other is the ability, and also the knowledge of the issue to have media access.

(Minaya, 2010)

Media influence is fundamentally attached to media consumption; therefore, legislators were asked: "How many hours in a typical week, do you read or hear the following media for news information?" Table 5.5 shows that media consumption is relatively stable across media, with magazines being consumed the least.

Respondents were also asked to rate the same media according to their level of trust on a five-point scale (from least (1) to most (5) trusted source of news information). Table 5.5 shows that the radio is considered the most trustworthy source of news information, while television and newspapers are considered the least. These results have to be considered within a larger picture of distrust towards the media in general, where 83.7 percent of surveyed legislators do not trust them (Tagina, 2009).

The media, climate change, and policy making

This section discusses the conditions where media coverage, media consumption, and policymaking interact. Looking more closely into media consumption about climate change, we asked legislators: "How closely do you follow news stories about climate change?" Eighty six percent responded either fairly (56 percent) or very closely (30 percent), while only 14 percent said not too closely. The issue is relatively new to most of the interviewees who have been working recently on climate change-related projects. Most of the interviewees first learned about it from the media. Therefore, the influence of the media in providing a first perspective on the issue becomes more relevant. Two main topics emerged in the interviews in regard to the perceptions about the content of media coverage of climate change. First, there was a strong prevalence of the topic of climate change and melting glaciers, as an adviser discussed: "Only recently we are paying attention, mostly because we are losing glaciers, even the Arctic. All that mass of ice, it's melting" (Minaya, 2010). Second, there was a strong focus on international relations and the discussions surrounding the 2009 Copenhagen summit, as another adviser recognized:

> Before and after the Copenhagen event, all the press discussed the topic; and when referring to all the press, I mean radio, TV, newspapers, magazines, etc. And all have used the theme of looking for consensus so that the industrialized countries, who are the ones that contribute the most with greenhouse gas emissions, decrease.
>
> (Minaya, 2010)

Moreover, the media played another important role in creating interest in further researching policy issues when such themes align with personal interests. A legislative adviser (with formal education in environmental issues) working on a climate change bill, clearly described the reasons behind her decision to focus on climate change. She decided to revise the current national strategy of climate change because she perceived that there was an opinion flow at the international level via her consumption of local and international media outlets:

> There was information from international organizations, scientists talking about the models, the trends; therefore there was a lot of serious work. One of the newspapers that published these reports was El Comercio, and when I read this I would say 'there are really serious things behind all this.' I started getting more interested, and started to really find out what was behind it.
>
> (Minaya, 2010)

Others were explicit in recognizing the role of the media in helping them learn about the issue:

> Well, (I learned about climate change) through the themes in the press, the press being television or some radio shows. Also a lot through Internet, which deals with climate change, and a lot more due to the Copenhagen conference that was going to take place.
>
> (Minaya, 2010)

When asked about the accuracy of the reporting in respect of the perceived seriousness of climate change, 58 percent thought that the coverage was generally correct, 10 percent that it was generally exaggerated, and 26 percent that it was generally underestimated. On the other hand, the majority of interviewees perceived media coverage to be insufficient and inadequate. A legislator said:

It lacks scientific backing, it lacks a lot of backing, and the depth which is used to handle these themes is not the most adequate. For the purpose of documenting a research, it can't be used as frame of reference, right?

(Minaya, 2010)

These apparently conflicting results could suggest differences between those legislators involved in environmental policy and those who are not, as revealed throughout the interviews. Individuals working on environmental legislation might be more critical of the media because of their involvement and knowledge of the issue. Nevertheless, those interviewed criticized the media's reporting mostly based on their negative perception of Peruvian media as a whole, rather than based on the limitations discussed in the preceding sections. This seems to be consistent with Newton's (2006) proposition that more knowledge and firsthand experience of an issue creates more interest in media coverage, but those factors also make individuals more reliant on their own judgments and political predispositions over the media. When discussing climate change, knowledge has been found to be relatively less among politicians when compared to experts and journalists (Sundblad et al., 2009). However, individuals rely on the media as their main source of information and knowledge about climate change (Wilson, 1995), posing a paradox.

Other policy information gathering practices

Information seeking practices depend on previous knowledge about the issue in question (Newton, 2006; Yanovitzky, 2002). Most interviewees acknowledged that the Internet is their main source of policy information. For example, an adviser to a legislator member of the Special Committee on Climate Change and Biodiversity explained his position: "Our knowledge was incipient, basic, very basic on the issue. After that (the special committee) we became more aware of the issue, we started downloading information, but the committee did not have a lot of response" (Minaya, 2010). Policy makers claiming expertise or knowledge of the topic tend to seek information from established and credible sources, such as the IPCC, UNEP, the Ministry of the Environment, etc. These individuals are aware that the quality of the information from the Internet can vary greatly, nevertheless many do not have a systematic procedure to search for information or discern between these sources. An adviser who was assigned to work on a climate change bill provided another example:

I tell my secretary: 'Go to Internet, and download everything you can about climate change.' Then, the secretary does what she can, she goes to Google ... climate change ... and there are for example, presentations, books. I don't know, she downloads what she can. Then, that information gives me an idea; let's say global, very generic, to understand it.

(Minaya, 2010)

As discussed earlier, the results of the survey show an overwhelming belief that climate change is happening, and that media coverage does not present it as a polarized issue. However, in the case of the Internet, the availability of diverging information and opinions can create polarizing positions. This is more so if the information gathering processes are not well established and there is an under-supply of local reliable and accessible information.

Institutional constraints in Congress and other government institutions exacerbate such information-poor environments. For instance, the Peruvian Congress operates its own research center, which is in charge of producing thematic reports and research dossiers at the request of legislators. The office includes only six staff members, and is deeply under-resourced, according to its director (Minaya, 2010). On the other hand, the center is underutilized, as it has received very few requests on environmental issues and none about climate change. Additionally, before the creation of the Ministry of the Environment in 2008, technical and scientific information was highly scattered and not easily accessible among government institutions.[2] This lack of a systematized and reliable information system on climate change that includes local resources was one circumstance that allowed individuals to adopt a mechanism of information gathering that relied on alternative sources such as the media, the Internet, secondary information from other countries, and interpersonal connections.

Conclusions

This chapter has argued that specific instances of media influence at the individual level can have substantive effects in the policy-making arena of Congress. The results suggest that the media play an important role in helping legislators decide which issues to focus on, and how those issues are understood. In this case, institutional and contextual characteristics prevented specialized information from easily reaching policy makers with limited knowledge of environmental issues. This includes the inadequate institutional arrangement with the research center, limited involvement by non-governmental organizations (Takahashi & Meisner, 2012), and a scarcity of scientific institutions and universities working on the topic (Takahashi, 2010). In contrast, those individuals with some interest in climate change sought information from alternative sources, especially the media.

The results also suggest that issue attributes, the type of media, and the type of coverage influenced policy makers' understanding of the issue. These results are put into perspective by our finding that most media articles and sources are from outside Peru, and they mostly focus on issues of secondary concern to the country. Some policy makers decided to get involved in climate change legislation after hearing an international opinion in the media. This led them to seek more information, especially via the Internet, since access to local scientific information was very limited. However, their understanding was mostly in relation to the need to reduce greenhouse gas emissions.

Based on the interviews, it was possible to confirm that newspapers are considered to be the main agenda setters in Congress. Despite perceiving radio as more trustworthy and newspapers as comparatively less so, newspapers are thought of as having an influence on public opinion. Additionally, the type of coverage was reflected in the ways that the legislators and advisers understand the issue. For those less knowledgeable, the issue is perceived by many as a foreign problem with limited relevance when compared to immediate local issues, such as current socio-environmental conflicts. In order to provide local relevance, the media focused strongly on the melting of tropical glaciers. In this case, national legislators are not setting the media's agenda because they don't have much expertise, which partially explains their limited media access. The media agenda seems to be driven by discourses originating in international contexts. The evidence presented in this study points out that such discourses, which are filtered via editorial decisions at the newspapers, can influence the ways in which legislators generally think about climate change.

Moreover, most of the bills authored by the policy makers interviewed in this study tend to generalize the issue, focusing on broad aspects that seek to reduce greenhouse gas emissions, which are negligible in Peru, instead of focusing on relevant local issues. Also, the bills discussed appeared right after the spike in media attention during 2007–2008. Although it is not possible to determine any direct effect using only this data, the timing suggests that a relationship is present.

Conflicting positions, something common in countries such as the US (see McCright & Dunlap, 2003), the United Kingdom, and Australia, are completely absent from both media coverage and policy-making discussions in Peru. This reflects a consensus about the issue, both from scientific and policy perspectives, which is partially a function of the status of the country as a developing and highly vulnerable nation with limited greenhouse gas contributions. This is considerably different from the evidence presented by Fisher et al. (2013) from the US Congress, where legislative actions and discourses significantly differ between Republican and Democratic policy makers. On the other hand, the issue was not considered an immediate priority and it did not threaten in any way the political climate or the process of economic development of the country. Therefore, the political price of supporting climate change was extremely low among legislators, while giving them the opportunity to gain favorable feedback from a population that was becoming increasingly aware of the issue.

Furthermore, the coverage had an influence on specific policy behaviors that, although they did not influence the agenda of Congress, evolved into subsequent legislative proposals and the institutionalization of climate change as a policy issue (i.e., The Special Committee on Climate Change and Biodiversity). This influence could have been even stronger if other contextual factors, such as a focusing event, had occurred. Focusing events in agenda setting have immediate effects on public, media, and government attention (Birkland, 1997). Analogously, it might be possible to discuss individual level focusing events, where media events prompt a reaction that then can have a long-term effect on policy making.

Media effects research need not limit its understanding of media influence to its agenda-setting power or its contribution to policy alternatives at the macro level.

In summary, in this chapter we have discussed specific instances where the media have played an important role in explaining some climate policy actions, either in the form of a new committee or in the preparation of a bill. Second, media frames and the discourses used by policy makers to discuss climate change show similarities. Although a causal relationship cannot be established, media appear to play a role in legislators' understanding of the issue. In this respect, it is important to consider that the consumption of climate change information originating from the media is significant compared to other sources. The limited range of policy options discussed by policy makers is not the media's responsibility alone, but a more poignant reporting could create more attention and understanding, which could also lead to further information seeking behaviors.

Acknowledgement

This research was funded by the National Science Foundation's Decision, Risk and Management Sciences program (Grant no. SES-0962505).

Notes

1 Issues were selected based on the highest responses to a similar question posted by Alcántara Sáez (2008) in the latest survey with these legislators.
2 MINAM has made available the National System of Environmental Information (SINIA). See http://sinia.minam.gob.pe.

References

Alcántara Sáez, M. (Ed.). (2008). *Politicians and politics in Latin America*. Boulder, CO: Lynne Rienner Publishers.

Bartels, L. (1996). Politicians and the press: Who leads, who follows? Paper presented at the American Political Science Association, San Francisco, 1996.

Baumgartner, F., Jones, B. D., & Leech, B. L. (1997). Media attention and congressional agendas. In S. Iyengar & R. Reeves (Eds.), *Do the media govern?* (pp. 349–363). Thousand Oaks, CA: Sage.

Birkland, T. A. (1997). *After disaster: Agenda setting, public policy, and focusing events*. Washington, DC: Georgetown University Press.

Boykoff, M. T. (2007). Flogging a dead norm? Newspaper coverage of anthropogenic climate change in the United States and United Kingdom from 2003 to 2006. *Area*, 39(4), 470–481.

Boykoff, M. T. (2008). The cultural politics of climate change discourse in UK tabloids. *Political Geography*, 27(5), 549–569.

Boykoff, M. T. (2009). We speak for the trees: Media reporting on the environment. *Annual Review of Environment and Resources*, 34, 431–457.

Boykoff, M. T. & Boykoff, J. M. (2004). Balance as bias: Global warming and the US prestige press. *Global Environmental Change Part A*, 14(2), 125–136.

Boykoff, M. T. & Boykoff, J. M. (2007). Climate change and journalistic norms: A case-study of US mass-media coverage. *Geoforum*, 38(6), 1190–1204.

Brooks, N., Adger, W. N., Bentham, G., Agnew M., & Eriksen, S. (2004). *New indicators of vulnerability and adaptive capacity*. Tyndall Centre for Climate Change Research, Vol. Technical Report 7.

Brossard, D., Shanahan J., & McComas, K. (2004). Are issue-cycles culturally constructed? A comparison of French and American coverage of global climate change. *Mass Communication & Society*, 7(3), 359–377.

Bybee, C. R. & Comadena, M. (1984). Information sources and state legislators: Decision-making and dependency. *Journal of Broadcasting & Electronic Media*, 28(3), 333–340.

Chatterjee, R. (2009). The road to REDD. *Environmental Science & Technology*, 43(3), 557–560.

Chong, D. & Druckman, J. N. (2007). Framing public opinion in competitive democracies. *American Political Science Review*, 101(04), 637–655.

Conaghan, C. M. (2005). *Fujimori's Peru: Deception in the public sphere*. Pittsburgh, PA: University of Pittsburgh Press.

Cosa Seria Este Clima. (2007). *Panorama del cambio climático en la comunidad andina*. Lima: Comunidad Andina.

Elmelund-Præstekær, C., Hopmann, D. N., & Nørgaard, A. S. (2011). Does mediatization change MP – media interaction and MP attitudes toward the media? Evidence from a longitudinal study of Danish MPs. *The International Journal of Press/Politics*, 16(3), 382–403.

Entman, R. M. (1989). How the media affect what people think: An information processing approach. *The Journal of Politics*, 51(2), 347–370.

Estado de la Opinión Pública. (2009). *El estado de la opinión pública*. Lima: Medio Ambiente, IOP-PUCP.

Estado de la Opinión Pública. (2011). *El estado de la opinión pública*. Lima: Instituto de Opinión Pública, PUCP.

Fisher, D. R., Waggle, J., & Leifeld, P. (2013). Where does political polarization come from? Locating polarization within the US climate change debate. *American Behavioral Scientist*, 57(1), 70–92.

Green-Pedersen, C. & Stubager, R. (2010). The political conditionality of mass media influence: When do parties follow mass media attention? *British Journal of Political Science*, 40(03), 663–677.

Hajek, F., Ventresca, M. J., Scriven, J., & Castro, A. (2011). Regime-building for REDD+: Evidence from a cluster of local initiatives in south-eastern Peru. *Environmental Science and Policy*, 14(2), 201–215.

Helms, L. (2008). Governing in the media age: The impact of the mass media on executive leadership in contemporary democracies. *Government and Opposition*, 43(1), 26–54.

Howarth, A. (2010). Contested processes, contested influence: A case study of genetically modified food in Britain. In S. Koch-Baumgarten & K. Voltmer (Eds.), *Public policy and mass media* (pp. 143–161). New York: Routledge.

Jones, B. D. & Baumgartner, F. R. (2005). *The politics of attention*. Chicago, IL: The University of Chicago Press.

Jones, B. D. & Wolfe, M. (2010). Public policy and the mass media: An information processing approach. In S. Koch-Baumgarten & K. Voltmer (Eds.), *Public policy and mass media* (pp. 17–43). New York: Routledge.

Jones, M. D. & McBeth, M. K. (2010). A narrative policy framework: Clear enough to be wrong? *Policy Studies Journal*, 38(2), 329.

Kepplinger, H. M. (2007). Reciprocal effects: Toward a theory of mass media effects on decision makers. *Harvard International Journal of Press/Politics*, 12(2), 3–23.

Kingdon, J. W. (2003). *Agendas, alternatives, and public policies*. New York: Longman.

Koch-Baumgarten, S. & Voltmer, K. (2010). Conclusion: The interplay of mass communication and political decision making – policy matters! In S. Koch-Baumgarten & K. Voltmer (Eds.), *Public policy and mass media* (pp. 215–227). New York: Routledge.

Lahsen, M. (2007). Trust through participation? Problems of knowledge in climate decision making. In M. E. Pettenger (Ed.), *The social construction of climate change: Power, knowledge, norms, discourses* (pp. 173–196). Aldershot: Ashgate Publishing Limited.

Lanegra, I. K. (2008). *El (ausente) estado ambiental*. Lima: CDE.

Laplante, L. J. & Phenicie, K. (2009). Mediating post-conflict dialogue: The media's role in transitional justice processes. *Marquette Law Review*, 93, 251–283.

Lewis, B. J. & Ellefson, P. V. (1996). Evaluating information flows to policy committees in state legislatures. *Evaluation Review*, 20(1), 29–48.

Liu, X., Lindquist, E., & Vedlitz, A. (2011). Explaining media and congressional attention to global climate change, 1969–2005: An empirical test of agenda-setting theory. *Political Research Quarterly*, 64(2), 405–419.

Mayo, C. M. & Perlmutter, D. D. (1998). Media use and disuse by state legislators: The social construction of innovation. *Journal of Business and Technical Communication*, 12(1), 71–88.

McComas, K. & Shanahan, J. (1999). Telling stories about global climate change: Measuring the impact of narratives on issue cycles. *Communication Research*, 26(1), 30–57.

McCright, A. M. & Dunlap, R. E. (2003). Defeating Kyoto: The conservative movement's impact on US climate change policy. *Social Problems*, 50(3), 348–373.

Minaya, E. L. (2010). Personal Interview, June 18.

Newton, K. (2006). May the weak force be with you: The power of the mass media in modern politics. *European Journal of Political Research*, 45(2), 209–234.

Olausson, U. (2009). Global warming-global responsibility? Media frames of collective action and scientific certainty. *Public Understanding of Science*, 18(4), 421–436.

Pump, B. (2011). Beyond metaphors: New research on agendas in the policy process. *Policy Studies Journal*, 39, 1–12.

Reeher, G. (1996). *Narratives of justice: Legislators' beliefs about distributive fairness*. Ann Arbor, MI: University of Michigan Press.

Reeher, G. (2006). *First person political: Legislative life and the meaning of public service*. New York: NYU Press.

Robinson, P. (2001). Theorizing the influence of media on world politics. *European Journal of Communication*, 16(4), 523–544.

Selin, H. & VanDeveer, S. D. (2009). Global climate change: Kyoto and beyond. In N. J. Vig & M. E. Kraft (Eds.), *Environmental policy: New directions for the twenty-first century* (pp. 265–285). Washington, DC: CQ Press.

Shanahan, E., McBeth, M., Hathaway, P., & Arnell, R. (2008). Conduit or contributor? The role of media in policy change theory. *Policy Sciences*, 41(2), 115–138.

Shoemaker, P. J. & Reese, S. D. (1996). *Mediating the message: Theories of influence on mass media content*. White Plains, NY: Longman.

Sonnett, J. (2010). Climates of risk: A field analysis of global climate change in US media discourse, 1997–2004. *Public Understanding of Science*, 19(6), 698–716.

Sundblad, E. L., Biel, A., & Garling, T. (2009). Knowledge and confidence in knowledge about climate change among experts, journalists, politicians, and laypersons. *Environment and Behavior*, 41(2), 281–302.

Tagina, M. L. (2009). El vínculo entre los parlamentarios Latinoamericanos y los medios de comunicación. Un análisis de la confianza y la influencia en la toma de decisiones. *Boletín Datos de Opinión, Elites Parlamentarias Latinoamericanas*. Salamanca: Universidad de Salamanca.

Takahashi, K. (2010). Cambio climático, investigación e incertidumbre. In A. Martínez & S. Pérez (Eds.), *Cambio climático en la cuenca del río Mantaro: Balance de 7 años de estudio*. Lima: Instituto Geofísico del Perú.

Takahashi, B. (2011). Framing and sources: A study of mass media coverage of climate change in Peru during the VALCUE. *Public Understanding of Science*, 20(4), 543–557.

Takahashi, B. & Meisner, M. (2011). Comparing influences on Peruvian climate change policy: Information, knowledge, and concern among political elites. *Journal of Intercultural Communication Research*, 40(3), 177–198.

Takahashi, B. & Meisner, M. (2012). Environmental discourses and discourse coalitions in the reconfiguration of Peru's environmental governance. *Environmental Communication: A Journal of Nature and Culture*, 6(3), 346–364.

Takahashi, B. & Meisner, M. (2013). Climate change in Peruvian newspapers: The role of foreign voices in a context of vulnerability. *Public Understanding of Science*, 22(4), 427–442.

Trumbo, C. (1996). Constructing climate change: Claims and frames in US news coverage of an environmental issue. *Public Understanding of Science*, 5(3), 269–283.

Ungar, S. (2000). Knowledge, ignorance and the popular culture: Climate change versus the ozone hole. *Public Understanding of Science*, 9(3), 297–312.

Van Aelst, P., Brants, K., Van Praag, P., De Vreese, C., Nuytemans, M., & Van Dalen, A. (2008). The Fourth state as superpower? An empirical study of perceptions of media power in Belgium and the Netherlands. *Journalism Studies*, 9(4), 494–511.

Vliegenthart, R. & Walgrave, S. (2011). When the media matter for politics: Partisan moderators of the mass media's agenda-setting influence on parliament in Belgium. *Party Politics*, 17(3), 321–342.

Vuille, M., Francou, B., Wagnon, P., Juen, I., Kaser, G., Mark, B. G., & Bradley, R. S. (2008). Climate change and tropical Andean glaciers: Past, present and future. *Earth-Science Reviews*, 89(3–4), 79–96.

Walgrave, S. (2008). Again, the almighty mass media? The media's political agenda-setting power according to politicians and journalists in Belgium. *Political Communication*, 25(4), 445–459.

Walgrave, S. & Lefevere, J. (2010). Do the media shape parties' agenda preferences? An empirical study of party manifestos in Belgium (1987–2003). In S. Koch-Baumgarten & K. Voltmer (Eds.), *Public policy and mass media* (pp. 44–64). New York: Routledge.

Walgrave, S., Soroka, S., & Nuytemans, M. (2008). The mass media's political agenda-setting power. *Comparative Political Studies*, 41(6), 814–836.

Walgrave, S. & Van Aelst, P. (2006). The contingency of the mass media's political agenda setting power: Toward a preliminary theory. *Journal of Communication*, 56(1), 88–109.

Wilson, K. M. (1995). Mass media as sources of global warming knowledge. *Mass Comm Review*, 22(1), 75–89.

Wilson, K. M. (2000). Drought, debate, and uncertainty: Measuring reporters' knowledge and ignorance about climate change. *Public Understanding of Science*, 9(1), 1–13.

Wood, B. D. & Vedlitz, A. (2007). Issue definition, information processing, and the politics of global warming. *American Journal of Political Science*, 51(3), 552–568.

Workman, S., Jones, B. D., & Jochim, A. E. (2009). Information processing and policy dynamics. *Policy Studies Journal*, 37(1), 75–92.

Yanovitzky, I. (2002). Effects of news coverage on policy attention and actions: A closer look into the media-policy connection. *Communication Research*, 29(4), 422–451.

COMMENTARY ON PART II

Climate change – media

Joe Smith

The media help shape what people think, feel, and do about environmental issues. They also hold public accounts of the actions or inactions of the main players in these dramas. From *The New York Times* pieces on the hazards of X-rays in the early 1900s, and the TV documentaries on population, pollution, and conservation in the 1970s and 1980s, through to digital and social media representations of climate change in the present, the quality of media storytelling has informed the nature and extent of public and political responses.

The three chapters in this section all address storytelling in one form or another. They consider the communication of high politics in the form of international climate summit journalism; the inter-relations between media and policy that shape climate change stories and policies in one developing country (Peru), and the work of US weathercasters in their own very specialized form of storytelling. The chapters all perform very valuable services in bringing novel empirical material to some vital questions about the formation and circulation of climate change storytelling. One of the things that is evident when read as a whole is that climate change mediations are strongly informed by the nature of the relationships amongst media storytellers, and between storytellers, their characters, and 'the people formerly known as the audience.' There are two contextual factors that are more or less present in each of the chapters. One is the dynamism and novelty of climate change politics. The issue generates a distinctive cultural politics, with six identifiable, often inter-relating features. These include: its global pervasiveness; its far reaching uncertainties; the interdependencies between human and non-human; the reverberations of history, above all post-colonial dimensions; the centrality of interdisciplinary knowledge; and the very distinctive play of temporality across the issue (Smith, 2011, 2013). These six features provide the hidden conceptual scaffolding beneath climate change stories across all media forms.

The chapters also indicate, however, how the conditions of media decision-making and news consumption are now undergoing more rapid and far-reaching changes than at any time since the birth of broadcasting. These changes have consequences, positive and negative, for the ways in which knowledge about climate change is sought, circulated, and debated. It is immensely demanding to make sense of the inter-relations between the shifting cultural politics of climate change and the dynamic developments in media culture and practice, technology, and political economy. It is noteworthy that in one form or another each set of authors in this section has coped with these challenges by focusing on particular venues or nodes in order to gather research data, and to tell revealing and well-informed stories about the storytellers.

Mainstream media concentration and competition: quality challenged

A review of media performance and influence in relation to climate change in the latter years of the last century would have focused exclusively on broadcast and print news and factual television. Such a research task would have been demanding, including tricky questions about advertiser or owner influence and varied forms of censorship, but at least there were some relatively tidy boundaries around types of media and the nature and contexts of media consumption. But many aspects of media consumption and production have changed significantly with the emergence of the Internet and digital media. Perhaps the one really persistent element is the sustained and central importance of the notion of 'story,' and the authority of the storytellers. The relationship between the two is another theme that runs through the three chapters gathered in this section.

The role of the storyteller, and the nature of the story, is inevitably informed by the nature and perspective of the patron. It is significant that one of the clearest trends of the last two decades has been the concentration of media ownership into a smaller number of increasingly international corporations. For example, in the US, the top five firms accounted for 13 percent of the mass media sector in 1984. Within a decade that share had doubled and the trend of concentration and consolidation continues (Noam, 2009). Digital media have seen parallel, often overlapping, processes of consolidation. This increases the influence of a small number of proprietors.

Intensifying competition for media consumer share, and apparently insuperable challenges to previous funding models for non-public service news provision are constantly driving down the funds available to support the practice of mainstream journalism. In 2009, online advertising revenues reached $24.2 billion, while print advertisement revenues stood at $24.8 billion (PWC, 2010). Taking the UK as a case study, Internet advertising in 2011 saw 12 percent growth while newspaper advertising saw an 8 percent drop in the same year (PWC, 2012). Researchers have shown how the amount of time available for the practice of journalism has narrowed. It was found that in 2006 the number of public relations executives in the UK exceeded the number of journalists for the first time (Davies, 2011).

In this context, media outlets tend to be less willing or able to invest in specialist journalists. With no time to research stories and intense pressure to fill space, investigative journalism has become an increasingly rare practice. Similarly, journalists have little time to research the background to complex stories that relate to academic research papers, evaluations of the scientific evidence, or policy or professional gray literatures. These developments have a number of negative consequences for mainstream coverage of demanding topics such as climate change.

There is far greater incidence of 'churnalism,' with press release content reproduced with little modification (Davies, 2011). Well-established NGOs and corporate interests, as well as the better resourced university and research institutions can more easily gain space for their content. But there is only limited interrogation of this content by mediators (journalists or editors), and the chances are increased of contradictory stories being run concurrently rather than cohesive and discursive pieces that have been carefully developed by a journalist. There is nothing new about corporate influence over journalism. Oreskes & Conway (2010) plot a history of the inter-relations between corporate interests and media representations of both health impacts of tobacco and climate change by powerful tobacco and oil interests. However, competition and concentration of ownership are making it yet more difficult to generate well researched and rounded media content on demanding topics within the mainstream media. Takahashi and Meisner's piece identifies the heavy reliance on a mix of national and local print outlets and international Internet sources for climate information on the part of, in their case Peruvian, legislators. The hazards of these routes to new knowledge are clear in a news environment that is almost universally seeing reduced investments in time, craft, and expertise.

Here comes everybody?

Social media, including blogging and micro blogging, create new practices, wherein production, consumption and sharing blend in entirely novel ways. Tegelberg et al. offer a close investigation of the relationship between social and mainstream media in their study of #climatenews. These developments have very mixed consequences for complex research or policy issues, but their chapter does serve to balance the generally negative accounts of mainstream media changes. There are more opportunities for unmediated knowledge exchange and debate between lay people and professionals/specialists (including lay specialists).

The opportunity for cheap generation, sharing, and responsiveness to a much more diverse body of content is opening up new media spaces around environmental risks, spanning hyper-local to global concerns. Niche communities can be convened on the web cheaply and quickly in ways that mainstream media could rarely achieve. Shirky (2010) explains how most leisure time of the late twentieth century was given over to the 'part-time job' of watching TV. He points to the extraordinary opportunities presented by the 'cognitive surplus' generated by educated populations with time available, and the novel tools of digital media before them. The hazards of this open media terrain may be managed by new forms of etiquette or social expectation. Linking to sources, avoiding anonymity except where conditions require it (above all whistleblowing) and online reputational signals may all serve to develop the depth and authority of online content. But such practices are far from becoming a dominant trend, and cannot be formalized in the manner of media governance or embedded in the form of professional journalistic norms of the pre-Internet era.

Mixed media

In different ways the three chapters all usefully perturb the idea that there is a 'right way' to tell the climate change story, or indeed to research it. Tegelberg et al.'s fine-grained account of the mingling of alternative and professional journalism in the context of climate summits reveals complex networks that "introduce hybridity into the news system by further blurring boundaries between information, news, and entertainment" (Papacharissi & Oliveira, 2012, p. 3, cited in Tegelberg et al.). Takahashi and Meisner bring fresh insights to the understanding of the knowledge politics of developing world climate policy-making through analysis of media-policy relations in Peru. Schweizer et al.'s study of weathercasters' views on climate science, policy, and communication demonstrates why researchers need to work harder to understand the underlying roots of conflict around science-based storytelling. Their sensitive approach to research design, and to the positioning of their research respondents, has generated important insights into the formation of attitudes and communication behaviors among an influential body of journalism professionals.

Such pluralism and innovation will be needed as researchers continue on the task of integrating understanding of three key trends and areas of analysis, that is: the political economy of the media, including concentration of ownership and blurring of mainstream and online; the political sociology of media consumption and production in the context of digital and social media and, third, the distinctive cultural politics of climate change. Shirky gives some hint of the complexity faced by the researcher, but also some of the opportunities presented to society more widely, by the new circumstances:

> All media can now slide from one to the other. A book can stimulate public discussion in a thousand places at once. An email conversation can be published by its participants. An essay intended for public consumption can anchor a private argument, parts of which later become public. We move from public to private and back again in ways that weren't possible in an era when public and private media, like the radio and the telephone, used different devices and different networks.

(Shirky, 2010, p. 56)

This 'sliding' will play out in interesting ways around issues that depend on the sharing and testing of knowledge claims about environmental change. In the past the incompleteness of search and retrieval made "possible, even plausible, the existence of undiscovered public knowledge" (Swanson, 1986, p. 103). The Internet and social media change that situation significantly. Organizations, networks, and individuals who are well motivated to understand or debate a particular point that in the past would not have won any media attention can now gather online with ease. It is not simply that more knowledge is available publicly: that alone would not allow 'undiscovered public knowledge' to be worked with. This can have difficult and confusing consequences for public debate, including the clustering of 'climate contrarians' who regularly generate highly selective and often distorted accounts that reject climate science. Nevertheless, the interaction of searching, sharing, linking, and commenting, paired with the sliding from one media form to another (public and private; mass and micro; global and hyper-local) creates opportunities for Shirky's cognitive surplus to contribute to understanding, debate and action on difficult new knowledge such as climate change.

However, mainstream media remain the main sources or origins of news media for most people, most of the time, and the trends are generally negative in terms of the resources and will to tackle demanding and complex topics such as climate change. Silverstone argues that the hazards presented by current changes in the media ecosystem call for an international structure of regulation for both public and commercial providers of content. His analogy is a fitting reference point for this volume, for he goes as far as to suggest:

> the equivalent of a Kyoto for the media. And notwithstanding the weaknesses of that particular accord, it provides a possible blueprint for a way forward in dealing with the palpable pollution and erosion of the global media environment, an environment which ironically is entirely man-made, but at the same time invisible as such in these structural terms … It is time for the global media environment to have its own movement if we are to be confident in humanity's capacity to secure the future of the planet.
>
> (Silverstone, 2006, pp. 176–177)

Silverstone and Shirky share the same object of study, that is, the media, and the relationships that diverse publics have with media platforms, products, and institutions. It is a mark of how far and fast the media environment has changed that the conclusions of two such different readings can be accepted by a reader simultaneously. The introduction to this volume cites Hall's concern to explore how discourses are tethered to "material realities, perspectives, and social practices" (Hall, 1997). However, the material realities, perspectives and social practices of media consumption and production have not simply been reconfigured by the Internet and digital and social media: they have been set in constant motion by them. 'Tethering' is perhaps no longer an appropriate metaphor as researchers take on the task of making sense of the varied flows of ideas and values that make up the cultural politics of climate change. The three chapters in this section all paused at venues, or nodes, in order to understand specific sets of relations at particular moments that have wider significance. In doing so they have helped indicate not simply how these processes might best be interpreted, but also clarified how climate change communications might also become more plural and dynamic in future.

References

Davies, N., (2011). *Flat Earth news: An award-winning reporter exposes falsehood, distortion and propaganda in the global media.* London: Random House.

Hall, S. (1997). *Representation: Cultural representation and signifying practices.* Thousand Oaks, CA: Sage.

Noam, E. M. (2009). *Media ownership and concentration in America.* New York: Oxford University Press.

Oreskes, N. & Conway, E. M. (2010). *Merchants of doubt: How a handful of scientists obscured the truth on issues from tobacco smoke to global warming*, 1st edition. New York: Bloomsbury Press.

Papacharissi, Z. & Oliveira M. (2012). Affective news and networked publics: The rhythms of news storytelling on #Egypt. *Journal of Communication*, 62(2), 266–282.

PWC. (2010). *Global entertainment and media outlook: 2011–2015.* PwC network. Retrieved June 1, 2013: http://www.pwc.co.uk/entertainment-media/issues/global-entertainment-and-media-outlook-2011-to-2015.jhtml.

PWC. (2012). *Global entertainment and media outlook: 2012–2016.* PwC network. Retrieved June 1, 2013: http://www.ukmediacentre.pwc.com/News-Releases/The-end-of-the-digital-beginning-The-challenge-for-media-companies-now-lies-in-how-to-implement-their-digital-strategies-1260.aspx.

Shirky, C. (2010). *Cognitive surplus: Creativity and generosity in a connected age.* London: Penguin Books.

Silverstone, R. (2006). *Media and morality: On the rise of the mediapolis*, 1st edition. Oxford: Polity Press.

Smith J. (2011). Why climate change is different: six elements that are shaping the new cultural politics. In R. Butler, E. Margolies, J. Smith & R. Tyszczuk (Eds.), *Culture and Climate Change: Recordings*, Cambridge: Shed, pp. 17–22.

Smith, J. (2013). Mediating tipping points: The search for a balanced story. In T. O'Riordan & T. Lenton (Eds.), *Addressing tipping points for a precarious future*, British Academy, Royal Society series. Oxford: Oxford University Press.

Swanson, D. R. (1986). Undiscovered public knowledge. *The Library Quarterly*, 56(2), 103–118.

PART III
Climate politics and policy

6

CLIMATE SCIENCE, POPULISM, AND THE DEMOCRACY OF REJECTION

Mark B. Brown

This chapter considers what popular distrust of climate science might tell us about the politics of democracy in the United States. I argue that such distrust can be usefully understood as part of a long tradition of popular suspicion of organized power. Whereas this tradition has usually focused on governmental power, those rejecting climate science take aim at the power of science. To be sure, they are usually mistaken in their scientific claims, they offer few constructive proposals, and their populist rhetoric echoes a broader anti-democratic tendency in contemporary politics. But unlike many climate policy advocates, climate science rejectionists have helped call attention to the economic and political dimensions of climate science and its role in public policy. In these respects, the rejection of climate science both illuminates and exacerbates contemporary dilemmas of democracy.

Introduction

What does climate change mean for democracy? According to many commentators, climate change is giving democracy a serious thrashing. For former US Vice President Al Gore, global warming is "the biggest failure of democratic governance in history" (Gore, 2009, p. 303). Famed British scientist James Lovelock suggests that climate change may require that we "put democracy on hold for a while" (Hickman, 2010). And philosopher Philip Kitcher calls the failure of climate policy "a huge failure of worldwide democracy" (Kitcher, 2011, p. 243). For many today, democracy is an inappropriate and ineffective political system for responding to climate change (Shearman & Smith, 2007).

Although the question of whether and how democracies can effectively tackle climate change is crucially important (Held & Hervey, 2010), it often obscures the equally important question of how the science and politics of climate change may be shaping what democracy means to people around the globe. As Mike Hulme (2009a), Clark Miller (2004), Sheila Jasanoff (2010), and others have argued, climate change has become an arena of controversy in which the meaning of various values and ideas is being worked out. Climate change is not just a policy problem, nor just a geophysical phenomenon, but a site of cultural and conceptual change. Both climate science and climate policy are intertwined with implicit and explicit conceptions of what democracy is or should be. Whether or not climate policy needs democracy, it is likely to transform it.

Focusing on the United States, this chapter shows how popular distrust of climate science and policy has become intertwined with the politics of democracy. I argue that those who reject mainstream climate science call attention to political dimensions of science often obscured by climate policy advocates. At the same time, however, rejectionists are often seriously misinformed about climate science, and they offer few constructive proposals for how science might better inform policy making. They also tend to embrace a corrosive populism, implausibly claiming to be the sole authentic spokesperson of the people. Climate science rejection thus both illuminates and exacerbates some of the key dilemmas associated with the politics of climate change.

More specifically, the views of many climate policy advocates and their critics on three key concepts – democracy, representation, and science advice – often amount to different sides of the same coin. They disagree over what democracy entails, but each assumes a partial and incomplete view of democracy that arguably depends on the other. They disagree over who truly speaks for the people, but they share a populist conception of political representation. And they disagree over whether climate science should be allowed to influence political decisions, but each assumes a linear conception of the relation between science and politics.

By arguing that climate policy advocates and their critics share several key assumptions, I do not mean to suggest that their views are equally well justified, nor to dispute the need for serious policies to address climate change. Rather, the aim of this chapter is to cast an alternative light on familiar dilemmas, thus opening up new questions for analysis. My goal is not to describe or explain the rise of climate science rejection or the anti-environmental movement. Others have carefully documented the loose network of fossil fuel interests, conservative foundations, think tanks, mass media outlets, and contrarian scientists that have long sought to create a false appearance of scientific debate over the basic facts of global warming (Dunlap & McCright, 2011; Jacques, 2009; Oreskes & Conway, 2010). Rather than repeating their efforts, I want to briefly explore the meaning of climate science rejection for how we think about democracy and democratic responses to climate change.

Climate science rejection

Scientific knowledge and scientific experts have long played an ambiguous role in the environmental movement, and different branches of environmentalism have adopted very different perspectives on the natural sciences (Beck, 1992, pp. 24–27, 163; Bocking, 2006; Yearly, 2010). On one hand, environmentalists have been among the most trenchant critics of the humanist arrogance and technocratic ambition often associated with modern science and engineering. Environmentalists have offered powerful arguments against the reduction of distinctly moral and political issues to technical problems of risk analysis and management. On the other hand, environmentalists have relied on the environmental sciences in at least two ways. First, effectively addressing a wide range of environmental problems depends in part on science. Many environmental problems, including nuclear radiation, toxic pollution, and climate change, cannot be directly perceived by the human senses, so without science we would not know about them in the first place. People can see climate change impacts, of course, ranging from shorter winters to shifts in animal habitats, but to see them *as* the (partial and possible) result of climate change requires climate science. Second, and of primary concern here, environmentalists have often relied on science to design, justify, and promote policy responses to climate change.

The 2007 report of the Intergovernmental Panel on Climate Change (IPCC, 2007) concluded that the existence of global warming is 'unequivocal,' and that it is more than 90 percent likely that the global warming observed during the past 50 years is largely caused by human activity. The world's major scientific institutions concur. Significant uncertainties persist about the timing and extent of local impacts, as well as the precise role of deep ocean warming, atmospheric aerosols, water vapor, and other factors. But there is widespread scientific consensus on the basics. Nonetheless, in the United States, beliefs on global warming vary widely according to self-identified political affiliation. In a 2011 poll, when asked whether global warming is happening, majorities of Democrats (78 percent), Independents (71 percent), and Republicans (53 percent) said yes, but that view was shared by only 34 percent of self-identified supporters of the libertarian-conservative Tea Party. (For non-US readers, the Tea Party is not an official political party, but a loosely organized and highly influential network of activists that rose to national prominence in early 2009.) A substantial majority of Democrats (62 percent) said that global warming is caused mostly by human activities, but that view was shared by a minority of Republicans (36 percent) and even fewer Tea Party supporters (19 percent) (Leiserowitz et al., 2011, p. 7). A more recent survey (Leiserowitz et al., 2013) found that 70 percent of Americans believe that global warming is real and should be addressed, but 30 percent are either 'doubtful' (uncertain whether global warming is occurring, but if so, they say it is due to natural causes: 13 percent), 'disengaged' (unaware of the issue: 9 percent), or 'dismissive' (convinced that global warming is not occurring: 8 percent). Outside the US, the situation looks rather different. According to a 2010 opinion survey of 111 countries, "People nearly everywhere, including majorities in developed Asia and Latin America, are more likely to attribute global warming to human activities rather than natural causes" (Ray & Pugliese, 2011).

Many commentators see the distrust of climate science among US conservatives as one manifestation of a larger phenomenon of 'denialism,' loosely defined as the rejection of mainstream science for ideological purposes (Diethelm & McKee 2009; Dunlap & McCright, 2011; Specter, 2009). Like all labels, the term 'denialism' is problematic (Boykoff, 2011, pp. 159–164; Lahsen, 2013; Wihbey, 2012). It polemically evokes the case of Holocaust deniers, and commentators often apply it indiscriminately to anyone critical of mainstream science. As one author aptly remarks, "Denial is the secular form of blasphemy; deniers are scorned, ridiculed and sometimes prosecuted" (Skidelsky, 2010). Moreover, most of those who accept mainstream climate science do so without any more critical investigation than those who reject it. In this chapter, I use the less polemical if still imperfect phrase 'climate science rejection' – or for convenience 'rejectionism' – to identify people who entirely reject the notion of anthropogenic climate change.

Commentators have offered various explanations for climate science rejection. Some see the primary cause in naked economic interest. The oil and coal industries have long funded bogus studies on climate change, copying earlier efforts by tobacco companies to 'manufacture doubt' about mainstream science (Jacques, 2012; Oreskes & Conway, 2010). Another plausible explanation is religious and cultural affiliation: many Christian conservatives link their rejection of climate science to a similar rejection of evolutionary theory, and such rejections may be best understood not as epistemic claims but as expressions of group identity (Revkin, 2011).[1] Similarly, research on 'cultural cognition' suggests that people with hierarchical and individualist values who tend to reject government regulation also reject climate science, because they assume a close link between them (Kahan, 2010). Others see denialism as a psychological defense mechanism for coping with troubling facts; it is not primarily a matter of 'denying' climate change, but of being 'in denial' about it – a phenomenon apparent not only among those who reject climate science but also those who accept it but fail to respond in any serious way (Norgaard, 2011; Lertzman, 2008). Despite their different explanations of what causes climate science rejection, most commentators agree that it threatens the effective resolution of complex public problems. Without disputing that view, I want to consider the possibility that rejectionism can also tell us something about the relationship between climate change and democracy.

Climate science and democracy

Scholars who study wealthy democracies have long observed a decline in citizen participation in formal state institutions like elections and political parties, coupled with a decline in public trust in government. But such distrust does not amount to citizen apathy, as many assume. Rather, a combination of high public expectations and low governmental performance produces 'critical citizens' who are frustrated with mainstream politics precisely because they are *not* apathetic (Norris, 2011; Lertzman, 2008). Today's skeptical, critical citizens express their demands in a highly diverse, de-centered political landscape, including non-electoral state institutions like public hearings, stakeholder processes, and courts; non-state civil society associations like religious organizations or environmental groups; and non-institutionalized forms of participation associated with social movements, such as protests, demonstrations, strikes, boycotts, online activism, and so on (Dalton, 2004; Rosanvallon, 2008, pp. 18–22; Warren, 2003).

A useful framework for making sense of this diverse participatory landscape appears in Pierre Rosanvallon's distinction between three elements of modern democracy: electoral-representative government, public deliberation, and 'counter-democracy' (Rosanvallon, 2008, pp. 313–316). Democratic theorists have devoted intense effort to studying public deliberation, while empirical political scientists have tended to focus on electoral democracy, or what Rosanvallon calls the 'democracy of proposition': the pursuit of collective goals through the delegation and exercise of power. Taking these two elements, a common view of democracy focuses on the electoral authorization and accountability of representatives, informed by various kinds of public deliberation. But equally important is what Rosanvallon calls counter-democracy or the 'democracy of rejection' (Rosanvallon, 2008, p. 15). Rather than constructive efforts at collective self-government, counter-democracy involves attempts to monitor, block, or evaluate such efforts. Through various forms of public oversight, prevention, and judgment, citizens limit and constrain the same public officials they authorize through elections. Indeed, the term 'counter-democracy' is potentially misleading, since the practices in question do not oppose democracy as such but are actually a key part of it.

Counter-democratic institutions and practices have a long history, predating the establishment of modern representative democracy. Consider the medieval maxim of popular consent: 'That which is the concern of all must be approved by all.' Today this notion is usually conceived in terms of positive consent, as a matter of popular sovereignty and universal suffrage. But it was long understood in negative terms, such that consent was taken to consist in the absence of popular opposition, rather than citizen approval of public officials or policies.

> All politics was thus organized around the idea of *prevention*. It was the power to say no, the potential to remove the Prince or his administrators that informed the earliest conception of legitimate and viable social intervention in the political realm.
>
> (Rosanvallon, 2008, p. 127)

Or consider the key role of popular judgment in ancient Athens, where a citizen was expected not only to participate in the Assembly, which discussed and adopted laws and policies, but also in randomly selected political juries. The latter evaluated citizens accused of corruption, negligence, or impiety, as well as those charged with promoting laws later deemed imprudent or against the public interest (Rosanvallon, 2008, pp. 195–202). More recent examples of counter-democratic institutions include the traditions of parliamentary opposition and investigation, internal and external audit and evaluation mechanisms, whistleblowing, mass media scrutiny, and judicial review.

The democracy of rejection is thus far from new, but it has become especially prevalent in today's advanced democratic societies. Most relevant here is the rise of critical social movements and civil society organizations. To be sure, social movements generally involve both critical and constructive elements. They denounce racism, sexism, or environmental destruction, for example, while also promoting more enlightened practices. But many recent protest movements, while perhaps advocating a broad vision of social change, show little interest in promoting their goals through established political institutions. According to one journalist's account, many protesters today exhibit a "wariness, even contempt, toward traditional politicians and the democratic political process they preside over" (Kulish, 2011). The recent Occupy movement is a case in point. Commentators differ on whether it is a weakness or strength of the movement that it lacks a unified policy agenda or a strategy for building alliances with public officials, but it seems clear that Occupy activists reject politics as usual (Gitlin, 2012). Indeed, as Rosanvallon points out (2008, pp. 14–15, 183–185), oppositional movements have a structural advantage: it is easier to mobilize citizens to reject a policy or institution than to agree on one. Blocking a proposed policy offers a clear victory, while the criteria for successful policy are far more ambiguous.

Now, what happens when the democracy of rejection is directed not against public officials, institutions, or policies, but against scientists and scientific knowledge? Rosanvallon does not consider popular rejection of mainstream science as an example of counter-democracy, but it offers a powerful illustration of his argument. Those who reject climate science are not best understood as anti-democratic, but as implicitly embracing a particular element of democracy.

Modern science has served a wide range of functions in the construction of liberal-democratic states (Ezrahi, 1990). In the eighteenth century, for example, public demonstrations of experimental science offered a model of rational discussion that played a key role in constituting the liberal-democratic public sphere. The practical application of the same scientific principles to diverse situations seemed to vindicate the liberal-democratic faith in human equality. Those who reject mainstream climate science implicitly accept this longstanding view of science as constituting political life – if they didn't, they wouldn't need to challenge climate science and the political aims associated with it. Indeed, rejectionists seem acutely aware of the political stakes associated with climate science. Whereas environmentalists tend to emphasize normative questions regarding future generations, vulnerable populations, and threatened ecosystems, rejectionists often highlight normative questions associated with climate science itself.

One set of questions involves potential conflicts of interest among climate scientists. Anti-environmentalists have long argued that climate change is little more than a cash cow for climate scientists and their liberal allies, above all the jet-setting Al Gore. In August 2011, for example, Texas Governor Rick Perry told an audience, "I do believe that the issue of global warming has been politicized.

I think there are a substantial number of scientists who have manipulated data so that they will have dollars rolling into their projects" (O'Sullivan, 2011). Perry offered no evidence for this charge, and of course he said nothing about the interest conflicts of those who dispute mainstream climate science while funded by the fossil fuel industry. Nonetheless, the question of conflicts of interest among climate scientists is important. When the InterAcademy Council examined the policies and procedures of the IPCC in the wake of the 'climategate' e-mail scandal, it found that the IPCC lacked a conflict-of-interest policy. It also noted that questions had been raised "about the IPCC Chair's service as an adviser to, and board member of, for-profit energy companies ... and about the practice of scientists responsible for writing IPCC assessments reviewing their own work" (IAC, 2010, p. 53) The Council recommended the adoption of a rigorous conflict-of-interest policy, as well as a series of other reforms to ensure greater public accountability and transparency in climate science (IAC, 2010, p. 53; Beck, 2012).

Those rejecting climate science have also sometimes raised important questions about the economic stakes of proposed climate policies. Conservatives in the US have long argued that the entire notion of climate change is part of a left-wing scheme to undermine American free-market capitalism, economic growth, and national sovereignty (Dunlap & McCright, 2011). Analyses of the economic costs of climate change vary enormously, of course, in part because key variables are not subject to definitive analysis but depend on value questions. Calculating whether the future benefits of climate mitigation policies justify their current costs, for example, requires establishing a social discount rate, which involves an inherently contestable decision regarding the importance of current generations as compared to future generations (Hulme, 2009a, pp. 120–123). Those rejecting mainstream climate science have generally not promoted thoughtful debate about such questions, but they have occasionally put them on the table. For example, in a speech in April 2009 on the floor of the US House of Representatives, Representative Michele Bachman of Minnesota said,

> Carbon dioxide is ... not harmful. It is a part of Earth's life cycle. And yet we're being told that we have to ... reduce the American standard of living to create an arbitrary reduction in something that is naturally occurring in the earth.
>
> (Dade, 2011)

And Sarah Palin (who once supported policies to address climate change) wrote in 2009 that "we can't say with assurance that man's activities cause weather changes. We can say, however, that any potential benefits of proposed emissions reduction policies are far outweighed by their economic costs" (Palin, 2009; see also Robinson, 2009). With respect to such arguments, Naomi Klein rightly argues that "the left is going to have to learn from the right" (Klein, 2011, p. 13). Libertarian-conservatives are wrong to reject mainstream climate science.

But when it comes to the real-world consequences of those scientific findings, specifically the kind of deep changes required not just to our energy consumption but to the underlying logic of our economic system, [they] may be in considerably less denial than a lot of professional environmentalists, the ones who paint a picture of global warming Armageddon, then assure us that we can avert catastrophe by buying 'green' products and creating clever markets in pollution.

(Klein, 2011, p. 14)

As these examples suggest, and despite appearances to the contrary, the primary concern of those who reject mainstream climate science is usually climate policy rather than climate science itself (Forsyth, 2012, p. 20). Anti-environmentalists are clearly mistaken about climate science, but they sometimes highlight political aspects of the issue neglected by climate policy advocates. Unlike some environmentalists, they rightly portray climate change as a distinctly political problem that should not be reduced to implementing the conclusions of climate science. Consider Al Gore, who in September 2011 introduced his "Climate Reality Project" by saying, "Fossil fuel interests have money, influence, control. But together we have something they don't: reality" (Gore, 2011a). Gore here suggests that reality itself supports his policy proposals. Gore echoed this sentiment in his concluding remarks on the event, when he insisted, "Climate change is not a political problem. It is a human problem" (Gore, 2011b). Like the reality discerned by climate science, Gore here suggests that "human" problems are indisputable – and hence, non-political. Anti-environmentalists may be mistaken about everything else, but they are right to insist that climate change is a political issue. And by rejecting climate science, they implicitly embrace and expand the tradition of counter-democracy. In this respect, they suggest a different but no less valuable conception of democracy than environmentalists who focus on electoral politics and public deliberation.

Climate science and populist representation

The discussion so far suggests that conceiving climate rejection as a form of counter-democracy may help open up new and important questions for political discussion. In this respect, climate rejection might inadvertently promote the effectiveness and legitimacy of democratic institutions. At the same time, however, as a form of counter-democracy, climate rejection threatens democratic institutions when it becomes infused with populism (Rosanvallon, 2008, pp. 22–24, 267–273).

Populism is a much contested concept with an ambiguous relationship to democracy (Canovan, 2005; Laclau, 2005). As Rosanvallon conceives it, populism employs the fiction of a unified and homogenous people to bolster claims to be the people's sole authentic spokesperson. Populists thus attack 'foreigners,' 'immigrants,' and other supposed 'others,' as well as public officials and other elites. Although claiming to speak for the people, populism "strikes at the representative principle itself," because it tries to erase the incomplete and divided quality of representation in pluralist societies (Rosanvallon, 2008, p. 266). Like other recent theorists of representation (Urbinati & Warren, 2008), Rosanvallon argues that no particular representative claim should be taken as the authentic voice of the people. Anyone claiming to speak for others should not aim for direct correspondence between their claims and an allegedly unified public will. In democracies today, 'the people' is constructed in the process of representation. Populists attempt to short-cut the laborious and contentious process of constructing the people, portraying themselves as the people's only true representatives.

When infused with populism, counter-democracy's various modes of distrust become pathological. Critical oversight of public officials becomes "a compulsive and permanent stigmatization of the ruling authorities" (Rosanvallon, 2008, p. 268). Efforts to resist selected legislative acts expand into a compulsive desire to block any government action at all. And the people as judges become mired in vindictive accusations of public officials, welfare state recipients, illegal immigrants, and so on. The melding of populism and counter-democracy creates "a form of political expression in which the democratic project is totally swallowed up and taken over by counter-democracy" (Rosanvallon, 2008, p. 273). As a result, "The citizen is transformed into an ever more demanding political consumer, tacitly renouncing joint responsibility for creating a shared world" (2008, pp. 253–254).

Is the popular rejection of mainstream climate science populist in this sense? Although rejectionism as such may not constitute a political movement, it seems to be a key component of a loose network of conservative, libertarian, and Christian fundamentalist think tanks, foundations, public officials, and activists, concentrated in the United States but extending to other countries around the world (Jacques, 2009). And rejectionism seems to be associated with the typical markers of a certain version of populism. Those rejecting climate science appeal to everyday common sense, when they insist that a cold winter means that global warming cannot be happening. They present themselves as defending popular interests, when they argue that carbon-dioxide regulation kills jobs. They rely on celebrity politicians like Sarah Palin. And most importantly, they claim to be the authentic voice of the sovereign people or "real Americans," as Palin famously put it.

The Tea Party movement, for example, bears many trappings of populism, and it has been a key locus of climate rejection in the United States. Funded and promoted (some say created) by conservative foundations and political elites, a large percentage of Tea Party activists reject climate science, as noted previously. More generally, many Tea Partiers see skepticism toward experts as key to their participatory conception of democracy. "To guard against possible bamboozlement – and to demonstrate their own virtue and skill as informed democratic citizens – Tea Party members arm themselves for confrontations with their legislative representatives by reading particular bills themselves" (Skocpol & Williamson,

2012, p. 53). Tea Party activists have been excellent at organizing rallies, meetings, and newsletters, and they show a general willingness to learn the nitty-gritty of everyday politics. Whereas educated liberals know a lot about policy content, Tea Party activists know how Congress and their state legislatures work, how to work with local government boards and committees, and how to get public officials elected and policies adopted. "They know process, but flub content – the exact opposite of the academic liberals" (Skocpol & Williamson, 2012, p. 198). Tea Party activists link their activism and ignorance to counter-democratic attacks, not on government as such, but on the 'undeserving poor' (primarily immigrants and minorities) who they believe benefit from government programs at the expense of more deserving 'real Americans' like themselves. Like other populists, Tea Partiers claim to be the sole authentic spokespersons for the people.

What is especially interesting, however, is that this populist view of democracy appears not only among those who reject climate science, but within the broader discourse of climate change itself. The common framing of climate change in both global and apocalyptic terms (Nisbet, 2011) arguably fosters a sort of 'climate populism' (Swyngedouw, 2010). The global framing of climate change appears in the prevailing focus on long-term targets for global carbon-dioxide and average temperature levels, as well as the dominance of global circulation models as the primary scientific approach to understanding climate change (Bocking, 2006, pp. 111–116). Indeed, the very notion of climate as a global phenomenon rests in part on the painstakingly established legitimacy of global political institutions like the IPCC (Miller, 2004). By reducing global warming to a problem caused by the universal physical properties of greenhouse gases, the IPCC addresses climate change primarily at the global scale (Demeritt, 2001). The issue has often been framed as a matter of protecting a 'fragile planet,' not in terms of equity and justice among people or nations. And the global focus diverts attention from the national, regional, and local venues where democracy has historically been most vibrant.

The apocalyptic framing appears in the use of catastrophic imagery of sea-level rise and natural disasters to mobilize people to 'save the planet' (Hulme, 2009a, pp. 345–348). The film *Please Help the World* (Poulsene, 2009), shown to delegates at the 2009 Copenhagen Climate Change Conference, is one among many examples. Framing climate change this way obscures the enormous differences in vulnerability among different populations around the globe. Billions of poor people are *already* highly vulnerable to climate, regardless whether the climate is changing or not, and regardless whether any changes are caused by humans.

In each of these respects, as Erik Swyngedouw (2010, pp. 221–224) argues, the populist framing of climate change reduces the wide range of factors contributing to climate change to a single 'enemy of the people': carbon-dioxide. The enemy is conceived as an outsider, and the solution lies in its elimination, rather than in changing the sociotechnical systems that produce it. In contrast to conceptions of politics that emphasize conflicts of interest and call on particular constituencies to bring about a desired change, populist climate politics addresses itself to all people everywhere. Elites are asked to answer the 'call of the people,' but the vast differences in what people want or need around the world remain unaddressed. In this respect, populist climate politics "ultimately reinforce processes of de-politicization and the socio-political status quo" (Swyngedouw, 2010, p. 214).

Both advocates and critics of climate science have thus implicitly adopted a populist framing of climate change. Among the advocates, populism limits the scope of climate policy; among the critics, it undermines the possibility of any constructive political action at all. Rejectionists illuminate aspects of the politics of science neglected by many environmentalists, but they generally fail to offer proposals for building a shared world in light of the emerging dilemmas associated with climate change.

Climategate and the politics of science advice

In the fall of 2009, somebody either hacked or leaked over 1,000 e-mails written over 15 years by climate scientists at the University of East Anglia. Among other things, the e-mails showed leading climate scientists refusing to share their data with critics, evading Freedom of Information Act requests, and conspiring to manipulate peer review processes to keep their critics from being published in leading journals. Conservative commentators endlessly and misleadingly quoted a few select e-mails to argue that climate science was corrupt to the core, and hence, that global warming is a hoax. Environmentalists replied, correctly, that the e-mails did not cast doubt on the basic conclusions of mainstream climate science. After multiple governmental inquiries, the scientists involved were largely exonerated (Randerson, 2010; Tierney, 2009). What few noticed is that the e-mails revealed not only 'scientists behaving badly,' but also a particular image of democracy.

The scientists apparently worried that the minor uncertainties in their calculations, if revealed to the public and exploited by industry-funded critics, would undermine popular support for both climate science and climate policy. Given the history of the issue, their concerns were not unfounded. However, they appear to have mistakenly assumed that maintaining public support for *climate policy* requires eliminating uncertainties from public presentations of *climate science* (Hulme, 2009b; Sarewitz, 2010). In this respect, the climate scientists assumed a 'linear model' of science advice, a view that has long dominated science advisory processes (Pielke, 2007).

The linear model is the idea that science can solve social problems only if it remains insulated from society. It assumes a direct, straight-line connection between scientific knowledge and public policy. According to the linear model, scientific knowledge both precedes and remains independent of political decisions. The basic assumption is that science comes first, followed by policy. First get the facts straight, then act. Moreover, the linear model assumes that once scientists reach consensus, public policy flows directly from the science. The linear model of science and policy has long been a prominent part of the politics of climate change (Beck, 2011).

The linear model of science advice may be appropriate in certain contexts, when there is consensus on both scientific knowledge and political values (Pielke, 2007). In such cases, scientists can inform politicians about the best means for pursuing a given goal, and politicians can then simply implement the recommended means. But most policy problems today are not like that. There is an irresolvable uncertainty to much of the science involved in current policy debates (Sarewitz, 2004). There is no single best solution that is best according to all relevant criteria. Policy scholars call these 'ill-structured problems' or 'wicked problems' (Turner, 2003). In most sociotechnical controversies today, the combination of technical uncertainty and political disagreement means that public policies either cannot or should not be determined by experts alone.

Most importantly, when you're dealing with a wicked problem, and scientists or politicians adopt the linear model of science advice, they practically invite their opponents to attack the science (Pielke, 2007). If you offer science as the single best reason for your preferred policy, you create an incentive for those who disagree with you to find problems with the science. The result is that public debate focuses on whether the science is credible or not. Science becomes a proxy battleground for politics. The irony is that both sides in the debate share the assumption that science drives policy. What gets lost is an honest debate over competing values and interests.

We have seen this repeatedly with regard to climate change. When environmentalists make their case for climate policies, they usually point first of all to climate science. They emphasize the growing evidence that human actions are causing climate change; they point to the IPCC reports; they fret about public ignorance of climate science. They occasionally talk about social and political values, such as the responsibility of rich countries for past carbon-dioxide emissions, the right of poor countries to economic development, our obligations to future generations, and so on. But these sorts of 'soft' arguments often take a back seat to the 'hard' claims of climate science. Climate science seems to offer a hammer for smashing the opposition, and environmentalists have often found it difficult to resist.

So, despite taking opposite sides on climate policy, rejectionists and their critics often share a basic assumption: climate science provides the single best justification for climate policy. They disagree on whether the science tells us about reality. But they agree that *if* science gives us an accurate picture of reality, *then* it tells us what we need to do about it. This fixation on climate science has made easy work for those who oppose climate policies. All they have to do is create public doubt about climate science. Counter-democratic attacks on climate science partly disrupt this prevailing focus on science, insofar as they highlight moral and economic disagreements. But merely by engaging their opponents on the terrain of science, rejectionists reinforce the dominant approach. In this respect, climate science rejection is better understood as a symptom, not a cause, of the failure of climate policy (Goeminne, 2012).

The sad thing is that the entire debate over climate science is largely irrelevant. For over 30 years, there has been sufficient scientific evidence of human-induced climate change to justify 'no regrets' policies to reduce greenhouse gas emissions, promote energy research, and increase people's resilience to climate, among other things. Such policies can be justified with hybrid judgments that combine scientific and political considerations, and which remain defensible even if aspects of mainstream climate science turn out to be somewhat mistaken. Generally speaking, better climate policy does not require better climate science. Nor does it necessarily depend on better public understanding of climate science (even if that may be desirable for its own sake). Indeed, recent studies suggest that as people have come to better understand climate change, their expressed concern about it has actually decreased (Kellstedt et al., 2008). And despite the 30 percent of Americans who either reject or don't know about climate change, a recent survey found that 77 percent say global warming should be a 'very high,' 'high,' or 'medium' priority for the president and Congress. And 92 percent say that developing sources of clean energy is a 'very high,' 'high,' or 'medium' priority (Leiserowitz et al., 2012).

In other policy areas, democratic governments have adopted policies with far less scientific certainty than we have today about climate change. With regard to stratospheric ozone depletion, for example, the US Congress took steps to reduce it long before scientists had achieved consensus on the details of the science. Indeed, during the early years of research on the ozone hole, scientific uncertainties actually increased rather than decreased. But that did not deter policymakers from taking action (Pielke, 2010, pp. 25–28). With regard to climate, the economic and political stakes are much higher, and the resistance to action therefore much greater. But it is doubtful that such resistance can be overcome by harping on the science (Prins et al., 2010, p. 18).

Conclusion

The preceding discussion suggests that climate science rejection is not only an ideological tool for defending economic interests, a psychological defense mechanism, or a cowardly abandonment of reason and rationality. It may be all those things. But it is also part of a long tradition of popular distrust of power, in this case the power of science rather than government. And it is part of a tendency across the political spectrum to use science as a proxy battleground for politics. Rejectionism is not simply an unwillingness to face an 'inconvenient truth,' but a political reaction against those who would use truth to eliminate politics. In this respect, those who reject mainstream climate science may inadvertently promote a more democratic approach to climate science and policy.

It goes beyond the bounds of this chapter to outline such an approach, but it clearly depends on recasting the role of science in climate politics and policy. Scholars in the social studies of science, science communication, and related fields have developed many promising proposals, and climate policy advocates should pay more attention to their findings. Climate science is essential for understanding and responding to our changing climate, but it cannot determine which policies best represent the needs and values of diverse human communities around the globe. Those needs and values are often matters of dispute, and effective and legitimate responses to climate change depend on various modes of citizen participation and representation, facilitated by diverse institutions at the local, national, and global level (Brown, 2009).

If democracy becomes reduced to a populist democracy of rejection, then those who argue that climate change requires us to put democracy on hold may turn out to be right. We may reach a point where authoritarian governments are better able than democracies to promote greenhouse gas reduction, climate adaptation, and some aspects of social justice. But rather than simply denouncing climate science rejection, environmental advocates should take up the concerns it raises about the politics of science. More generally, we should be aware that climate change has implications, not only for global justice and the global environment, but also for democracy – not just whether it exists, but what it means.

Note

1 "Democrats are more likely to believe that human beings evolved from earlier species of animals (62 percent), compared to Independents (57 percent), Republicans (51 percent), and Tea Party members (34 percent)" (Leiserowitz et al., 2011, p. 6).

References

Beck, U. (1992). *Risk society: Towards a new modernity*, trans. Mark Ritter. London: Sage Publications.

Beck, S. (2011). Moving beyond the linear model of expertise? IPCC and the test of adaptation. *Regional Environmental Change*, 11(2), 297–306.

Beck, S. (2012). Between tribalism and trust: The IPCC under the "public microscope." *Nature and Culture*, 7(2), 151–173.

Bocking, S. (2006). *Nature's experts: Science, politics, and the environment.* New Brunswick, NJ: Rutgers University Press.

Boykoff, M. T. (2011). *Who speaks for the climate: Making sense of media reporting on climate change.* Cambridge: Cambridge University Press.

Brown, M. B. (2009). *Science in democracy: Expertise, institutions, and representation.* Cambridge, MA: MIT Press.

Canovan, M. (2005). *The people.* Cambridge: Polity.

Dade, C. (2011). *In their own words: GOP candidates and science.* NPR.org, September 6. Retrieved July 25, 2013: http://www.npr.org/2011/09/07/140071973/in-their-own-words-gop-candidates-and-science.

Dalton, R. J. (2004). *Democratic challenges, democratic choices: The erosion of political support in advanced industrial democracies.* New York: Oxford University Press.

Demeritt, D. (2001). The construction of global warming and the politics of science. *Annals of the Association of American Geographers*, 92(2), 307–337.

Diethelm, P. & McKee, M. (2009). Denialism: What is it and how should scientists respond? *European Journal of Public Health*, 19(1), 2–4.

Dunlap, R. E. & McCright, A. (2011). Organized climate change denial. In D. Schlosberg, J. Dryzek, and R. Norgaard (Eds.), *The Oxford handbook of climate change and society* (pp. 144–160). Oxford: Oxford University Press.

Ezrahi, Y. (1990). *The descent of Icarus: Science and the transformation of contemporary democracy.* Cambridge, MA: Harvard University Press.

Forsyth, T. (2012). Politicizing environmental science does not mean denying climate science nor endorsing it without question. *Global Environmental Politics*, 12(2), 18–23.

Gitlin, T. (2012). *Occupy nation: The roots, the spirit, and the promise to occupy Wall Street.* New York: It Books, HarperCollins Publishers.

Goeminne, G. (2012). Lost in translation: Climate denial and the return of the political. *Global Environmental Politics*, 12(2), 1–8.

Gore, A. (2009). *Our choice: A plan to solve the climate crisis.* Emmaus, PA: Rodale; New York: Melcher Media.

Gore, A. (2011a). What can change in a day? (2011, August 2). *USTREAM* (Online video). Retrieved July 25, 2013: http://www.ustream.tv/recorded/16396717.

Gore, A. (2011b). Hour 24: New York. (2011, September 15). *USTREAM* [Online video]. Retrieved July 25, 2013: http://www.ustream.tv/recorded/17294584.

Held, D. & Hervey, A. F. (2010). Democracy, climate change and global governance. *Policy Network Paper.* Retrieved July 25, 2013: http://www.policy-network.net/publications/publications.aspx?id=3406.

Hickman, L. (2010). James Lovelock: Humans are too stupid to prevent climate change. *The Guardian*, March 29. Retrieved: http://www.guardian.co.uk/science/2010/mar/29/james-lovelock-climate-change.

Hulme, M. (2009a). *Why we disagree about climate change: Understanding controversy, inaction and opportunity.* Cambridge: Cambridge University Press.

Hulme, M. (2009b). The science and politics of climate change. *Wall Street Journal*, December 2. Retrieved: http://online.wsj.com/article/SB10001424052748704107104574571613215771336.html.

IAC (InterAcademy Council). (2010). *Climate change assessments: Review of the processes and procedures of the IPCC.* Amsterdam: InterAcademy Council.

IPCC (Intergovernmental Panel on Climate Change). (2007). *Fourth Assessment Report: Climate Change 2007.* Retrieved: http://www.ipcc.ch/publications_and_data/ar4/syr/en/contents.html.

Jacques, P. J. (2009). *Environmental skepticism: Ecology, power and public life.* Farnham: Ashgate.

Jacques, P. J. (2012). A general theory of climate denial. *Global Environmental Politics*, 12(2), 9–17.

Jasanoff, S. (2010). A new climate for society. *Theory, Culture & Society*, 27(2–3), 1–27.

Kahan, D. M. (2010). Fixing the communications failure. *Nature*, 463 (January 21), 296–297.

Kellstedt, P. M., Zahran, S., & Vedlitz, A. (2008). Personal efficacy, the information environment, and attitudes toward global warming and climate change in the USA. *Risk Analysis*, 28(1), 113–126.

Kitcher, P. (2011). *Science in a democratic society.* Amherst, MA: Prometheus Books.

Klein, N. (2011). Capitalism vs. the climate. *The Nation*, November 28, 11–21.

Kulish, N. (2011). As scorn for vote grows, protests surge around globe. *New York Times*, September 27. Retrieved July 25, 2013: http://www.nytimes.com/2011/09/28/world/as-scorn-for-vote-grows-protests-surge-around-globe.html?pagewanted=all.

Laclau, E. (2005). *On populist reason.* London, UK: Verso.

Lahsen, M. (2013). Anatomy of dissent: A cultural analysis of climate skepticism. *American Behavioral Scientist*, 57(6), 732–753.

Leiserowitz, A., Maibach, E., Roser-Renouf, C., & Hmielowski, J. D. (2011). *Politics and global warming: Democrats, republicans, independents, and the Tea Party.* Yale

University and George Mason University. New Haven, CT: Yale Project on Climate Change Communication.

Leiserowitz, A., Maibach, E., Roser-Renouf, C., Feinberg, G., & Howe, P. (2012). *Public support for climate and energy policies in September, 2012*. Yale University and George Mason University. New Haven, CT: Yale Project on Climate Change Communication.

Leiserowitz, A., Maibach, E., Roser-Renouf, C., Feinberg, G., & Howe, P. (2013). *Global warming's six Americas, September 2012*. Yale University and George Mason University. New Haven, CT: Yale Project on Climate Change Communication.

Lertzman, R. (2008). The myth of apathy. *Ecologist*, 19(6), 16–17.

Miller, C. A. (2004). Climate science and the making of a global political order. In S. Jasanoff (Ed.), *States of knowledge: The co-production of science and social order* (pp. 46–66). London: Routledge.

Nisbet, M. C. (2011). Public opinion and political participation. In D. Schlosberg, J. Dryzek, and R. Norgaard (Eds.), *The Oxford handbook of climate change and society* (pp. 355–368). Oxford: Oxford University Press.

Norgaard, K. M. (2011). *Living in denial: Climate change, emotions, and everyday life*. Cambridge, MA: MIT Press.

Norris, P. (2011). *Democratic deficit: Critical citizens revisited*. Cambridge: Cambridge University Press.

Oreskes, N. & Conway, E. M. (2010). *Merchants of doubt*. New York: Bloomsbury Press.

O'Sullivan, J. (2011). Perry tells N.H. audience he's a global-warming skeptic. *National Journal*, August 17. Retrieved July 25, 2013: http://www.nationaljournal.com/politics/perry-tells-n-h-audience-he-s-a-global-warming-skeptic-with-video-20110817.

Palin, S. (2009). Sarah Palin on the politicization of the Copenhagen Climate Conference. *Washington Post*, December 9. Retrieved July 25, 2013: http://www.washingtonpost.com/wp-dyn/content/article/2009/12/08/AR2009120803402.html.

Pielke, Jr., R. A. (2007). *The honest broker. Making sense of science in policy and politics*. Cambridge and New York: Cambridge University Press.

Pielke, Jr., R. A. (2010). *The climate fix: What scientists and politicians won't tell you about global warming*. New York: Basic Books.

Poulsene, M. P. (Director). (2009). *Please Help the World* (video). Shown at the opening ceremony of the United Nations Climate Change Conference 2009 (COP15), Copenhagen, Denmark, December 7. Retrieved July 25, 2013: http://www.youtube.com/watch?v=NVGGgncVq-4.

Prins, G., Galiana, I., Green, C., Grundmann, R., Korhola, A., Laird, F., Nordhaus, T., Pielke, Jr., R. A., Rayner, S., Sarewitz, D., Shellenberger, M., Stehr, N., & Hiroyuki, T. (2010). *The Hartwell paper: A new direction for climate policy after the crash of 2009*. London: Institute for Science, Innovation & Society, University of Oxford; LSE Mackinder Programme, London School of Economics and Political Science. Retrieved July 25, 2013: http://www.lse.ac.uk/collections/mackinderProgramme/theHartwellPaper.

Randerson, J. (2010). Climate researchers 'secrecy' criticised – but MPs say science remains intact. *The Guardian*, March 31. Retrieved July 25, 2013: http://www.guardian.co.uk/environment/2010/mar/31/climate-mails-inquiry-jones-cleared.

Ray, J. & Pugliese, A. (2011). *Worldwide, blame for climate change falls on humans. Americans among least likely to attribute to human causes*. Gallup Poll, April 22. Retrieved July 25, 2013: http://www.gallup.com/poll/147242/Worldwide-Blame-Climate-Change-Falls-Humans.aspx.

Revkin, A. C. (2011). A fundamental republican science problem. *New York Times*, Dot Earth blog. Retrieved July 25, 2013: http://dotearth.blogs.nytimes.com/2011/08/22/a-fundamental-republican-science-problem.

Robinson, E. (2009). Sarah Palin's flip-flop on climate change. *Washington Post*, December 15. Retrieved July 25, 2013: http://www.washingtonpost.com/wp-dyn/content/article/2009/12/14/AR2009121402712.html?hpid%3Dopinionsbox1&sub=AR.

Rosanvallon, P. (2008). *Counter-democracy: Politics in an age of distrust*, trans. Arthur Goldhammer. Cambridge: Cambridge University Press.

Sarewitz, D. (2004). How science makes environmental controversies worse. *Environmental Science and Policy*, 7(5), 385–403.

Sarewitz, D. (2010). Curing climate backlash. *Nature*, 464(4), 28.

Shearman, D. & Smith, J. W. (2007). *The climate change challenge and the failure of democracy*. Westport, CT: Praeger.

Skidelsky, E. (2010). Words that think for us: The tyranny of denial. *Prospect*, 167, January 27. Retrieved July 25, 2013: http://www.prospectmagazine.co.uk/2010/01/words-that-think-for-us-3.

Skocpol, T. & Williamson, V. (2012). *The Tea Party and the remaking of Republican conservatism*. Oxford and New York: Oxford University Press.

Specter, M. (2009). *Denialism: How irrational thinking hinders scientific progress, harms the planet, and threatens our lives*. New York: Penguin.

Swyngedouw, E. (2010). Apocalypse forever? Post-political populism and the spectre of climate change. *Theory, Culture & Society*, 27(2–3), 213–232.

Tierney, J. (2009). E-mail fracas shows peril of trying to spin science. *New York Times*, November 30. Retrieved July 25, 2013: http://www.nytimes.com/2009/12/01/science/01tier.html?_r=3&n=Top/News/Science/Columns/Findings.

Turner, S. P. (2003). *Liberal democracy 3.0: Civil society in an age of experts*. London and Thousand Oaks, CA: Sage Publications.

Urbinati, N. & Warren, M. E. (2008). The concept of representation in contemporary democratic theory. *Annual Review of Political Science*, 11, 387–412.

Warren, M. E. (2003). A second transformation of democracy? In B. E. Cain, R. J. Dalton, & S. E. Scarrow (Eds.), *Democracy transformed? Expanding political opportunities in advanced industrial democracies* (pp. 223–249). Oxford: Oxford University Press.

Wihbey, J. (2012). *'Denier,' 'alarmist,' 'warmist,' 'contrarian,' 'confusionist,' 'believer'*. The Yale Forum on Climate Change and the Media, August 16. Retrieved July 25, 2013: http://www.yaleclimatemediaforum.org/2012/08/denier-alarmist-warmist-contrarian-confusionist-believer.

Yearly, S. (2010). Science and the environment in the twenty-first century. In M. Redclift & G. Woodgate (Eds.), *The new international handbook of environmental sociology* (pp. 212–225). Cheltenham: Edward Elgar.

7

EXPLAINING INFORMATION SOURCES IN CLIMATE POLICY DEBATES

Dallas J. Elgin and Christopher M. Weible

The societal impacts from climate change are grave and encompassing. The high stakes have resulted in political debates over the certainty and causes of climate change and appropriate public policy responses. The political debates have been visceral, with denials and distortions of scientific claims and arguably unethical behavior among individuals on both sides seeking an edge in shaping public knowledge and opinion. Some have claimed that conservatives have waged a war on science about truthfulness of climate change (Mooney, 2005) or that scientific mandarins – working for industry – have clouded the issue (Oreskes & Conway, 2010). Others accuse climate change supporters of cooking their data and engaging in a conspiracy (Parris, 2007).

The content of the debates is fueled by information about topics ranging from the predicted impacts on food and water supplies to the economic impacts of carbon taxes and cap and trade policies. This information is most likely used by actors in the policy process at different frequencies and from different sources. However, any conclusions drawn about the patterns of information use by policy actors in climate change debates are largely speculative. Many unanswered questions remain, including: To what extent are policy actors engaged in climate change issues using information from similar sources? Are climate change deniers relying more on information from their own organization or from industry? Are climate change supporters more likely to rely on academic research or on research from government agencies and non-profits? Or, perhaps, are individuals choosing information sources that reflect their level of training, their organizational needs, and technical needs in doing their job? Developing an improved understanding of the information sources utilized by policy actors and the factors determining their use may help provide a better understanding of their positions as well as contribute, even in the smallest of ways, to more constructive arguments and decision-making processes.

This chapter reports on the effect of four rival factors – pro-climate change beliefs, individual capacity, the professional use of various analytical and collaborative tools and techniques, and organizational capacity – in understanding the choice and frequency in the use of information sources in climate-related issues in Colorado. We focus on both the types of information sources and the frequency of use to provide a greater understanding of how policy actors utilize information to inform their work on climate and energy issues.

Factors that shape patterns of information use

Almost every public policy topic involves a multitude of policy responses, and climate change policy has a number of common policy responses ranging from climate action plans and regulatory instruments that advocate action to rhetorical statements and inaction. These policy responses are embedded within ongoing processes of interactions among individuals seeking to influence government decisions and societal outcomes. These individuals, called 'policy actors,' include officials from all levels of government as well as individuals working in non-profits, businesses, academia, consulting firms, and the news media (Zaller, 1992). Policy actors possess a level of expertise within a specific policy domain and utilize their expertise in an attempt to influence the policy domain over an extended period of time (Sabatier & Weible, 2007). To influence policy, policy actors utilize information along with other available resources in an attempt to sway decision makers, influence public opinion, recruit individuals to support a policy objective, or attract additional resources (Sabatier & Weible, 2007).

The literature on policy actors in political debates has generated a number of expectations and findings about the factors that affect patterns of information use. Some of these expectations derive from a model of the individual rooted in bounded rationality where cognitive limitations force policy actors to select and interpret information based on a variety of heuristics including their beliefs and interests (Simon, 1947). These heuristics lead to the conscious or unconscious selection and interpretation of information (Festinger, 1957; Lord et al., 1979). Information sources consumed might be interpreted through the prism of a priori beliefs and used to reinforce a worldview, mobilize supporters, and shape government agendas and policy (Sabatier & Jenkins-Smith, 1993). We, therefore, expect that policy actors' beliefs about climate change will affect their sources of information as well as their frequency of use.

Another explanation, policy analytical capacity, is related to the capacity of individuals and their organizations to acquire and utilize information in the policy process (Howlett, 2009). At the individual level, policy analytical capacity is comprised of several dimensions, including level of training, and access and use of tools and techniques commonly used within a profession (Wellstead et al., 2009). Level of training is defined by the formal level of education and professional preparation of a policy actor. It might include an individual's level of education or the ability to conduct applied research, statistical methods, policy analysis or evaluation, trends analysis, and modeling of various scenarios. Formal trainings provide opportunities and constraints in problem solving and arguably require different sorts of information. We would, therefore, expect that the formal training that policy actors have received in various analytical techniques will affect both the sources of information they use as well as the frequency of use.

In addition to level of training, policy actors also utilize a variety of tools and techniques in doing their job. Tools are used to help achieve specific objectives from making sense of the world through a particular form of data analysis to guiding an approach for gathering original data as might be conducted through facilitating focus groups. The tools and techniques used by policy actors encompass both analytical tools that utilize an analytical approach to examine and evaluate information (Lindblom, 1959; Weimer & Vining, 2010) as well as collaborative approaches that utilize techniques focused on engaging stakeholders and building consensus (deLeon, 1992; Fischer, 2003). Samples of analytical tools can include environmental impact analysis, risk analysis, economic and financial analysis, modeling, and political feasibility analysis. Samples of collaborative tools can include facilitation and consensus building, collaborating with those with similar or dissimilar beliefs, and other informal tools and techniques. We expect that the relative use of analytical and collaborative tools by policy actors will affect their sources of information as well as their frequency of use.

At the organizational level, policy analytical capacity relates to the organizational support available to policy actors, including an organization's priority in addressing a particular issue as well as its willingness to devote resources to the issue (Craft & Howlett, 2012; Howlett & Oliphant, 2010). The argument is one of resource dependency (Pfeffer & Salancik, 1978), that is, the organizations provide policy actors' assets and deficiencies in shaping public policy debates. We, therefore, expect that organizational capacity, in the form of an organization's willingness to prioritize action on climate change and willingness to devote the necessary resources, will affect policy actors' sources of information as well as their frequency in use.

Case study

The context for this study is climate and energy issues in Colorado, United States. Colorado provides an effective case study to examine climate and energy policies due to the state's vast traditional energy resources, the rise of its renewable energy sector, and its vulnerability to climate change. Colorado has long been a major producer of traditional energy with several major fossil fuel-rich basins, major production of coalbed methane, and vast reserves and high levels of natural gas production (US Energy Information Administration, 2012). In recent years, Colorado's renewable energy sector has grown partly in response to the state's renewable energy portfolio standard via ballot initiative in 2004 and a further strengthening of the standard by the legislature in 2010 (Database of State Incentives for Renewables & Efficiency, 2010). Colorado has been identified as vulnerable to both current and predicted impacts of climate change, including shorter and warmer winters and increased periods of drought (Ritter, 2007). Scientists project that in the ensuing decades, climate change in Colorado will produce temperature increases of 3 to 4 degrees Fahrenheit, longer and more intense wildfires during the summer, and an increase in water shortages.

In an effort to address the predicted impacts of climate change, former Colorado Governor Bill Ritter launched the Colorado Climate Action Plan in November of 2007. This plan called for a 20 percent reduction of the state emission of greenhouse gases by 2020. The state's adoption of a climate action plan is representative of climate policy at the state level (EPA, 2011; ICLEI, 2011) and indicative of a country where climate policies are absent at the national level (Lachapelle et al., 2012).

Methodology

A web-questionnaire was administered in the spring of 2011 to policy actors in Colorado actively involved in climate and energy issues (see Elgin & Weible, 2013; Weible & Elgin, 2013). The sample was collected through a modified snowball sample technique targeting those individuals involved in Colorado climate and energy issues by first searching the Internet for government and nongovernment organizations and the people therein. As a second step, newspapers and online publications were also searched to identify names of individuals not identified in the initial search. In the final step, preliminary interviews were conducted with five policy actors involved with Denver and Colorado climate and energy issues and interviewees were asked for the names of individuals that should be included in the sample. The total sample identified through these efforts was 793 individuals. Of the total population sampled, 272 people returned fully completed surveys for a response rate of 34 percent. Only the fully completed surveys were analyzed for this chapter. Compared to the total population, the response rate ranged from 26 to 86 percent for all categories of government and nongovernment policy actors. The sample is not representative of members of the media, where only two completed the survey out of 53. Due to the low response rate, members of the media are excluded from this study.

Operational measures

Dependent variable

Information sources. We asked survey respondents to report the frequency in use of various information sources: reports from their own organization, reports from non-profits, reports from city and state governments, reports from consultants, reports from industry, and academic research. For each source, respondents were asked, "How often do you use the following types of information in your climate and energy-related policy work?" Respondents could answer on a five-point Likert scale consisting of 'daily,' 'weekly,' 'monthly,' 'yearly,' and 'never.' The items were coded in order ranging from 5 = daily through 1 = never, respectively. An information frequency scale was then created by averaging the means of the six information sources (Cronbach's alpha = 0.70).

Independent variables

Climate beliefs. We asked survey respondents to report their beliefs on the severity of climate change, its causes, and possible policy approaches for mitigating carbon emissions, including carbon taxes, cap and trade systems, and policies promoting renewable energy generation. Respondents were asked to use a five-point scale ranging from –2 = Strongly disagree to +2 = Strongly agree. These individual questions were then aggregated by their means into a single-scaled item called 'Pro-climate change beliefs.'[1]

Formal training. To measure formal training in analytical techniques, respondents were asked, "In which of the following areas have you received formal training?" Responses included 'applied research,' 'modeling,' 'policy analysis,' 'policy evaluation,' 'statistical methods,' and 'trends analysis and/or forecasting.' The formal training questions were then aggregated by their means into a single-scaled 'Sum of formal training' variable.

Tools and techniques used. To measure the tools and techniques used by policy actors, respondents were asked the following question: "How often have you used the following tools and techniques as part of your work in the past year?" Choices included 'political feasibility analysis,' 'risk analysis,' 'modeling,' 'collaborating with those who you agree with,' 'collaborating with those you disagree with,' 'environmental impact analysis,' 'facilitation and consensus building,' 'economic analysis,' and 'informal tools and techniques.' Respondents were asked to respond using a scale coded from 5 to 1 consisting of daily, weekly, monthly, yearly, and never. We created two scales via confirmatory factor analysis from the nine questions. The first scale consists of analytical tools and techniques, including modeling, environmental impact analysis, economic analysis, risk analysis, and political feasibility analysis. The second scale consists of collaborative tools and techniques, including collaborating with those you agree with, collaborating with those you disagree with, facilitation/consensus building, and informal tools/ techniques. Cronbach's alpha scores for both scales were 0.80.

Organizational capacity. We asked respondents three questions pertaining to their organizational priorities, organizational resources, and ability to engage in long-term planning on climate change. Measuring climate and energy issues as an organizational priority was done by asking respondents: 'Compared with other issues that your organization responds to, how much of a priority are climate-related issues and energy policies?' The sample was asked to respond using a five-point Likert scale consisting of 'much higher,' 'higher,' 'about the same,' 'lower,' and 'much lower.' For the question on organizational resources, we asked respondents: "Compared to similar organizations, does your organization have adequate knowledge, skills, and people to respond to climate-related issues and energy policies?" The sample was asked to respond using a five-point scale consisting of 'very high capacity,' 'high capacity,' 'medium capacity,' 'low capacity,' and 'very low capacity.' To measure the ability of the organization to engage in long-term planning processes that are associated with climate change adaptation, we asked respondents their level of agreement or disagreement with the following statement: "Urgent day-to-day issues seem to take precedence over thinking 'long-term.'" The sample was asked to respond using a five-point scale consisting of 'strongly disagree,' 'disagree,' 'neutral,' 'agree,' and 'strongly agree.' Scales in the three questions were coded from 5 to 1. An organizational capacity scale was then created by taking the mean of the three variables (factor loading = 0.88, Cronbach's alpha = 0.70).

In addition to the four categories of variables above, we also control for the number of years the policy actors were involved in climate related issues and their organizational affiliation. For years of involvement, respondents were asked "How many years have you been involved in climate-related issues and/or energy policy?" Responses ranged from 1 = 'Less than 1 year',' 2 = '1–5 years,' 3 = '6–9 years,' 4 = '10–14 years,' 5 = '15–20 years,' or 6 = 'Greater than 20 years.' To determine organizational affiliation, we asked respondents "Which of the following best describes your organization?" Responses included 'academic/ research,' 'business/private sector,' 'government,' and 'non-profit.'

Results

We present the results in two parts. The first part (Tables 7.1 through 7.4) presents the descriptive results for information source use, climate beliefs, individual capacity, use of analytical and collaborative tools and techniques, and organizational capacity. The second part (Table 7.5) presents the explanatory results from the ordered logit models and the ordinary least squares (OLS) regression models used to explain the variation in the frequency of use for climate and energy information sources.

Descriptive analysis

Table 7.1 lists the mean frequency of use for six types of information sources: reports from a policy actor's own organization, reports from non-profits, reports from city and state governments, reports from consultants, reports from industry, and academic research. The results show that policy actors engaged in Colorado climate and energy policy issues utilize information at an average rate of a

TABLE 7.1 Mean responses for information sources

Reports from own organization	Reports from non-profits	Academic research	Reports from city & state governments	Reports from consultants	Reports from industry	Information frequency scale
3.24	3.01	3.31	3.14	3.01	3.25	3.16

Exact wording: "How often do you use the following types of information in your climate and energy related policy work?" (5 = 'Daily,' 4 = 'Weekly,' 3 = 'Monthly,' 2= 'Yearly,' 1= 'Never').

monthly basis, regardless of source. The information frequency scale, which was created to reflect the frequency of use across all information sources, shows that policy actors tend to use these information sources on a monthly basis (mean of 3.16, median= 3.17).

Table 7.2 lists the correlation coefficients between information sources and climate beliefs and individual capacity as well as the total means for the variables in the column on the far right.[2] The top portion of the table presents six measured items for climate beliefs as well as the combined scale (from –2 = Strongly disagree to +2 = Strongly agree). Overall, policy actors expressed concern for climate change issues and tepid support for various government responses. Policy actors tend to disagree when asked if the severity of climate change has been overstated and if the market is the suitable venue for handling climate and energy decisions. In contrast, they agreed that humans caused climate change, were equivocal about the need for cap and trade policies (mean = 0.05), and supported policies for renewable energy and a carbon tax (means of 1.21 and 0.55, respectively). The climate beliefs scale is the mean value of the measured items (with two items reversed) and underscores the tendency for respondents in this dataset to agree about the severity of climate change and with plausible responses. Overall, no discernible patterns emerge between climate beliefs and the frequency of use for various information sources. Reports from non-profits showed the most consistent and strongest correlations (significant on 4 of the 6 belief measures as well as with the climate beliefs scale), while the other information sources had tepid correlations with climate beliefs (no more than two statistically significant correlations).

The middle and bottom portions of Table 7.2 present the data for years of involvement and formal training. Policy actors report a mean level of involvement of 6–9 years. Level of involvement was found to have a positive correlation with the frequency of use of information sources, with statistically significant associations in four of the seven information sources examined (significant at $p<0.05$). As a result, policy actors with higher years of involvement are found to utilize various information sources less frequently. In regard to formal training, policy actors reported varying levels of training with approximately a quarter of respondents trained in policy analysis to nearly a half (46 percent) trained in policy evaluation (see column on far right of Table 7.2). Policy actors reported a mean of having received training in 2.16 of the areas, meaning that most report training in a least two areas. Overall, the majority of relationships with formal training were statistically non-significant, though policy analysis demonstrated a positive correlation in five of the variables examined ($p<0.05$), indicating that actors trained in these areas utilized information more frequently.

Table 7.3 presents the data for use of tools and techniques. Policy actors reported differing frequencies of use for various tools and techniques. Actors most frequently collaborated with individuals they agreed with, on a weekly basis. Actors reported using informal tools, economic and financial analysis, and collaborating with those they disagreed with on a monthly basis. Environmental impact analysis, risk analysis, modeling, and political feasibility analysis were

TABLE 7.2 Individual characteristics and information sources

	Information source correlation coefficients							Total means
	Reports from own organization	Reports from non-profits	Academic research	Reports from city and state governments	Reports from consultants	Reports from industry	Information sources scale	
Climate beliefs								
Severity of predicted impacts is not overstated (Reversed)	0.07	-0.11	-0.07	0.05	0.02	0.09	0.00	1.88
Human behavior is the principal cause	-0.08	0.13*	0.06	0.00	-0.01	-0.11	0.01	1.00
Decisions on climate & energy are not best left to the market (Reversed)	0.10	-0.10	0.02	0.05	0.05	0.13*	0.06	1.87
Carbon tax is required	-0.08	0.16**	0.09	-0.05	0.00	-0.08	0.03	0.55
Cap & trade is required	-0.12*	0.02	0.05	0.03	-0.01	-0.04	-0.01	0.05
Renewables policy is required	-0.14*	0.23***	0.15*	0.07	0.03	-0.06	0.08	1.21
Pro-climate change beliefs scale	-0.12	0.17**	0.09	0.00	-0.02	-0.10	0.01	0.84
Years of involvement	0.15*	0.22***	0.12	0.09	0.13*	0.11	0.20**	3.23
Formal Training								
Training in applied research	0.05	-0.02	0.19**	-0.03	-0.02	-0.03	0.03	0.34
Modeling	0.13*	0.00	0.01	-0.04	-0.04	-0.06	0.00	0.24
Policy analysis	0.05	0.17**	0.14*	0.06	0.19**	0.13*	0.16*	0.45
Policy evaluation	0.06	0.12	0.08	0.00	0.11	0.11	0.11	0.42
Statistical methods	-0.09	-0.13*	-0.05	-0.08	-0.10	-0.07	-0.12*	0.46
Trends analysis	0.01	-0.09	-0.01	-0.02	-0.03	0.01	-0.02	0.25
Sum of formal training	0.05	0.01	0.12	-0.03	0.03	0.03	0.04	2.16

Policy core beliefs scale: –2= 'Strongly disagree,' –1 = 'Disagree,' 0= 'Neither agree nor disagree,' +1 = 'Agree,' +2= 'Strongly agree.'

***p<0.001, **p<0.01, *p<0.05

TABLE 7.3 Use of tools and techniques and information sources

Frequency of use of tools and techniques	Information source correlation coefficients							Total means
	Reports from own organization	Reports from non-profits	Academic research	Reports from city and state governments	Reports from consultants	Reports from industry	Information sources scale	
Collaborate with those you agree	0.33***	0.40***	0.42***	0.29***	0.35***	0.29***	0.48***	3.92
Collaborate with those you disagree	0.23***	0.23***	0.31***	0.34***	0.29***	0.31***	0.38***	3.08
Facilitation/consensus Building	0.18*	0.39***	0.30***	0.33***	0.36***	0.31***	0.43***	2.54
Informal tools	0.28***	0.39***	0.32***	0.39***	0.39***	0.36***	0.50***	3.39
Modeling	0.37***	0.30***	0.35***	0.23***	0.28***	0.17**	0.39***	2.16
Environmental impact	0.18*	0.24***	0.28***	0.24***	0.25***	0.22***	0.30***	2.39
Economic/financial analysis	0.27***	0.31***	0.26***	0.32***	0.32***	0.31***	0.39***	2.70
Risk analysis	0.20***	0.19*	0.27***	0.26***	0.24***	0.20***	0.29***	2.21
Political feasibility	0.17**	0.35***	0.24***	0.30***	0.28***	0.29***	0.36***	1.77
Sum of collaborative tools	0.33***	0.45***	0.41***	0.42***	0.45***	0.39***	0.57***	3.22
Sum of analytical tools	0.33***	0.40***	0.42***	0.38***	0.40***	0.35***	0.50***	2.23

***p<0.001, **p<0.01, *p<0.05

the least used by policy actors, with respondents reporting yearly use. Overall, tools and techniques were found to have a positive correlation with the use of information sources with statistically significant associations ($p<0.01$) across all tools and techniques and information types, indicating that actors with higher levels of use of tools and techniques utilize information more frequently. Policy actors reported using collaborative tools and techniques on a monthly basis (mean of 3.22) and using analytical tools and techniques on a yearly basis (mean of 2.23). Both tools and techniques scales showed a positive correlation with the use of information sources, with statistically significant associations ($p<0.001$) across all information types.

Table 7.4 lists the correlation coefficients between information sources and organizational variables. Policy actors represented a variety of different organization types, with the business/private sector (32.7 percent) being the most highly represented and followed closely by government (31.3 percent), with lower levels of representation for non-profit (20.2 percent) and academic/research organizations (10.3 percent). Organizational affiliation had a mixed level of correlation with the frequency of information sources. The majority of relationships were statistically non-significant, though government demonstrated a positive correlation in three of the six information types ($p<0.05$), indicating that government organizations utilized information more frequently. Policy actors reported that their organizations on average made climate and energy issues a higher priority (mean of 3.71). Actors reported that their organizations possessed a high capacity (mean of 3.69) in regard to having adequate knowledge, skills, and people to respond to climate-related issues and energy policies. These variables indicated a positive correlation with statistically significant relationships ($p<0.01$) across all information sources. When asked whether urgent, day-to-day issues took precedence over long-term planning on climate change, policy actors reported that they agreed (mean of 2.17). There was no significant association between the prominence of urgent, day-to-day issues and use of information sources. An organizational capacity variable comprised of the organizational priority, skills, knowledge and people, and long-term planning variables were constructed to better understand the relationship between organizational capacity and information sources. Policy actors held a mean organizational capacity of 3.19 on a scale of 1 to 5, with 5 representing the highest level of capacity. Organizational capacity had a positive correlation with information sources, with statistically significant relationships across all information types ($p<0.001$), indicating that high levels of organizational PAC resulted in more frequent use of information sources, across all types.

Explanatory analysis

Table 7.5 presents the multivariate analysis explaining the variation in the frequency of use for climate and energy information sources. Ordinal logit models were conducted for each information source variable with the dependent variables

TABLE 7.4 Organizations' characteristics and information sources

	Information source correlation coefficients							Total means
	Reports from own organization	Reports from non-profits	Academic research	Reports from city and state governments	Reports from consultants	Reports from industry	Information sources scale	
Organizational affiliation								
Government	−0.11	−0.18**	−0.16**	−0.07	−0.10	−0.17**	−0.16*	31.3%
Business	0.11	−0.15*	−0.11	0.04	0.13*	0.21***	0.05	32.7%
Non-profit	−0.08	0.28***	−0.01	0.05	0.03	0.04	0.05	20.2%
Academic/research	0.06	0.11	0.30***	−0.04	−0.15*	−0.08	0.05	10.3%
Organizational priority	0.28***	0.30***	0.21***	0.19**	0.24***	0.25***	0.35***	3.71
Adequate knowledge, skills, and people	0.34***	0.22***	0.22***	0.19**	0.22***	0.25***	0.35***	3.69
Urgent day-to-day issues take precedence	0.07	0.03	0.09	0.04	−0.01	−0.02	0.05	2.17
Organizational capacity scale	0.34***	0.27***	0.25***	0.21***	0.22***	0.23***	0.36***	3.19

***p<0.001, **p<0.01, *p<0.05

TABLE 7.5 Explanatory analysis of information sources

	Own org's reports	Non-profit reports	Academic research	City and state government reports	Consultant reports	Industry reports	Sum of information sources
Pro-climate change beliefs scale	-0.37*	0.21	0.03	-0.26	-0.22	-0.43***	-0.08
Organizational capacity scale	0.82***	0.46*	0.66**	0.29	0.36	0.36	0.23***
Sum of formal training	-0.04	0.07	0.07	-0.14	0.03	-0.05	0.00
Business	-0.20	-0.17	-0.35	-0.19	0.29	0.86*	0.06
Non-profit	-0.76*	1.31***	-0.30	-0.19	-0.11	0.34	0.01
Consultant	-0.05	0.19	1.34	-0.36	0.14	-0.01	0.14
Academic	-0.03	0.96*	1.82***	-0.40	-1.10*	-0.71	0.02
Years of involvement	0.11	0.16	0.07	0.04	-0.03	-0.03	0.04
Collaborative tools scale	0.64***	0.87***	0.77***	1.02***	1.09***	0.97***	0.41***
Analytical tools scale	0.34	0.66**	0.63**	0.59*	0.58*	0.49*	0.24***
Constant							0.47
Pseudo R^2 / R^2	0.11	0.17	0.16	0.12	0.14	0.13	0.50
Prob>Chi^2 / F-Stat	0.00	0.00	0.00	0.00	0.00	0.00	0.00

Note: Models are ordinal logit analysis with robust standard errors except for the 'Sum of Information Sources' dependent variable where ordinary least square regression was used (coefficients omitted from exhibit, for the collaborative technique scale the constant = 0.50 and for the analytical techniques scale the constant = 0.17).

***p<0.001, **p<0.01, *p<0.05

organized by climate beliefs scale, organizational capacity scale, the sum of an individual's formal training, organizational affiliation, years of involvement, and sum of collaborative and analytical tools. The models show moderate fit, with chi^2 probability from 0.000 to 0.001 and Pseudo R^2 scores ranging from 0.11 to 0.17. The results of an OLS regression analysis for the information sources scale shows a good fit with the adjusted R^2 equaling 0.47[3]. All coefficients in Table 7.5 are unstandardized.

Table 7.5 indicates that respondents who frequently use various information sources tend to use both collaborative and analytical tools and report high levels of organizational capacity to deal with climate change issues. Organizational capacity and the use of collaborative and analytical tools and techniques are consistent and positive determinants of the use of informational sources. Collaborative tools were significant across all seven information types, while analytical tools were significant for five of the six information types. Organizational capacity was a less strong determinant compared to collaborative and analytical tools, with statistical significance in four of the information types ($p<0.05$).

The other variables were not as consistent in their effect on the dependent variables. The more likely respondents reported pro-climate change beliefs, the less likely they used information from their own organization, city/state governments, consultants, and industry. Each of the organization types had both positive and negative coefficients with no more than three statistically significant relationships ($p<0.05$). Formal training and years of involvement had no explanatory power in the models, with neither of the variables providing statistically significant relationships with any of the information sources.

Discussion

The purpose of this chapter is to provide insight into the patterns of information use to better understand the debate of climate and energy issues with Colorado as the case study. Whereas debate on climate and energy issues can be understood through the divergent beliefs of the policy actors on the different sides of the debate, the results in this chapter suggest that climate beliefs have little impact on information use. Alternately, the debate over climate and energy issues can be interpreted to originate from the level of personal knowledge and insight into the science. But the results of this study show that patterns of information use were independent of the level of formal training possessed by policy actors.

Rather than beliefs or formal training, the results of this chapter revealed that analytical and collaborative tools were the strongest determinants of the frequency of use of information sources. Collaborative and analytical tools were found to increase the frequency that information sources were used. The use of collaborative tools resulted in more frequent use across all sources and the use of analytical tools resulted in more frequent use for all sources except a policy actor's own organization. Organizational capacity also affects the frequency of use among information sources. Though not as strong a determinant as collaborative and analytical tools, organizational capacity increased the frequency of use across four of the seven information sources examined.

The climate and energy political landscapes of the states can vary considerably, from supportive landscapes that result in a state enacting progressive climate policies (Mark & Lynd Luers, 2010; Rabe, 2007) to unsupportive landscapes that result in an inability or unwillingness to enact climate policies. It can be argued that the climate and energy political landscape of Colorado as well as a number of other states could be characterized as occupying a middle ground that is neither entirely supportive nor unsupportive of climate and energy policy. Along with more than 30 other states, Colorado has completed a climate action plan that outlines a collection of steps for mitigating the state's carbon emissions and adapting to the impacts of climate change. While Colorado provides an effective case study and it could be argued that the state is representative of other states engaged in climate and energy policy, generalizing these results to other states should be done with caution for the generalizability of this study to other states is ultimately an empirical question. Academics and practitioners should carefully consider the context of a different state prior to drawing lessons.

Conclusion

This chapter contributes to our understanding of how climate and energy policy actors acquire and utilize information by exploring the relative roles of beliefs, individual and organizational capacity, and information-related tools and techniques. In their quest to translate their policy beliefs into governmental policies, climate and energy policy actors within Colorado utilized information from a variety of sources at a similar rate of frequency. The frequency in use of information is most strongly affiliated with the frequency of tool use in their work and their organizational capacity. Among the tools, analytical types (e.g., risk analysis, modeling, and financial analysis) were just as important as collaborative types (e.g., collaboration, facilitation). These findings provide a better understanding about the role of information in climate-related politics and policy. Commonly, information is seen as a vital resource among policy actors in their efforts to realize their climate and energy policy objectives. These empirical findings demonstrate that policy actors use a variety of information sources at similar frequencies despite possessing a wide range of climate change beliefs, individual experience and training, organizational resources, and use of various information-related tools. Most importantly, these findings demonstrate that a policy actor's decision to utilize various sources of information in their policy activities is largely driven by their organizational resources and their use of analytically focused and collaboratively based tools and much less so on their beliefs about climate change.

Previous research has investigated how coverage of the media, values, and information inform climate change debates (Boykoff & Boykoff, 2007; Elgin & Weible, 2013; Ingold, 2011; Leiserowitz, 2006). This chapter contributes to this effort by verifying a few unsurprising patterns, such as the inverse relationship between pro-climate change beliefs and seeking reports from industry sources. However, this chapter also suggests that future research agendas should shift efforts to factors understudied in the literature, in particular, the analytical and collaborative tools used by policy actors. These tool types provide the means for making sense of the world and likely serve as another way for understanding and simplifying climate change issues and, achieving policy-related objectives. The implication is not that information sources are unimportant in climate change debates but rather that scholars and practitioners should not ignore the analytical and collaborative tools that are being used by policy actors in their professional jobs. In addition, this chapter also suggests that future research agendas should focus on the role of information sources and collaborative and analytical tools in policy actor strategies. While this chapter has provided insight into how policy actors involved in climate and energy policy utilize information and information-related tools, future research should build upon these findings by examining how they are incorporated into the strategies employed by policy actors to achieve their climate and energy policy goals. Developing an improved understanding of the information sources, tools, and strategies used by policy actors may help provide policy actors with a better understanding of their positions as well as contribute, even in the smallest of ways, to more constructive arguments and decision-making processes. If policy actors were to better understand their positions as well as the positions of their opponents, they might be able to identify new opportunities for reaching agreement on climate and energy policy solutions.

Notes

1 Respondents were asked to express their level of agreement and disagreement with the following questions: (1) "The severity of predicted impacts on society from climate change are vastly overstated" (reversed, factor loading = 0.88); (2) "Human behavior is the principal cause of climate change" (factor loading = 0.82); (3) "Decisions about energy and its effect on climate are best left to the economic market, and not to government" (reversed, factor loading = 0.687); (4) "An energy and/or carbon tax is required to combat climate change" (factor loading = 0.800); (4) "A cap and trade system of permits for the emission of greenhouse gas is required to combat climate change" (factor loading = 0.698); (5) "Government policies to promote renewable energy generation are required to combat climate change" (factor loading = 0.795). The mean of the five items was calculated to create the pro-climate change belief scale (Cronbach's alpha = 0.870).
2 Point-biserial correlation coefficients were calculated for the association between level of involvement and individual level PAC, Kendal Tau b coefficients were calculated for the association between level of involvement and organizational capacity, Spearman Rank Order correlation coefficient for level of involvement and pro-climate change beliefs. Results from Exhibit 2 are robust across different measures of correlations.
3 Results of an ordinal logit regression with the information sources variable found significant positive coefficients for organizational resources and collaborative tools, and a significant negative coefficient for policy core beliefs. The model has a Pseudo R2 of 0.12 and was significant from the 0.000 to 0.001 level.

References

Boykoff, M. T. & Boykoff, J. M. (2007). Climate change and journalistic norms: A case-study of US mass-media coverage. *Geoforum*, 38(6), 1190–1204.

Craft, J. & Howlett, M. (2012). Subsystem structures, shifting mandates and policy capacity: Assessing Canada's ability to adapt to climate change. *Canadian Political Science Review*, 6(1), 3–14.

Database of State Incentives for Renewables and Efficiency. (2010). *Colorado incentives/ policies for renewables & efficiency*. Retrieved November 9, 2012: http://www.dsireusa. org/incentives/incentive.cfm?Incentive_Code=CO24R.

deLeon, P. (1992). The democratization of the policy sciences. *Public Administration Review*, 52(2), 125–129.

Elgin, D. J. & Weible, C. M. (2013). A stakeholder analysis of Colorado climate and energy issues using policy analytical capacity and the advocacy coalition framework. *Review of Policy Research*, 30(1), 114–133.

EPA (Environmental Protection Agency). (2011). *Climate change action plans*. Retrieved November 9, 2012: http://www.epa.gov/statelocalclimate/state/state-examples/action-plans.html.

Festinger, L. (1957). *A theory of cognitive dissonance*. Stanford, CA: Stanford University Press.

Fischer, F. (2003). *Reframing public policy: Discursive politics and deliberative practices*. Oxford: Oxford University Press.

Howlett, M. (2009). Policy analytical capacity and evidence-based policy-making: Lessons from Canada. *Canadian Public Administration*, 52(2), 153–175.

Howlett, M. & Oliphant, S. (2010). Environmental research organizations and climate change policy analytical capacity: An assessment of the Canadian case. *Canadian Political Science Review*, 4(2–3), 18–35.

ICLEI (Local Governments for Sustainability). (2011). *Members*. Retrieved November 9, 2012: http://www.iclei.org.

Ingold, K. (2011). Network structures within policy processes: Coalitions, power, and brokerage in Swiss climate policy. *Policy Studies Journal*, 39(3), 435–459.

Lachapelle, E., Borck, C. P., & Rabe, B. (2012). Public attitudes toward climate science and climate policy in federal systems: Canada and the United States compared. *Review of Policy Research*, 29(3), 334–357.

Leiserowitz, A. (2006). Climate change risk perception and policy preferences: The role of affect, imagery, and values. *Climate Change*, 77(1–2), 45–72.

Lindblom, C. E. (1959). The science of muddling through. *Public Administration Review*, 19(2), 79–88.

Lord, C. G., Ross, L., & Lepper, M. R. (1979). Biased assimilation and attitude polarization: The effects of prior theories on subsequently considered evidence. *Journal of Personality and Social Psychology*, 37(11), 2098–2109.

Mark, J. & Lynd Luers, A. (2010). Policy in California. In S. H. Schneider, A. Rosencranz, M. D. Mastrandrea, & K. Kuntz-Duriseti (Eds.), *Climate change science and policy* (pp. 356–363). Washington, DC: Island Press.

Mooney, C. Z. (2005). The politics of morality policy: Symposium editor's introduction. *Policy Studies Journal*, 27(4), 675–680.

Oreskes, N. & Conway, E. M. (2010). Defeating the merchants of doubt. *Nature*, 465(10), 686–687.

Parris, T. M. (2007). Climate change skeptics: Disagreement, hot air, or conspiracy? *Environment: Science and Policy for Sustainable Development*, 49(2), 3–7.

Pfeffer, J. & Salancik, G. R. (1978). *The external control of organizations*. New York: Harper & Row.

Rabe, B. (2007). Environmental policy and the Bush era: The collision between the administrative presidency and state experimentation. *Publius*, 37(3), 413–431.

Ritter, Jr., B. (2007). *Colorado climate action plan: A strategy to address global warming*. Colorado Department of Public Health and Environment. Retrieved November 9, 2012: http://www.cdphe.state.co.us/climate/ClimateActionPlan.pdf.

Sabatier, P. A. & Jenkins-Smith, H. C. (Eds.). (1993). *Policy change and learning: An advocacy coalition approach*. Boulder, CO: Westview Press.

Sabatier, P. A. & Weible, C. M. (2007). The advocacy coalition framework: Innovations and clarifications. In P. A. Sabatier (Ed.), *Theories of the policy process* (pp. 189–220). Boulder, CO: Westview Press.

Simon, H. A. (1947). *Administrative behavior*. New York: The Free Press.

US Energy Information Administration. (2012). *Colorado energy fact sheet*. Retrieved November 9, 2012: http://www.eia.gov/state/state-energy-profiles-print.cfm?sid=CO.

Weible, C. M. & Elgin, D. J. (2013). Contrasting capacities from city to international levels of involvement in climate and energy issues. *Cityscape*, 15(1), 171–187.

Weimer, D. & Vining, A. R. (2010). *Policy analysis: Concepts and practice*, 5th edition. London: Longman.

Wellstead, A. M., Stedman, R. C., & Lindquist, E. A. (2009). The nature of regional work in Canada's federal public service. *Canadian Political Science Review*, 3(1), 34–56.

Zaller, J. R. (1992). *The nature and origins of mass opinion*. Cambridge: Cambridge University Press.

8

NAVIGATING CONTROVERSIES IN SEARCH OF NEUTRALITY

Analyzing efforts by public think tanks to inform climate change policy

Jason Delborne

Introduction

In a time when our political process is becoming more and more partisan, many actors look to the provision of expert advice as one way to break stalemates and move toward public policy based on 'sound science.' Yet, simultaneously, expert advice itself is seen as partisan and more 'politicized' – in the sense of conclusions being driven or heavily influenced by political preferences. One of the few bastions of non-partisan expert advice to the political process in the United States would seem to reside in "the public think tanks, joined institutionally to the policy process but vested with no political authority of [their] own" (Bimber, 1996, p. x), such as the Congressional Research Service (CRS) and the Government Accountability Office (GAO). These organizations, housed in the legislative branch, advertise themselves as non-partisan, objective, balanced, and neutral providers of expert advice, and they exhibit a mix of structural, procedural, and rhetorical strategies to achieve these goals.

Not surprisingly, US policymakers who have faced the 'wicked' problem of climate change – so called because of its persistence, complexity, and uncertain causes and effects (Van Bueren et al., 2003) – have tasked the GAO and CRS to produce numerous reports on climate change science and policy. Whether such requests represent a genuine desire to compile accurate information to guide policy, or whether they represent a delay tactic (i.e., commissioning a study in order to put off making a political decision), the resulting reports do not translate neatly into policy proposals or political action; in fact, measuring their influence with any degree of precision would seem impossible in light of theories of the policymaking process that emphasize its non-linearity (Kingdon, 2002; Stone, 2012). Nevertheless, public think tank (PTT) reports serve as the formal representations of complex engagement processes – among elected officials, political staff, agency personnel, technical experts, interest groups, and less frequently, lay persons. Equally important, they inhabit the realm of political discourse and become resources for policy arguments by a variety of actors (e.g., Nixon, 2012; Pear, 2010). Thus, they deserve the attention of those who wish to understand the communication of the science of climate change between experts and policymakers.

This chapter interrogates efforts by PTTs to navigate controversies in climate change science and policy – analyzing how expertise becomes consolidated, translated, and communicated for explicitly political purposes. Broadly speaking, this follows a long tradition in science and technology studies (STS) of investigating the dynamic relationship between politics and expertise (Collins & Evans, 2002; Epstein, 1996; Jasanoff, 1990; Kinchy & Kleinman, 2005; Latour, 2004). Specifically, I explore the rhetorical strategies employed by the CRS and GAO to navigate the mix of scientific and political controversies surrounding climate change within an institutional context that demands at least the appearance of 'objectivity' and 'non-partisanship.' I ask how PTTs have invoked 'strategies of neutrality' (Bimber, 1996) in their published reports with some combination of efforts to reflect the balanced treatment of controversy, engage heterogeneous expertise to discern 'truth,' and accumulate evidence to bolster claims.

Defining public think tanks

The universe of 'public think tanks' might include hundreds or thousands of organizations, depending on one's interests, perspectives, and definition of 'public' (for thoughtful treatments of think tanks in general, see Medvetz, 2012; Rich, 2004). For example, well-known nonprofit think tanks such as the Cato Institute or the Center for American Progress claim to offer expert advice in the public interest, but are widely understood to reflect certain ideological commitments. Public universities, with less obvious partisan leanings, produce policy-relevant expertise in the form of research, but other organizations with explicit policy agendas often function to filter such information into the policymaking process with strategic intent. Many government agencies occupy a clearer role in directly providing expert advice to the policymaking process, including federal regulatory agencies (e.g., the Environmental Protection Agency) and national laboratories (e.g., the National Renewable Energy Laboratory). Such agencies, while marshaling expertise to serve the public interest, also exist institutionally under unavoidably partisan leadership: appointments from the executive branch. Where, then, might we find a truly 'public' think tank – an organization funded by public monies that draws upon diverse sources of expertise to serve the public interest, unfiltered through a partisan agenda?

While a number of potential organizations present themselves as possibilities (e.g., the National Research Council, the RAND Corporation), for methodological reasons I follow the work of others who have examined issues of science advice to the legislative process at the federal level (Bimber, 1996; Morgan & Peha, 2003). These organizations, funded solely by public monies as part of the legislative branch's budget, are ruled by majorities at any given time, but always include powerful minorities that threaten to become the majority in the next election cycle. Thus, as Bimber (1996) argues, public think tanks that directly serve the legislative branch operate in a highly partisan environment – so partisan and dynamic that public think tanks must develop neutral reputations to be valued over time as congressional majorities shift. Excluding the Congressional Budget Office, which operates on the more narrow charge of conducting economic analyses, this chapter focuses on two PTTs: the Congressional Research Service and the Government Accountability Office.

The Congressional Research Service (CRS) serves congressional committees and Members of Congress by providing analyses at all stages of the legislative process. Their services include "reports on major policy issues, tailored confidential memoranda, briefings and consultations, seminars and workshops, expert congressional testimony, [and] responses to individual inquiries" (Library of Congress, 2012). While CRS reports are widely available online and have been made public for many years by various non-governmental organizations (e.g., see http://opencrs.com/ or http://www.fas.org/sgp/crs/index.html), CRS does not officially make their reports available to the public. Instead, the Congress has historically reserved its right to control and disseminate CRS reports and products under the principle that CRS works exclusively for the Congress (Brudnick, 2011).

The Government Accountability Office (GAO), formerly the General Accounting Office, employs nearly 3,300 people across the country, staffed with a variety of professionals including economists, social scientists, accountants, public policy analysts, attorneys, and experts in a range of fields. The US Comptroller General heads the agency, appointed to a 15-year term, distinguishing the position as the longest-term government appointment after Supreme Court Justices. GAO's primary work products are reports (or 'blue books') and testimony before Congress. Some reports are required by law, others are initiated in-house under GAO's own authority, but most result from requests by members of Congress and especially committee chairpersons. Unlike the CRS, GAO provides its reports directly to the public (www.gao.gov).

While these organizations clearly differ in many respects – timescale of projects, leadership structure, freedom to pursue ideas generated 'in-house,' transparency to the public – it remains beyond the scope of this chapter to conduct the fine-grained analysis required to contrast their strategies to navigate controversies surrounding climate change. Instead, I will focus on their similar institutional position and demonstrate commonalities in their strategies of translating expertise into policy-relevant reports.

Commitments to 'neutrality'

Focusing first on their most important commonality, both the CRS and GAO present themselves as providing objective, neutral, balanced, and non-partisan advice to the policymaking process. The GAO website states, "We provide Congress with timely information that is objective, fact-based, nonpartisan, nonideological, fair, and balanced" (US Government Accountability Office, 2012). While such terms flirt with redundancy, they indicate a clear goal of presenting the GAO's analysis in the character of traditional science – facts over and before values (Pielke, Jr., 2007; Sarewitz, 1996). GAO goes on to describe its strategy for achieving such a non-partisan and neutral perspective: "Our independence as an agency is further safeguarded by the fact that our workforce consists of career employees hired on the basis of their knowledge, skills, and ability" (US Government Accountability Office, 2012). In other words, GAO distinguishes itself from government agencies that have significant turnover with each change in the political majority or presidential administration, which bolsters their claim to operate above the partisan fray. Likewise, according to the CRS website, "CRS is well-known for analysis that is authoritative, confidential, objective and nonpartisan," and these terms are listed as 'core values' of the organization. Their website further explains that "CRS approaches complex topics from a variety of perspectives and examines all sides of an issue" (Library of Congress, 2012), reassuring us that their methods of employing expertise create no bias.

While presenting a full critique of this framing is beyond the scope of this chapter, scholarship in STS offers a number of critical perspectives. First, claims for pure objectivity in science are in themselves problematic (e.g., Daston, 1999; Haraway, 1999; Latour, 1987; Longino, 1990; Wynne, 1991). Not only does the choice of topics studied by PTTs require political decisions largely determined by values preferences, but all expert knowledge comes from one point of view or another. If expertise is situated, social, and partial, one would be hard-pressed to argue that the compilation of expertise – the task of the PTT – could be purely objective. Second, the PTTs' descriptions of themselves resonate with narratives favoring the scientization of politics – "attempts to turn all policy-making into technical exercises that obviate the need for political debate" (Pielke, Jr., 2007, p. 34) – and the "myth of authoritativeness" – the belief that expertise translates unproblematically into policy choices (Sarewitz, 1996, pp. 71–96). While science can inform policy choices, it is rarely deterministic in the sense of determining an outcome without politics playing any sort of role.

Other criticisms stem from empirical arguments about the actual practices of PTTs. Hill (2003, p. 108), for example, states:

> CRS makes limited use of external sources of information and even less of external analysis. Its approach tends to be reportorial rather than analytical. It tends to present the views of all interested parties as if they were of comparable validity, rather than to analyze each view skeptically so as to arrive at the best available understanding of an issue.

These accusations undermine the 'authoritative' core value of the CRS by suggesting that analysis remains incomplete and partial. More subtly, the critique exposes the Achilles heel of a balanced approach to analysis: the risk that a balanced perspective misleads an audience by implying the existence of multiple truths with equal probability. This perspective informs my analysis below by helping to define one particular 'strategy of neutrality.' Finally, in quite an interesting twist, CRS has historically engaged the practice of 'directed writing,' in which CRS removes all traces of its own authorship for documents written for a Member of Congress. Such work not only sheds the veneer of non-partisanship, but also undermines any accountability for CRS to stay true to its stated core values. Unfortunately, the invisibility of 'directed writing' also makes it a difficult phenomenon to study, and thus it remains beyond the scope of this chapter.

Public think tanks and political controversy

Scholarship on PTTs has thus far focused on how they have navigated political controversy. As boundary organizations, they inhabit a space between communities of experts (e.g., scientists and engineers) and communities of policymakers (e.g., congressional staff, congressional committees). In bridging these worlds, they offer a place to examine questions about how these worlds influence one another.

Bimber (1996) explores the case of the Office of Technology Assessment (OTA), a PTT that Congress stopped funding in 1993, to challenge the standard assumption that "expertise located in government institutions is believed to exhibit a secular trend toward greater politicization" (1996, p. 16). This standard assumption stems from the belief that political leaders seek passionate commitment rather than objective, neutral, expert advice. The history of the Office of Management and Budget (OMB) exemplifies this narrative. As Bimber explains, OMB began as a fairly neutral and objective source of expert advice for the executive branch, but political pressures soon transformed OMB into a voice of and for the presidential administration. Would we not expect the same results – the politicization of expertise – from PTTs associated so closely with the legislative branch?

Instead, Bimber (1996) argues that the history of the OTA demonstrates a key difference for PTTs that serve Congress. Because Congress is never completely uniform in its partisan identity, the structural pressures for objective and non-partisan advice endure in ways not experienced by the OMB.

> Some institutional settings tend to elicit greater degrees of politicization from experts than others, regardless of the character of political decision-makers for whom the expertise is produced and regardless of the political inclinations of the experts themselves ... [S]tructure does indeed shape action ... Congress, I argue, shows how an institution with a highly pluralistic distribution of power tends to reward experts who provide broadly applicable, politically uncommitted expertise.
>
> (1996, p. 7)

Specifically, Bimber shows how OTA leadership gradually settled upon a series of 'strategies of neutrality' in order to survive as an institution serving Congress with the provision of expert advice. Here 'neutrality' describes the substance, or at least appearance, of political neutrality. OTA's strategies of neutrality included:

1 Despite OTA taking direction from committee chairs (who always represent the majority party), OTA would share requests with ranking minority members.
2 In order to avoid creating enemies – who might react strongly to published reports that supported their political opponents – OTA would 'offer a little something for everyone' in their reports.
3 OTA followed a procedure of informing rival committees and sub-committees and coordinating joint press releases so as not to enter turf wars of jurisdiction.
4 OTA's panel review system included both technical and political experts.
5 OTA refused steadfastly to endorse a specific policy action, instead providing a range of policy options for Congress to consider.

(1996, pp. 57–66)

Following these strategies helped OTA survive a highly politicized environment for nearly 20 years. Ultimately, OTA's demise had less to do with their failure to maintain neutrality, and more to do with the incoming Republican majority needing to demonstrate a willingness to downsize government in their own legislative branch according to their 'Contract with America' – a move made less painful by the fact that OTA remained fairly small and had not built up an important political constituency (Bimber, 1996; Margolis & Guston, 2003).

While Bimber's (1996) account provides important insight into the structural pressures on the politicization of expertise in PTTs within the legislative branch, it remains less clear how and if PTTs navigate controversy on the opposite boundary – within the scientific community.

Public think tanks and scientific controversy

Given PTTs' rhetorical commitment to objective, neutral, non-partisan advice, and the structural pressures on the CRS and GAO to maintain a degree of the same with respect to a pluralistic Congress, I assume that the existence of scientific controversies – debates between experts over the quality, interpretation, and significance of data – poses a key challenge to PTTs. They must somehow demonstrate their own expertise by interpreting scientific controversies for policymaking audiences while simultaneously avoiding the pitfall of 'taking a side' that benefits a partisan outcome. Perhaps this is an impossible task, but PTTs have maintained their status and their budgets through a procession of unfolding scientific controversies and multiple shifts in majority control of Congress. They must be doing something 'right,' even if we must interpret their success as organizational survival rather than the realization of the myth of perfectly neutral advice to the policymaking process.

Analyzing reports – a first step in analysis

As discussed above, reports represent a major outcome of the work of PTTs. They are more enduring and more publicly accessible than the informal communications and constructed networks of experts and policymakers that result from PTT research and negotiation with congressional staff and members. As such, PTT reports are political artifacts worthy of study, but I do so mindful that they may not be the most powerful outcome, nor do they necessarily faithfully represent the less formal conclusions and communications that PTT staff entertain among themselves or during off-the-record interactions with policymakers.

In fact, scholars warn of reifying the significance of the written report in relation to the "value of the spoken word" (Bimber, 1996, p. 96). Referencing work by Smith (1992), for example, Morgan & Peha (2003, p. 14) comment:

> Science advisors who are effective … almost always operate in the pragmatic rationalist mode … They may choose to write a report using the rhetoric of the utopian rationalist, but they will almost always have subtly negotiated the terms of what they will say so as to mesh with the goals of their clients.

In other words, reports are a type of performance that is orchestrated for an audience, and we cannot take such performances at face value (for dramaturgical analyses of scientific controversies, see Delborne, 2011; Hilgartner, 2000). Guston (2003, p. 81) notes:

> [E]mphasis on social learning, communication, and the process of assessment leads to different ways of evaluating assessments [by PTTs]. It displaces attention from the bound volume of the report to the greater variety and forms of communication, including interactions that produced the report in the first place.

Analyzing reports thus represents just a first step in analysis, but one that both stands on its own as well as informs future efforts. First, while the reports may not faithfully represent the complex analysis and communication involved in each research assignment, they live as political artifacts referenced – as they are written – by diverse political actors. How the reports navigate scientific controversy matters because the reports are treated as valuable and credible. Second, understanding the mix of rhetorical strategies contained within the reports informs a set of questions and hypotheses to bring to a subsequent phase of more textured, ethnographic research.

Methodology

I completed a textual analysis of ten recently published reports by the GAO and CRS that addressed issues of climate change science and policy.[1] I used Atlas.ti (qualitative data analysis software) to code the reports, first looking for any text referring to or addressing implicitly a scientific controversy. Codes began as free descriptions of how the language characterized and/or navigated a controversy (e.g., 'presents both sides evenly'). The second phase of analysis involved grouping similar codes into categories. This technique permitted the categories to emerge from the data rather than imposing a priori categories – a methodology known as grounded theory (Glaser & Strauss, 1967). Eventually, I settled upon five categories that were sufficient to describe almost every example I had found. I then analyzed the relative frequencies of categories to gain a sense of whether some strategies were more dominant than others. Lastly, I performed a qualitative, contextual analysis to discern the significance of the various strategies in the reports.

Strategies for navigating scientific controversy

My analysis of CRS and GAO reports reveals five primary strategies for navigating scientific controversy around climate change science:

1 showcase scientific uncertainty
2 reveal scientific disagreement
3 simulate journalistic balance
4 provide qualitative judgments
5 discern consensus.

These categories do not have neat and precise boundaries, but the following descriptions and examples reveal my aim to notice key strategic differences in the ways that PTTs navigate scientific controversy.

Showcase scientific uncertainty

The most banal treatment of scientific controversy involves the simple recognition of scientific uncertainty (see Box 8.1). In such cases, scientific controversy may or may not be actively occurring, but the uncertainty prevents the PTT from offering an informed judgment to policymakers. At times, the language is quite explicit:

> Driven by concerns about scientific uncertainty with respect to global climate, the George H. W. Bush Administration – against the wishes of most environmentalists and some vocal Members of Congress – refused to commit to a binding agreement to reduce the nation's CO_2 emissions by a specific date.
>
> (Parker et al., 2011, p. 3)

In this case, CRS navigates the political controversy around global climate change policy by emphasizing the much less politically charged scientific uncertainty to justify a particular action, or inaction, by the first Bush Administration. This

---

BOX 8.1 Textual examples of showcasing scientific uncertainty (excerpted from analyzed CRS and GAO reports)

- "It is not clear whether ..."
- "It is not clear why ..."
- "[T]he record of observations may not be long enough to determine ..."
- Citation of a NOAA study showing that "a claim of attribution ... is thus problematic, although it does not exclude" a future claim with additional evidence
- Rulings by the EPA "have raised questions about the carbon neutrality of biopower"
- "It could be argued that ..."
- "As an unproven concept ..."
- "Little research has been done ..."
- "Peer-reviewed literature is scant"
- "impacts ... are uncertain"
- "Studies have yet to demonstrate ..."
- "Further research is likely needed to answer numerous questions including ..."
- "A paucity of literature exists ..."
- "The lifecycle carbon benefit has not been calculated."
- "The long-term implications ... are not yet fully understood."
- "Several questions have yet to be answered ..."

---

strategy gives a degree of political cover for any decisions or non-decisions made – by suggesting that scientific certainty *would* lead to a more definitive policy decision. Yet, the subtext implied by the controversy between President Bush and "environmentalists and some vocal Members of Congress" challenges whether the scientific uncertainty represents something unknown, unknowable, or simply not proven to a particular standard that might stem more from political commitments than adherence to expert methodologies of proof. In a different report, the CRS highlights more specific uncertainties around climate change: "Given scientific uncertainties about the magnitude, timing, rate, and regional consequences of potential climatic change, what are the appropriate responses for US and world decision makers?" (Justus & Fletcher, 2006, Summary). Here the scientific uncertainties are specified, creating a very different valence from the previous quote invoking scientific uncertainty at the more general level. By posing the question of action in the face of scientific uncertainties – rather than justifying political inaction – the CRS positions uncertainty as a challenge rather than a barrier to policy decisions.

At other times, the technical uncertainty appears as more of a statement of the extent of complexity. In discussing the benefits of a carbon offset program within a cap-and-trade strategy for greenhouse gas emissions, the GAO comments that, "The extent of any savings is uncertain and would depend on many factors, including the design of the regulatory and offset programs" (Trimble, 2011, p. 2). Here, one might imagine further modeling of various policy scenarios to calculate economic benefits, but the language directs the reader to pay greater attention to the policy variables rather than the technical analysis. In other words, unlike the invocation of scientific uncertainty surrounding climate change to justify the Bush Administration's policy preference, the uncertainty identified here by the GAO is political rather than technical. In the same report, the GAO points to technical limitations as a source of a related uncertainty: "emissions reductions from some types of offset projects, particularly soil and forestry projects, can be difficult to measure" (Trimble, 2011, p. 7). Thus, the debate over the wisdom and impacts of offsets – a policy decision – connects to different flavors of scientific uncertainty.

Reveal scientific disagreement

Explicitly foregrounding the existence of some degree of scientific controversy, strategies that highlight scientific disagreement go beyond acknowledging uncertainty to suggest that knowledge contests exist among experts (see Box 8.2). CRS, for example, states, "Experts disagree, however, on the timing, magnitude and patterns of future climate changes" (Legget, 2009, Summary). Although this quote identifies similar types of uncertainty as the 2006 CRS report quoted above, the explicit attention to disagreement highlights a more politically charged question. This strategy thus allows the report to acknowledge a controversy

---

BOX 8.2 Textual examples of showcasing scientific disagreement (excerpted from analyzed CRS and GAO reports)

- "nor do scientists agree on the relationship between …"
- "studies … using similar data have produced different results" [footnote references two example studies in the peer-reviewed literature]
- "multiple assertions … have been put forth," with four listed as bullets
- Discussion of two distinct sign-on letters from scientists to Members of Congress regarding the carbon neutrality of biomass
- "Different LCA [life-cycle assessment] time frames can lead to radically different, even contradictory, results"
- "The debate about … the LCA … was controversial"
- Two-page table, "Scientific Underpinnings for Different Perspectives on Geoengineering," with columns of "Primary Concern," "Arguments in Favor," and "Arguments Against"
- "[T]here is controversy whether carbon accumulation continues or peaks.

explicitly without taking a side. In other words, revealing scientific disagreement does not require the PTT experts to weigh the evidence and offer an informed opinion on which experts *should be believed.*

In another example, GAO advertises its careful research into a controversy with opposing experts. The authors describe debates over the Clean Development Mechanism (CDM) as a compliance program for carbon offsets: "Several studies on the CDM also suggest that a substantial number of non-additional projects have received offsets,[15] although some experts reported that the CDM has improved the quality of its offsets significantly in recent years[16]" (Trimble, 2011, p. 8). Footnote 15 (in the original GAO report) describes two published studies, examining 93 and 226 CDM projects respectively, that found rates of non-additionality of 40 and 26 percent; although the same note acknowledges that the two studies do "not reflect recent program improvements." Footnote 16 describes direct conversations between the report's authors and CDM officials, suggesting that these experts have greater optimism in avoiding non-additionality. Again, GAO takes no position on which experts should be believed, but their report reflects the disagreement as analyzed.

Simulate 'journalistic' balance

A related strategy that also acknowledges expert disagreement simulates the practice in journalism of giving a 'balanced' report on a contentious issue. The difference is subtle, but calls attention to the careful management of conflicting perspectives – giving each equal attention and credibility without making a judgment about what position represents the majority view. A CRS report on biopower states:

> Many views exist about whether biopower is carbon neutral. Some contend that biopower is carbon neutral because the carbon released during bioenergy production comes from a carbon neutral feedstock – biomass. Some argue that biopower is not carbon neutral because the amount of GHG emissions released per unit of energy during simple biopower combustion may be higher for certain biomass fuels than for fossil fuels; or, if the GHG emissions from certain biomass fuels are lower than fossil fuels, they are still not zero. These perspectives are often based on differing assumptions, technologies, and time frames.
>
> (Bracmort, 2011, p. 1)

This excerpt demonstrates a very careful treatment of a significant scientific controversy – whether biopower is carbon neutral – that includes a mix of technical assumptions, values, perspectives, and horizons of analysis. What is notable is the politeness and balance given rhetorically to the conflicting positions. No judgment is made – for example, the author does not weigh in on which "assumptions, technologies, and time frames" would be most appropriate for policymakers to consider.

An even more striking example mimics journalistic balance by indirectly assigning competing perspectives to well-known actors in climate change policy debates. Again, addressing the carbon neutrality of biomass, CRS provides sequential paragraphs that communicate the opposing positions. Each paragraph is exactly nine lines and uses frank, clear, measured language. The first paragraph references and draws upon a Natural Resources Defense Council blog, "Scientists to Congress & Obama: Count the Carbon in Biomass"; the second paragraph quotes a press release from the American Forest & Paper Association, "EPA's Tailoring Rule Undermines Renewable Energy From Biomass, Harms Rural Communities, and Puts American Jobs at Risk," and cites a personal communication with the CEO of the Biomass Power Association (Bracmort, 2011, pp. 8–9). While it is possible that the nine-line symmetry is a coincidence, the overall effect presents a nearly perfectly balanced perspective on a scientific controversy, letting some of the strongest advocates speak for their positions.

Provide qualitative judgments

As an incremental step beyond providing a balanced perspective on controversy, PTT reports sometimes include a qualitative judgment about the likelihood of certain outcomes or the weight of opposing arguments. For example, addressing the "Observed Impacts of Climate Changes," CRS states that "Anthropogenic warming over the last three decades has *likely* had a discernible influence at the global scale on observed changes in many physical and biological systems [emphasis mine]" (Legget, 2009, p. 7). Mirroring their description of the 2007 report by the Intergovernmental Panel on Climate Change (IPCC), the CRS authors stop short of claiming an authoritative position in the scientific controversy over anthropogenic climate change. Nor do they simply present the controversy in a balanced manner or emphasize qualities of uncertainty or disagreement on the issue.

An earlier CRS report on the same subject made a similar qualitative judgment based on rough numbers of opposing scientists:

> A large number of scientists believe that human activities, which have increased atmospheric concentrations of carbon dioxide (CO_2) by 35% from preindustrial values of 280 parts per million (ppm) to 378 ppm over the past 150 years, are leading to an increase in global average temperatures. Global temperatures have already risen 0.6 °C (0.9 °F) in the last 100 years, and, according to model projections, might rise anywhere from as little as 1.8 °C to as much as 7.1 °C (2.7 °F to 10.7 °F) over the next 100 years. However, the science of "global warming" is not without challengers, who argue that scientific proof is incomplete or contradictory, and that there remain many uncertainties about the nature and direction of Earth's climate.
>
> (Justus & Fletcher, 2006, pp. 1–2)

This text, while presenting the existence of some uncertainty and disagreement, does not characterize the controversy as balanced. Specifying that "a large number of scientists believe ..." gives greater credibility by designating a majority opinion in relation to "challengers," who are marginalized by the analysis, although not excluded entirely. Later discussion within the same report describes the position of "Many climate scientists" in a detailed, 26-line paragraph with multiple ranges of likely estimates for sea level rise, followed by a generic, five-line paragraph that mentions how "Skeptics of the global warming theory have called into question the reliability of the computer climate models ... They also challenge some scientists' assertions that recent episodic weather events may seem more extreme in nature" (Justus & Fletcher, 2006, pp. 3–4). Again, the controversy is laid bare and not dismissed out of hand, but the space allotted to the different views and the labels used to identify the actors ("Many climate scientists" vs. "Skeptics") portray a strong qualitative judgment. Nevertheless, in the spirit of including "a little something for everyone" identified by Bimber (1996), the text would still allow selective citation to support the minority view on climate change.

Other reports include language such as: "one of the clearest trends ..." (Folger, 2011, p. 9), "Researchers generally expect ..." (2011, p. 10), and "Most interested observers agree that ..." (Bracmort et al., 2011, p. 3). My point here is not to call attention to a lack of quantitative comparison (e.g., criticizing the use of qualitative language such as 'most' rather than specifying a precise ratio), but rather to highlight a strategy that begins to make a judgment within the context of controversy. Qualitative statements by PTTs give greater confidence to one position over another without entirely dismissing the marginal position.

Discern consensus

A rationalistic view of the purpose of PTT reports would expect them to exhibit constant efforts to discern expert consensus in the face of scientific controversies. After all, if the goal is to inform policymakers on highly complex, technical, and controversial issues, should we not expect that groups of objective, non-partisan, neutral analysts (within PTTs) would "get to the bottom" of technical disputes and translate the consensus view to policymakers, who presumably possess little capacity to wade through opposing technical arguments? Such a goal connects directly to visions of the scientization of politics discussed previously, wherein hard facts and expert advice can and should resolve policy dilemmas. Instead, as suggested by the previous strategies of navigating scientific controversy, PTTs rarely make clear claims in their reports about the 'right' answers. Some examples exist, however, and are worth exploring.

One strategy involves making claims at the general level rather than discerning consensus within a more significantly controversial subject. For example, GAO defines, with limited specificity, the evaluative criteria for carbon offsets: "While definitions vary, our review of the literature points to five general criteria for assessing offset quality – an offset must be additional, real, verifiable, permanent, and enforceable" (Trimble, 2011, p. 3). Note that GAO justifies its claim with their "review of the literature," calling attention to the expertise they bring to the controversial topic. The report goes on to define each of these terms, but one could argue that the controversy is in the details rather than the identification of general criteria for evaluation.

A second strategy relies upon the credibility of cited sources, especially those that review multiple studies on a controversial topic. For example, CRS states, "Based on a review of more than 25 LCAs [Life Cycle Assessments], biopower is in the top tier of bioenergy pathways that avoid the most GHG emissions and replace the largest amounts of fossil energy[14]" (Bracmort, 2011, p. 5). Footnote 14 (in the original text) lists a chapter in an edited volume published by Routledge that includes a table with "[i]nformation regarding the feedstocks, conversion processes, end products, system boundaries, allocation methods, and impact metrics for each LCA." Thus, while CRS shows a willingness to make a relative claim about biopower as a "top tier" solution, they justify this position with a direct citation rather than conducting an independent analysis.

Conclusion

The CRS and GAO strategies for navigating climate change controversies identified in this chapter represent a continuum proportional to the degree of political risk faced by the PTT. Showcasing scientific uncertainty hints at scientific controversy, but can also serve as a rhetorical tool to mask political controversy or to highlight the shortcomings of technical analysis. Revealing scientific disagreement acknowledges the existence of scientific controversy more explicitly, but involves no judgment. Simulating journalistic balance introduces stakeholders into the conversation, letting their voices advocate for partisan interpretations of expertise, but still avoids decisions about which experts or perspectives deserve the most attention. Providing qualitative judgments begins to weigh in on the question of majority views or more likely scenarios, but simultaneously maintains some amount of text that partisans could use as 'ammunition' through selective quotations. Discerning consensus represents the most political risk as it attempts to sort through a scientific controversy and declare a winning position or perspective.

Perhaps not surprisingly, PTTs more frequently engage in less risky strategies of navigating climate change controversies in their reports. To be clear, less risky in this context does not refer to probabilities of being proven wrong but to the institutional risk of being perceived by political actors as straying from their mission to provide neutral advice to the policymaking process. As such, explicit attention to scientific uncertainty and disagreement occur much more frequently than the provision of qualitative judgments. While more extensive analysis is required to explore additional attempts at discerning consensus, those studied thus far suggest that the consensus discerned fails to reflect bold analysis and may rely primarily upon other published and credible research.

These somewhat preliminary findings position PTTs as paradoxical actors. On one hand, the CRS and GAO advertise their analytical prowess and its incorporation into the policymaking process, presumably adding expertise and rationality along the way. They thus present themselves in service of the scientization of politics, a vision judged by many scholars as highly problematic within debates over climate change (Hulme, 2009; Meyer, 2011; Pielke, Jr., 2010; Sarewitz, 1996). On the other hand, at least within the context of their published reports, PTTs appear to avoid making the 'tough calls' within the context of controversies in climate science. Their reports demonstrate a propensity to showcase uncertainty and disagreement rather than adjudicate among conflicting views for the benefit of policymakers (who presumably lack the expertise to do so themselves). As a result, and perhaps due to their central commitment to maintaining neutrality in a highly partisan environment, they partly undermine the rationality project of scientizing political discourse.

Furthermore, the lack of serious discernment of consensus within scientific controversies provides evidence that PTTs do not and cannot occupy a central place in steering climate change policy. Interested parties, stakeholders, and competing experts will have a strong voice when controversy exists, and more likely than not, their voices will appear within PTT reports with little editorial comment. As such, except in rare cases, PTT reports may serve as vehicles for the formal inclusion of partisan expertise into policy debates on climate change.

Undoubtedly, this topic deserves more careful attention through further exploration. First, a study of the informal communication within PTTs and between PTT staff and policymakers as they navigate scientific controversies might reveal heretofore hidden processes of negotiation and discernment. If so, we might conclude that the political value of PTT research lies within the research process rather than the products (i.e., published reports). Second, by focusing on the texts of the reports, this chapter has not analyzed their impacts on policy discourse. Further research might explore how political actors use PTT reports on climate change both within formal Congressional debates and in broader media. One could study the ways in which political debates explicitly reference the reports or their findings, or how experts associated with the reports become targets to mobilize in the service of political advocacy. Third, CRS's practice of 'directed writing' offers an opportunity for comparative work. If one could gain access to the products or processes of anonymous research and writing conducted by CRS personnel in the service of Members of Congress, one could compare such analyses with the more formal reports that bear the CRS name. Such a comparison might reveal a new set of strategies of navigating controversies in climate change science when neutrality is no longer required.

Note

1 Cameron Nazminia, a graduate student from Colorado School of Mines, assisted me in collecting the reports and conducting a preliminary analysis.

References

Bimber, B. (1996). *The politics of expertise in Congress: The rise and fall of the Office of Technology Assessment.* New York: State University of New York Press.

Bracmort, K. (2011). *Is biopower carbon neutral?* Congressional Research Service. Retrieved April 30, 2012: http://www.fas.org/sgp/crs/misc/R41603.pdf.

Bracmort, K., Lattanzio, R., & Barbour, E. (2011). *Geoengineering: Governance and technology policy.* Congressional Research Service. Retrieved April 30, 2012: http://www.fas.org/sgp/crs/misc/R41371.pdf.

Brudnick, I. A. (2011). *The Congressional Research Service and the American legislative process.* Congressional Research Service. Retrieved April 31, 2012: http://www.fas.org/sgp/crs/misc/RL33471.pdf.

Collins, H. M. & Evans, R. (2002). The third wave of science studies: Studies of expertise and experience. *Social Studies of Science*, 32(2), 235–296.

Daston, L. (1999). Objectivity and the escape from perspective. In M. Biagioli (Ed.), *The science studies reader* (pp. 110–123). New York: Routledge.

Delborne, J. A. (2011). Constructing audiences in scientific controversy. *Social Epistemology: A Journal of Knowledge, Culture and Policy*, 25(1), 67–95.

Epstein, S. (1996). *Impure science: AIDS, activism, and the politics of knowledge*, A. Scull, ed., Berkeley, CA: University of California Press.

Folger, P. (2011). *Severe thunderstorms and tornadoes in the United States.* Congressional Research Service. Retrieved: http://assets.opencrs.com/rpts/R40097_20100202.pdf.

Glaser, B. G. & Strauss, A. L. (1967). *The discovery of grounded theory: Strategies for qualitative research.* Chicago, IL: Aldine.

Guston, D. H. (2003). Insights from the Office of Technology Assessment and other assessment experiences. In *Science and Technology Advice for Congress* (pp. 77–89). Washington, DC: Resources for the Future.

Haraway, D. (1999). Situated knowledges: The science question in feminism and the privilege of partial perspective. In M. Biagioli (Ed.), *The science studies reader* (pp. 172–188). New York: Routledge.

Hilgartner, S. (2000). *Science on stage: Expert advice as public drama.* Stanford, CA: Stanford University Press.

Hill, C. T. (2003). An expanded analytical capability in the Congressional Research Service, the General Accounting Office, or the Congressional Budget Office. In *Science and Technology Advice for Congress* (pp. 106–117). Washington, DC: Resources for the Future.

Hulme, M. (2009). *Why we disagree about climate change: Understanding controversy, inaction and opportunity.* New York: Cambridge University Press.

Jasanoff, S. (1990). *The fifth branch. Science advisers as policymakers.* Cambridge, MA: Harvard University Press.

Justus, J. J. & Fletcher, S. R. (2006). *Global climate change.* Congressional Research Service. Retrieved April 30, 2012: http://fpc.state.gov/documents/organization/67128.pdf.

Kinchy, A. J. & Kleinman, D. L. (2005). Democratizing science, debating values: New approaches to 'politicized' science under the Bush administration. *Dissent*, Summer, 54–62.

Kingdon, J. W. (2002). *Agendas, alternatives, and public policies*, 2nd edition. London: Longman Classics.

Latour, B. (1987). *Science in action: How to follow scientists and engineers through society.* Cambridge, MA: Harvard University Press.

Latour, B. (2004). *Politics of nature: How to bring the sciences into democracy*. Cambridge, MA: Harvard University Press.

Legget, J. A. (2009). *Climate change: Science highlights*. Congressional Research Service. Retrieved April 30, 2012: http://www.fas.org/sgp/crs/misc/RL34266.pdf.

Library of Congress. (2012). About CRS. Retrieved April 31, 2012: http://www.loc.gov/crsinfo/about.

Longino, H. E. (1990). *Science as social knowledge*. Princeton, NJ: Princeton University Press.

Margolis, R. M. & Guston, D. H. (2003). The origins, accomplishments, and demise of the Office of Technology Assessment. In *Science and Technology Advice for Congress* (pp. 53–76). Washington, DC: Resources for the Future.

Medvetz, T. (2012). *Think tanks in America*. Chicago, IL: University of Chicago Press.

Meyer, R. (2011). The public values failures of climate science in the US. *Minerva*, 49(1), 47–70.

Morgan, M. G. & Peha, J. M. (2003). *Science and technology advice for congress*. Washington, DC: Resources for the Future.

Nixon, R. (2012). Bill would expand insurance for crops. *The caucus: The politics and government blog of The Times*. Retrieved April 25, 2012: http://thecaucus.blogs.nytimes.com/2012/04/20/bill-would-expand-insurance-for-crops.

Parker, L., Blodgett, J., & Yacobucci, B. D. (2011). *US global climate change policy: Evolving view on cost, competitiveness, and comprehensiveness*. Congressional Research Service. Retrieved April 30, 2012: http://assets.opencrs.com/rpts/RL30024_20110224.pdf.

Pear, R. (2010). Baffled by health plan? So are some lawmakers. *The New York Times*, April 13. Retrieved April 25, 2012: http://www.nytimes.com/2010/04/13/us/politics/13health.html.

Pielke, Jr., R. A. (2007). *The honest broker: Making sense of science in policy and politics*. Cambridge: Cambridge University Press.

Pielke, Jr., R. A. (2010). *The climate fix: What scientists and politicians won't tell you about global warming*. New York: Basic Books.

Rich, A. (2004). *Think tanks, public policy, and the politics of expertise*. Cambridge and New York: Cambridge University Press.

Sarewitz, D. (1996). *Frontiers of illusion: Science, technology and the politics of progress*. Philadelphia, PA: Temple University Press.

Smith, B. L. R. (1992). *The advisors: Scientists in the policy process*. Washington, DC: Brookings Institution.

Stone, D. (2012). *Policy paradox : The art of political decision making*, Third Edition. New York: W.W. Norton & Co.

Trimble, D. C. (2011). *Climate change issues: Options for addressing challenges to carbon offset quality*. Government Accountability Office. Retrieved April 30, 2012: http://www.gao.gov/new.items/d11345.pdf.

US Government Accountability Office (2012). About GAO. Retrieved August 31, 2012: http://www.gao.gov/about.

Van Bueren, E. M., Klijn, E.-H., & Koppenjan, J. F. M. (2003). Dealing with wicked problems in networks: Analyzing an environmental debate from a network perspective. *Journal of Public Administration Research & Theory*, 13(2), 193.

Wynne, B. (1991). Knowledges in context. *Science, Technology, & Human Values*, 16(1), 111–121.

COMMENTARY ON PART III

Beyond polarization – the limits to technocratic and activist approaches to climate politics

Matthew C. Nisbet

As the chapters in this section emphasize, policy debate over climate change presents us with a troubling paradox. The more divisive our disagreements over policy have become, the more that each side has turned to science, economics, and other forms of technocratic expertise as the perceived antidote to this division. Yet rather than overcoming polarization, this strategy seems to only deepen disagreement.

Mike Hulme, writing in the *Guardian* in 2007, perhaps summed up the driver behind this predicament best:

> Too often with climate change, genuine and necessary debates about these wider social values – do we have confidence in technology; do we believe in collective action over private enterprise; do we believe we carry obligations to people invisible to us in geography and time? – masquerade as disputes about scientific truth and error.

Mark Brown in his chapter provides ample evidence in support of Hulme's observation. He details how values-based debates over policy options and technologies have too frequently been equated with arguments over climate science. He also critiques the strong focus on international negotiations and atmospheric targets as the ultimate political objectives. Such a focus, Brown notes, conflicts with the need to act nationally and locally and to pursue adaptation and resilience measures. The approach can also lead to authoritarian views of governance and leave the public with a feeling of hopelessness in the face of an apparently intractable, global-scale problem.

Focusing on Colorado, Dallas Elgin and Christopher Weible in their chapter find that non-profit staffers working on climate change in the state were likely to rely on information from other non-profit organizations rather than from academic or business sources. These latter groups were similarly likely to rely on information sources from within their own domains or sectors. This suggests that in considering ways to address climate change and forge collaborations, that the state's most highly skilled professionals are unlikely to look beyond their like-minded colleagues unless new forums, incentives, and approaches are taken, a topic I return to at the end of this commentary.

In his own chapter, Jason Delborne shows that independent, non-partisan technocratic agencies such as the US General Accountability Office and the Congressional Research Service may in fact actually enhance political gridlock. Instead of serving as the basis for agreement, his analysis of the process by which agency reports are produced suggests that partisan voices often shape the content of reports and that once released, the reports are selectively interpreted to serve partisan and advocacy ends.

Designed to win: engineering social change?

The findings from these three chapters complement my own research on how major US foundations bet heavily on the ability of technocratic expertise to overcome political differences on climate change and in the process pursued a relatively narrow set of policy goals and technologies (Nisbet, 2011). In 2006, several of the country's wealthiest foundations hired a consulting firm to comprehensively survey the available scientific literature and to consult more than 150 leading climate change and energy experts. The result of this intensive undertaking was the 2007 report *Design to Win: Philanthropy's Role in the Fight Against Global Warming*.

Leading the report was the recommendation that 'tempering climate change' required a strong cap and trade policy in the US and the European Union, and a binding international agreement on greenhouse gas emissions. The report predicted that passage of cap and trade legislation would "prompt a sea change that washes over the entire global economy." The authors included little to no discussion of the role of government in directly sponsoring the creation of new energy technologies. The report was additionally notable for the absence of any meaningful discussion of social, political, or cultural dimensions of the challenge. Instead, the authors offered a decidedly optimistic outlook: "The good news is that we already have the technology and know-how to achieve these carbon reductions – often at a cost savings."

To understand how this planning document shaped the investment strategies of major foundations, I analyzed available records as of January 2011 for 1,246 climate change and energy-related grants distributed by nine aligned foundations between 2008 and 2010. These aligned foundations were among the wealthiest in the country, included several of the top funders of environment-related programs, and were either sponsors of the *Design to Win* report or described themselves as following its recommendations.

Approximately $368 million was distributed across the 1,246 individual grants. The funding provided by the nine foundations reflected a pattern of support focused on achieving a clear set of policy objectives as outlined in the *Design to Win* report. Funding included $39 million associated with activities in support of cap and trade policies; $32 million associated with efforts at reaching an international agreement or influencing the policies of a specific country; and $18.7 million associated with efforts at limiting or opposing coal-fired power plants.

Funding patterns also reflected the *Design to Win* report's framing of climate change as a physical threat that required primarily scientific and economic expertise to solve rather than investments in communication, public participation, and political dialogue. More than $48 million in grants were associated with policy analysis or economic impact analysis; $17 million with environmental impact analysis; and $13 million given directly to support university-based programs.

In comparison, there was either very limited or no funding focused on the role of government in promoting innovation or on development of technologies favored by political conservatives like nuclear energy, carbon capture and storage, or natural gas fracking. Nor was there equivalent investment in important human dimensions of the issue, such as adaptation, health, equity, justice, or economic development. Similarly, very few grants supported initiatives designed to better understand public opinion, to evaluate communication strategies, and/or to promote media resources across states and regions.

From technocracy to grassroots activism

Following the failure of cap and trade legislation in 2010, much of the focus in the US has been on the need for philanthropists, environmentalists, and their allies to invest in grassroots activism. Yet still missing are similar investments in strategies designed to promote critical reflection, cross-cutting discussion, and ultimately broader based cooperation and collaboration.

In his 2007 book *Fight global warming now: The handbook for taking action in your community*, writer-turned-activist Bill McKibben was among the first to call for a shift from the technocratic approach to politics favored by big budget environmental groups: "The change we need is so sweeping and so rapid that only by mobilizing ourselves through our government will we be able to make enough progress in the time we have left." Recognizing the difficulty in mobilizing people around international negotiations and emissions targets, what was needed, he argued, were political activities that reflect "local affection and local history," since "a sense of place is invaluable for effective organizing and for creating a brighter future" (McKibben, 2007, p. 26).

Through his organization 350.org, McKibben and his co-founders have pioneered new methods of social protest. Their strategies combine traditional face-to-face organizing at the local level with the global potency of social media and the storytelling ability of McKibben as a best-selling author. The organization has applied these strategies most notably to oppose the Keystone XL oil pipeline and to urge divestment from fossil fuel companies.

350.org's focus on grassroots activism was bolstered most recently by the conclusions of Harvard University political scientist Theda Skocpol. In a January 2013 analysis, she argued that in order to pass comprehensive US climate legislation,

> several years of popular organizing would be needed to build alliances stretching into most states and congressional districts. Leaders and citizen activists would have to get involved. And not just the usual suspects in the environmental movement. A push for carbon taxes and dividends would need support from unions, women's groups, and community associations.
>
> (Skocpol, 2013a; Skocpol, 2013b)

As of 2012, 350.org employed 26 staff in the US and 11 abroad. According to IRS records, in 2011, 350.org generated $3 million in revenue, spent $1.8 million on program activities with $1.2 million – or two-thirds of its program expenditures – dedicated to grassroots field organizing. Much of the financial backing for 350.org has come from the Rockefeller Brothers Fund, a relatively small philanthropy that has adopted a very different approach from the Design to Win coalition, investing much of its portfolio in grassroots organizing, communication research, and media. The foundation, for example, is also the main financer behind the launch of Inside Climate News, which won a 2013 Pulitzer prize for its investigation of a Michigan pipeline spill of Canadian Tar sands oil (Nisbet, 2013a).

Billionaire Tom Steyer and Facebook co-founder Mark Hughes are among a newer generation of philanthropists who have prioritized grassroots activist strategies and specialized media as a means to pressure elected officials and promote policy action. In 2013, Steyer funded a super PAC to support the successful election to the US Senate of Massachusetts Representative Ed Markey, a leading advocate for climate action and a vocal opponent of the Keystone XL pipeline. Steyer also bankrolled a sophisticated social media campaign that targets Facebook, Twitter, and YouTube users with petitions, photos, and videos opposing the pipeline. Hughes has used the *New Republic* magazine, which he bought in 2012, to promote President Barack Obama's climate agenda (Bagley, 2013).

Yet as innovative as McKibben, these philanthropists, and their allies have been in promoting new approaches to activism, as I argued in a recent paper, their efforts can be criticized for continuing to advocate on behalf of conventional policy approaches such as a cap and dividend bill, a carbon tax, and a binding international agreement on emissions, while insisting that there can be absolutely no compromise on the Keystone XL pipeline or divestment. McKibben's climate movement is perhaps at even greater fault for downplaying the need for 'hard' technological approaches like nuclear energy or carbon capture and storage, and focusing almost exclusively instead on 'soft' technologies like solar, wind, and efficiency, since these favored technologies are unlikely to alter the dynamics of fossil-fuel energy use and dependency worldwide (Nisbet, 2013b).

An additional weakness of the movement is that 350.org and allies tend to target and mobilize a relatively like-minded and narrow segment of the public. As May Boeve, Executive Director of 350.org said in an interview conducted for a recent study:

> Our most consistent audience is the community of people who care about climate change and see it as a problem and are committed to do something about it. The metaphor we like to use is, yes, there's an issue of preaching to the choir, but imagine if you could have the choir all singing from the same song sheet.
>
> (Hestres, 2013)

Beyond wicked polarization

In a 2013 essay titled 'Wicked polarization,' Michael Shellenberger and Ted Nordhaus describe progress on climate change and other complex social problems as obstructed by experts and public intellectuals who have "come to frame virtually every national problem as a consequence of the irrationality, ignorance, and immorality of the political Other." As they continue:

> The problem is not that we are in a post-truth age but rather that we have not learned to adapt to it. Perhaps a good place to begin is by recognizing our own biases, perspectives, and agendas and attempting to hold them more lightly ... bringing an end to our ideological arms race will ultimately require that we force partisans out of their comfort zone by redefining those problems in ways to which partisans do not already know the answers.
>
> (Shellenberger & Nordhaus, 2013)

Along with efforts at grassroots activism, what we therefore need at the international, national, and local levels are public intellectuals, writers, media platforms, and public forums, which serve as bridges between discourses and perspectives on climate change. These voices and forums would help expand the policy actions and technologies considered and focus on a greater plurality of values and arguments.

On this function, "The idea here is not just to highlight points of communality and sites for compromise," write political scientists Hayley Stevenson and John Dryzek (2012), "but also to provide possibilities for contestation and the reflection it can induce." Similarly, as the University of Michigan's Andrew Hoffman concludes, what's needed are initiatives that offer 'broker frames,' discourses and contexts that expand, diversify, and blur perspectives on the issue, beyond the mostly left-leaning, affluent, older and white segment of Americans who are currently alarmed by climate change (Hoffman, 2012).

In the US, states and major metropolitan regions are the places, communities, and contexts where we can experiment, evaluate, and invest in communication initiatives that recast how we debate and talk about climate change policy. By focusing on the local and regional, we can also start to set the conditions for eventual change in national politics, by rewiring our expectations and norms relative to public debate; and by forging relationships and collaborations that span ideological differences. Research institutes and land grant universities can serve a vital function in this regard, by sponsoring media and public forums, by convening stakeholders and political groups, and by serving as a resource for collaboration and cooperation.

Many might argue that focusing on self-reflection and dialogue at this stage in the climate crisis is too little and far too late. Yet despite great financial resources spent over the past two decades, traditional technocratic approaches to politics have brought little progress, and have likely contributed to polarization. Continued investments in grassroots activism are important, but so too is investment in our civic capacity to learn, discuss, question, disagree, collaborate, and ultimately broker support for a range of policy actions.

References

Bagley, K. (2013). Wealthy donors in his corner as Obama comes out swinging on climate change. *Inside Climate News*, July 10. Retrieved September 5, 2013: http://insideclimatenews.org/news/20130710/wealthy-donors-his-corner-obama-comes-out-swinging-climate-change.

Hestres, L. (2013). Preaching to the choir: Internet-mediated advocacy, issue public mobilization and climate change. *New Media & Society*, April 1.

Hoffman, A. (2012). Climate science as culture war. *Stanford Social Innovation Review*, Fall. Retrieved September 5, 2013: http://www.ssireview.org/articles/entry/climate_science_as_culture_war.

Hulme, M. (2007). The appliance of science. *The Guardian*, March 13. Retrieved September 5, 2013: http://www.guardian.co.uk/society/2007/mar/14/scienceofclimatechange.climatechange.

McKibben, B. (2007). *Fight global warming now: The handbook for taking action in your community*. New York: Henry Holt and Company, LLC.

Nisbet, M. C. (2011). *Climate shift: Clear vision for the next decade of public debate*. Washington, DC: American University, School of Communication. Retrieved September 5, 2013: http://climateshiftproject.org/report/climate-shift-clear-vision-for-the-next-decade-of-public-debate/#climate-shift-clear-vision-for-the-next-decade-of-public-debate.

Nisbet, M. C. (2013a). The opponent: How Bill McKibben changed environmental politics and took on the oil patch. *Policy Options*, April/May, 29–41. Retrieved September 5, 2013: http://www.irpp.org/en/po/arctic-visions/the-opponent.

Nisbet, M. C. (2013b). *Nature's prophet: Bill McKibben as journalist, public intellectual, and activist*. Joan Shorenstein Center for Press, Politics, and Public Policy. Discussion Paper Series, D-78 March. Cambridge, MA: Kennedy School of Government, Harvard University. Retrieved September 5, 2013: http://shorensteincenter.org/2013/03/natures-prophet-bill-mckibben-as-journalist-public-intellectual-and-activist.

Shellenberger, M. & Nordhaus, T. (2013). Wicked polarization: How prosperity, democracy and experts divided America. *Breakthrough Journal*, Winter. Retrieved September 5, 2013: http://thebreakthrough.org/index.php/journal/issue-3/wicked-polarization.

Skocpol, T. (2013a). You can't change the climate from inside Washington. *Foreign Policy*, January 24. Retrieved September 5, 2013: http://www.foreignpolicy.com/articles/2013/01/24/you_can_t_change_the_climate_from_inside_washington_barack_obama.

Skocpol, T. (2013b). *Naming the problem: What it will take to counter extremism and engage Americans in the fight against global warming*. Scholars Strategy Network, February 14. Retrieved September 5, 2013: http://www.scholarsstrategynetwork.org/sites/default/files/skocpol_captrade_report_january_2013_0.pdf.

Stevenson, H. & Dryzek, J. (2012). The discourse democratization of global climate governance. *Environmental Politics*, 21(2), 189–210.

PART IV

Emerging research in climate politics and policy

9

GOVERNING SUBJECTIVITIES IN A CARBON CONSTRAINED WORLD

Matthew Paterson and Johannes Stripple

Introduction[1]

Routinized ways of eating, flying, driving, warming our homes, or consuming are 'regimes of practices' – relatively systematized ways of doing things – within which our carbon emissions are generated. Many of these practices have recently been called into question because of their contribution to climate change. The contestation of these practices are highly suggestive that one of the central questions for climate politics has become a question of subjectivity – what types of people (what sorts of desires, daily routines, and so on) we are and need to become to address climate change. We argue that a Foucauldian approach to power and government is extremely useful to addressing this focus since it conceptualizes government precisely in terms of subjectivity – as the 'conduct of conduct.' We will outline and exemplify how this sort of approach can recast familiar questions about climate change policy and governance. Our aim is to offer a new angle on 'climate governance' – an increasingly detached and empty concept – as being about the governing of ourselves and others in the context of climate change.

The chapter engages in a preliminary exploration of the rationalities and subjectivities by which a carbon constrained world is ordered, categorized, and represented. It seems to us that the research community has not yet grasped the way in which the climate issue is becoming interwoven in the fabric of modern societies. Long gone are the times when climate change was simply a question for international diplomacy, a sector to be covered by national regulatory authorities or an issue that mobilized a small set of highly motivated NGOs and businesses, such as large reinsurance firms or the renewable energy industry. Hulme (2010) has recently noted that personal engagement with the idea of climate change is unavoidable. In this chapter, we will draw attention to what we call the 'cultural politics of climate change,' which are processes of governing, or at least attempting to govern, that are usually under the radar of conventional policy analysis.

In this chapter, we understand government in the general Foucauldian sense of 'the conduct of conduct' – a form of activity aiming to shape, guide or affect the conduct of some person or persons (Gordon, 1991, p. 2). Government does not have to be tied to the state, but could be understood as any calculated and rational activity, undertaken by a multiplicity of authorities and agencies that shape our behavior according to particular norms for a variety of ends (Dean, 1999, p. 11). Central to Foucault's thinking on power and governance was the notion of 'self-government' – the ways in which particular forms of conduct could be accomplished through shaping the self and subject positions. Translating this into the realm of climate governance one could talk about the 'conduct of carbon conduct,' by which we mean a government that works through people's governing of their own greenhouse gas emissions (Paterson & Stripple, 2010, p. 347). In this chapter we pay particular attention to the form of person, self, and identity that is presupposed by different practices of 'climate governance,' and to identify what sorts of transformation these practices seek.

The chapter first outlines the key themes we take from Foucauldian scholarship. We develop the notion of problematization, which is key to understanding how phenomena, such as carbon-emitting practices, become objects of government. We then explore how government is accomplished through specific 'technologies' – the mundane and routinized ways in which different authorities seek to shape and normalize behaviors, actions and decisions of others. In both of these we provide illustrations of these processes in climate change politics. We then turn to how individual subjectivities have been problematized in relation to climate change, and to what sorts of technologies of government have been developed in order to (re)shape subjectivities towards various sorts of 'low-carbon subject.' Finally, we highlight that the construction of low-carbon subjects is a process that is subject to considerable contestation, that the process does not consist of a simple roll-out of climate governmental logics. The chapter is necessarily provisional and exploratory, since this is a fast-moving field and there is as yet only limited empirical work (including our own) on these sorts of climate governance initiatives. In particular, we should emphasize that the specific governance projects we explore cannot be evaluated according to their impacts on actual practices; they remain too embryonic for such an analysis. Instead, our focus is on their logics of governance: how they *attempt* to shape emissions through shaping subjectivity.

Governmentality and the problematization of carbon

According to Rose and Miller (1992, p. 181), government is a *problematizing* activity. By this they meant how the articulation of government is always tied to the identification of difficulties and failures of ways of governing: that "if the conduct of individuals or collectives appeared to require conducting, this was because something in it appeared problematic to someone" (Miller & Rose 2008, p. 14). Reflecting on their own research on governmentality, they described their own path as one about asking questions about how, and to what ends, socially legitimated authorities sought to interfere in the lives of individuals in sites as diverse as the school, the home, the workplace, the courtroom, etc. (2008, p. 1). Underpinning these problematizations were specific conceptions of the human being that are held at a particular time (as citizen, schoolchild, customer, worker, manager, etc.) (2008, p. 7). Hence, problems are not pregiven, but have to be constructed and made visible. Miller and Rose term this process 'problematization' – "issues and concerns have to be made to appear problematic, often in different ways, in different sites, and by different agents" (2008, p. 14).

Problematizations are done in relation to 'regimes of practices,' which can be understood as coherent and organized ways of doing things. As we live our lives, we engage in various acts of consumption that produce greenhouse gas emissions. Usually, all this is done without too much reflection. For many years we had no clue about what these routinized ways of living our lives implied for the Earth's climate.

However, these practices have now been increasingly problematized via a range of framings of climate change. We can readily think of a number of these. Climate change is a problem of increasing social and political insecurity, where sea-level rise, increased temperature extremes, agricultural impacts, and water scarcity, drive both social insecurity and political conflict (for just a few recent examples see Busby, 2008; German Advisory Council on Global Change, 2008; World Bank, 2012). Or it is problematized as the mismatch between an interstate political system and a global commons problem, where free-riding by states in the resolution of the collective action problem is the norm and new institutional forms – new 'architectures' – are required to generate adequate responses (see Aldy & Stavins, 2007; Barrett, 2005; Gupta et al., 2007; Sprinz & Luterbacher, 2001). For others, it is problematized in terms of radical global inequalities in emissions and climate impacts, where these inequalities both are understood to themselves be unjust and to generate new injustices via climate impacts, as well as to operate as significant obstacles to action on climate change (Agarwal & Narain, 1991; Okereke, 2010; Roberts & Parks, 2007). Others still see it as a problem of a globalized capitalism unable to check its systemically expansionist logic or to disentangle fossil energy from its core dynamics (Clark & York, 2005; Newell & Paterson, 2010; Panitch & Leys, 2007; Pelling et al., 2012).

It is thus possible to think about the history of 'climate government' as a history of specific problematizations, which emerge at different sites mobilizing different sorts of knowledges, actors, and practices. While the various problematizations outlined above are rather visible, they all tend to locate the sites of governance that ensue in states. But attempts to govern the climate have emerged in many other sites, reflecting different problematizations. Miller and Rose coined the term 'programs of government' to capture the designs put forward by "philosophers, political economists, physiocrats, and philanthropists, government reports, committees of inquiry, white papers, proposals and counterproposals by organizations of business, labour, finance, charities and professionals, that seek to configure specific locales and relations in ways thought desirable" (Miller & Rose, 2008, p. 63). It is therefore possible that 'programs of climate government' can be found among, say, a travel agency implementing an online carbon footprint calculator in order to enable their customers to offset the carbon emissions that their flight generates; or one might closely examine the various activities that the local authority have done for problematizing the casual use of car driving and instead cultivating people's rationales for biking to work (e.g., personalized weather reports, health advice, fast bike lanes, subsidized helmets and cycling clothes, fees on car in the city); or the research interests might be drawn to the International Standardization Organization's standard ISO14064 that facilitates measuring, reducing, and verification of greenhouse gas emissions and how that standard enables organizations to take part in emissions trading schemes.

Central to such problematizations are particular forms of knowledge and expertise, which define the 'right disposition of things' and hereby constitute and make visible problems of government. Central also are the sorts of people that are intended to emerge as low-carbon subjects. It might be worth emphasizing that in studies of governmentality there is neither a foundational, pre-existing starting point nor an endpoint in the constitution of subjectivities. Foucault once explained that the objective of his intellectual inquiry has been to "create a history of the different modes by which, in our culture, human beings *are made subjects*" (Foucault, 1982, p. 208, our emphasis). Foucault himself was particularly concerned with the social forms of knowledge that emerged with the constitution of the population as a domain of regulation and action in the late eighteenth-century Europe (Foucault, 1977). In a similar vein, we have seen in recent years a series of problematizations around dieting, obesity, and health on the grounds of a warming and carbon constrained world – a problematization that we explore later in this chapter. To look for this particular 'program of climate government' one has to venture in to the worlds of NGO campaigners, cookbook writers, urban designers, and health professionals who through invention, appropriation, and adaption of the carbon diet discourse have all contributed to a particular attempt to 'conduct carbon conduct.' The climate dieting discourse that we explore further on in this chapter is what Bridge (2010) would call, a new moral economy being construed through and around carbon.

Technologies of climate government

We have so far in this chapter mostly talked about how studies of governmentality encourage a focus on how problems become problematized and how particular rationalities inform the governing. However, for Foucault and particularly the body of research that has emerged out of his rather sketchy notes on governmentality, government is not only a matter representing a particular phenomenon, it is also a matter of intervening through technical means. The focus on what Dean (2010,

p. 42; see also Miller & Rose, 2008, p. 32) has called 'the techne of government' is important; by what means, mechanisms, procedures, instruments, and vocabularies is authority constituted and rule accomplished? Hence, the activity of ruling should be analyzed in terms of its 'governmental technologies'; i.e., the mundane mechanisms through which authorities of various sorts seek to shape and normalize the conduct, thought, and decisions of others (Miller & Rose, 2008, p. 32). Given that these technologies are highly specific (Walters, 2012, p. 58), there is thus *no climate governance in the general.*

A few examples help illustrate this point. We can think, for example, about technologies that enable the commodification of carbon, where it is today commonplace to talk about primary and secondary carbon products (e.g., futures, swaps, and options) as well as different carbon currencies such as European Union Allowances (EUAs), Certified Emission Reductions (CERs), Verified Emission Reductions (VERs). Or we could consider the increasingly complex assemblage of negotiations inside and outside the UNFCCC, which through e.g., 'negotiation tracks,' 'ad-hoc groups,' and 'networks of city mayors' today brings together issues as different as bunker fuels, urban energy issues, tropical deforestation and a work program to address loss and damage associated with climate change impacts in particularly vulnerable developing countries. Or we could think of the emergence of an EU renewable energy policy, which developed slowly from quite loose forms of cooperation in the 1980s toward a common policy framework in the recent climate and energy package. In this complex line of emergence, renewable energy has come to be seen variously as a solution to a triad of issues: environmental and climate change, security of supply, and economic competitiveness. Finally, we might explore the visions of various governments to install or require smart energy meters in all homes, where for example in the case of the UK, its roll-out is seen to play an important role in the UK's transition to a low-carbon economy by providing consumers and electricity grid managers with real-time information on energy consumption to help them control and manage their energy use, save money and reduce emissions.[2]

If studies of climate governmentality are to make analytical progress, then scholars must be able to identify those technologies of governance that follow the logics of an 'apparatus' or an 'assemblage' – heterogeneous elements that have been stabilized (to various degrees) to work in different domains. Lövbrand and Stripple (2011) have developed an 'analytics of carbon accounting' that draws attention to the calculative practices that turn stocks and flows of carbon into objects of governance. Carbon accounting as a rationality of government is concerned with the ways in which carbon can be measured, quantified, demarcated and statistically aggregated. Lövbrand and Stripple outline three different regimes of carbon accounting – 'the national carbon sink,' 'the carbon credit,' and 'the personal carbon budget' – to illustrate how stocks and flows of carbon are constructed as administrative domains amenable to certain forms of political and economic rationality, such as government regulation, market exchanges and self-governance by responsible individual subjects.

Personal carbon budgets are one technology aimed at forming low-carbon subjects. But there are many other such assemblages of technologies through which this process is governed. Low-carbon subjects may well be produced by specific technologies like smart meters that encourage a continual reflexivity about carbon-emitting practices. But they are also enabled by a range of general technologies, such as carbon footprint calculators, those general devices available in a range of forms – websites, smartphone apps, books and manuals – that enable a calculation of one's carbon emissions. These technologies then enable and are connected to other technologies, such as carbon offset systems, which enable subjects to 'self-govern' in relation to climate change via investing elsewhere to compensate for their own emissions (see Paterson & Stripple, 2010 for more detail).

Although such 'practices' (carbon accounting, carbon commodification, carbon footprints) function as mediums of thought that translate political rationalities into reality and hereby make government possible, we should not think of them as the extension of control from some central site of power (Dean, 1999). As has been indicated in the examples above, the search for 'programs of climate government' enables research to resituate and reconsider the role and place of the state in climate governance. When approaching government as the sum of all processes and activities that seek to shape, guide and affect the conduct of persons (Gordon, 1991, p. 2), climate government is no longer confined to the apparatus of the state *per se*. We turn now to looking at some of these attempts at climate government.

Constructing low-carbon subjects

As discussed in the previous sections, central to Foucault's thinking on governmentality was thus the notion of 'self-government' – the ways in which particular forms of conduct could be accomplished through shaping the self and subject positions. In recent years we have seen increased scholarly attention to subjectifications around climate change and carbon, as well as an explosion of initiatives precisely focused on shaping subject positions and practices (De Goede & Randalls, 2009; Paterson & Stripple, 2010; Rice, 2010; Rutland & Aylett, 2008). De Goede and Randalls (2009, p. 871) explore the different ways in which subjects are constituted through contemporary climate change policies; from the 'neurotic citizen,' which is promised the impossible, absolute security from climate change, to 'conscious consumers' knowledgeable about the carbon content of each purchase. In her study of greenhouse gas mitigation practices in Seattle, Rice (2010) shows how these are pursued as processes of subjectifications. In this urban setting, local governments engage individuals in their climate policies by appealing to 'the good carbon citizen.' Rice (2010, p. 930) illustrates how carbon accounting practices enable 'carbon territories,' which she defines as the "active creation and quantification of bounded and ordered spaces of carbon-producing activities and simultaneous reproduction of local government jurisdictional capacities." Rutland and Aylett (2008) argue that these territorial practices articulate the responsible, carbon-calculating individual. When individuals internalize the carbon metrics of the state, and "base their actions on these metrics, they become part of a network of self-regulating actors" (Rutland & Aylett, 2008, p. 631).

The explosion of projects designed to enable individuals to 'do their bit' in line with government and industry objectives to limit climate change can be regarded as one means through which such subject positions are enacted. Paterson and Stripple (2010) outline and compare five different contemporary practices that aim at calculating, measuring and accounting for emissions of greenhouse gases at the level of the individual (footprinting, offsetting, dieting, rationing and trading, either in Carbon Rationing Action Groups or through a system of Personal Carbon Allowances). What can be seen in these practices is an emergent government of carbon that entails the 'conduct of carbon conduct.' This 'carbon governmentality' molds and mobilizes individual subjects to govern their own emissions in various ways – as counters, displacers, dieters, communitarians, or citizens. Paterson and Stripple (2010) call this governmental rationality 'My Space' – individuals as agents managing their own carbon practice in relation to an articulated global public goal of minimizing climate change. The research community has just begun to explore the processes of subjectification around carbon, or "how the status of hydrocarbons or standing biomass as resources for the carbon economy hinges on people orienting themselves towards them in particular ways" (Bridge, 2010, p. 8). Most work has been on the subjectivities of end-users, those who consume fossil energy and produce emissions, although in principle it could similarly explore the construction of their subjectivities as workers, managers, voters, teachers, parents or many other dimensions of our subjectivities.

While there are numerous examples that could be explored, we use the 'carbon dieting' discourse here to illustrate the way such initiatives operate. Carbon dieting emerged in the mid-2000s as a term to get people to articulate themselves towards their practices that produce carbon emissions via the metaphor of a diet. Carbon emissions were problematized as a question of excess and gluttony, leading to ill-health and increased morbidity, and thus to be managed via the meticulous counting of individual carbon emissions much as the dieter counts calories. In publications developing this sort of approach, the world was figured itself as overweight, with a tape measure around its circumference in the manner of a waistline being measured (e.g., Harrington, 2008).

The initial problematization of carbon as over-eating has since diversified in a number of ways. Significantly, they have for the most part entailed a narrowing of the focus, from overall carbon emissions towards food and transport-related emissions. Religious organizations have taken it up and promoted the idea of carbon fasting, connecting carbon dieting to well-established religious practices and subjectivities (e.g., Woodiwiss, 2012). Public health officials have on the one hand moved into this space to promote a notion of what we call 'climate fitness' (e.g., Maibach et al., 2009), articulating climate change as an opportunity to reinvigorate campaigns for active lifestyles, especially via transport modes, reframed as 'low-carbon.' Chefs and food writers have joined them in this sort of framing, with various cookbooks emerging to promote a 'low-carbon diet' (e.g., Barnouin, 2010; Geagan, 2009; Heyhoe, 2009; Stec & Cordero, 2008). Public health officials have also, often combined with transport and urban planners, articulated connections between climate change and obesity, either through constructing overweight subjects as a problem for climate change, or problematizing low-density urban environments as origins of both problems of climate change and obesity (e.g., Delpeuch et al., 2009; Edwards & Roberts, 2009; Egger, 2008; Griffiths & Stewart, 2008; Reisch & Gwozdz, 2011). All of these variants share a focus on shaping subjects' orientations towards specific practices (eating, moving around, notably) in relation to climate change.

These initiatives attempt to govern via specific sorts of assemblages of technologies designed to engender low-carbon subjects. Some are highly individualist, with the combinations of carbon counters, low-carbon cookbooks, the exhortations of celebrity chefs, and via the register of guilt and reward typical of dieting systems. These often contain the sort of narcissistic subjectivity of many dieting regimes, with low-carbon subjects being motivated by the combination of the desire for the 'body beautiful' with the desire for some sort of virtuous practice, a virtuousness which is normally highly competitive with others, but which may also make connections to religious traditions and identities. It can be understood usefully in relation to Skoglund's account of 'Homo Clima' (Skoglund, 2011), which suggests the emergence of a new ideal citizen, one that invests in its own vulnerability, adaptability and changeability to amend as well as protect a climate authorized aestheticized life.

Others however involve different combinations of technologies. For example with those focused on the combinations of transport policy, planning systems and public health regimes, where the low-carbon subject is figured as an effect of broad shifts in these social systems, that are designed not only to produce low-carbon practices but to do so via the production of 'active subjects,' simultaneously healthier and lower-emitting. Here the subject is conceptualized as much more intimately connected to broader patterns of social relations.

These two variants in the sorts of low-carbon subjectivities can be seen to reflect what Rose (1996) has called to govern in an advanced liberal manner. Liberalism is understood here as a historically specific art of governing that "operates through dispersed forms and figures of expertise and practices that utilize and govern through the regulated freedoms and choices of individuals and groups, and the promotion of certain kinds of subjectivity" (Walters, 2012, p. 72). Miller and Rose argue that with liberalism comes a new specification of the subject of government – the actively responsible self. But this sort of actively responsible self is nevertheless enmeshed in networks of practice and social structure that constrain and shape how they engage the world – these initiatives encapsulate Dillon's account of such forms of government as focused on the "strategic orchestration of the self-regulating freedoms of populations" (Dillon, 2003, p. 135).

Contesting low-carbon subjects

But as in other areas of governance, attempts to construct low-carbon subjects encounter resistance. Exploring subjectivity as the focus of climate government also enables us to think through the political contestations around climate change in a novel manner. They suggest to us that at the heart of many contemporary struggles over climate change are struggles over the meanings of daily practices and the subjectivities they sustain. Recall the famous ad campaign in the run-up to the Kyoto Protocol, as part of an assault by the Global Climate Coalition (and its associated front organizations) on the UN negotiations and in particular on US participation in the proposed treaty, which had as its tagline "they're trying to take away my SUV." The figure of the threat posed by climate change here is the harried mother, committed to various activities related to family obligations, including to protect her children by driving a large (and by implication safe) vehicle. These sorts of images pervade the discourse of those hostile to action on climate change, and to the tensions amongst those who want to see action but resist those measures that they might see precisely as threatening to their existing subjectivities.

However, in contrast to other, more classic, forms of resistance politics, resistance to the politics of subject formation occurs via the ambivalences and multiple commitments and interests they have. Dowling (2010) cautions about reading too much of a neoliberal (read calculating, self-interested, rational) subject into the practices described in the previous sections, and that there is only rarely an alignment between governmental processes and the identifications of individuals. People are instead argumentative subjects and research must thus accommodate ambiguity and alternative subject positions. Resistance can be expected to occur through people's ambivalence regarding low-carbon subjectivities – they accept its basic premise but it conflicts with various other existing subject positions they hold – as in the 'soccer mom' example. Dowling's critique, which is aimed specifically at the construction of low-carbon subjects, is actually a rather common one in studies of governmentality. Walters (2012, p. 74, referencing O'Malley et al., 1997) notes that studies of governmentality have been criticized for making governance appear overly coherent, univocal and rational. Instead, scholars need to avoid taking the 'programmers view,' and to "reveal the immanent disjunction and dissonance between the 'programmer's view' and the logic of practices" (Dean 2007, p. 83). Similarly, Walters argues that more weight could, in studies of governmentality, be given to "questions about processes of transformation, dynamics of change and the difference made by political struggle" (Walters, 2012, p. 74). We agree, in order to contribute to an understanding of the political dynamics of responses to climate change, it is important to explore the character of the discursive conflicts over these attempts to construct subjectivities around climate change and carbon.

There seems to be a recent appreciation that many of the political conflicts over climate change have at their heart deep cultural and emotional attachments to particular sorts of daily practice and related identities that are called into question by decarbonization. Researchers have begun to explore how these attachments generate resistance to climate change responses and complicate the pursuit of decarbonization. One interesting example is the work of Hargreaves et al. (2010) who explored how UK householders interacted with feedback on their domestic energy consumption in a field trial of real-time displays or smart energy monitors. These technical devices enable householders to 'see' their energy use (and its associated carbon emissions) and thus take steps to reduce it. They show how the monitors are "domesticated into the physical domain, social relations and cultural practices of each household" (2010, p. 6118). The installment of the monitors in British households generated new patterns of both cooperation and contestation. In some cases, they were giving participants an increased sense of control and empowering them to take stronger action to reduce their own energy consumption. Energy savings appeared easier to achieve and became "a normal aspect of using energy in everyday life" (2010, p. 6119). But the monitors also seemed to "create a sense of fatalism, despondency, anxiety and even guilt among interviewees that what they could do was futile in the face of huge social, political and environmental problems" (Ibid., 2010, p. 6119). Governing energy use in the household through smart energy monitors, is a strategy, "that is only as good as the household, social and political contexts in which they are used" (2010, p. 6119). In a recent book chapter, Hargreaves (2013) situated the work on smart energy monitors within a governmentality framework arguing that although the monitors introduce new forms of surveillance and discipline to household practices these are mediated by pre-existing householder relations. Households specifically resist the monitors through appeals to ethics and aesthetics, but also through a partial rejection of the territorialization of climate change at the household level. Hargreaves (2013) therefore concludes that carbon dioxide appears to be a relatively weak rationality of government that is not challenging entrenched household practices.

This example is suggestive of the sorts of limits of subjectivity-focused climate governance. There is a longer-standing critique of 'green consumerism' (e.g., Luke, 1994), which argues that such individualistic responses fail to acknowledge the deep structural forces that drive emissions and that individuals in practice do not control the key decisions that affect 'their' emissions-producing consumption. Our critique here is connected, in that the resistance to the 'conduct of carbon conduct' does, as in Hargreaves' example, operate in part because people recognize their inability to change basic features that generate their emissions (the design of housing, the physical layout of cities, the electricity system). But it is different because thinking about such governance initiatives as assemblages shows that many operate via connections between these structural processes and daily practice. The contrast between the two sorts of carbon dieting assemblages (the one focused on individual virtue and self-control, versus the one focused on urban planning, transport policy and 'active lifestyles') outlined above is a good example that not all governance focused on subjectivity is necessarily hyper-individualist in character. Nevertheless, the resistance is likely still to be focused on the tensions between the shifts in practices envisaged by a low-carbon transition and the practices valued by contemporary societies.

Concluding remarks

Much of what is preceded might be taken as much as a research agenda than as an established body of knowledge. What we know about climate governance understood in terms of shaping subjectivity is fragmentary at best. As a consequence, as stated in the introduction, we are not in a position to make any serious claims about the effects of the various climate governance initiatives we discuss in this chapter. We explore instead their political logic as forms of governmentality – efforts to 'conduct carbon conduct.' Nevertheless, we argue here that focusing on the governing of cultural subjects is becoming and will remain a central aspect of climate politics, and thus to explore the forms of governance involved is an important exercise. As projects to reduce GHG emission become more serious and organized, they attempt to deal with the myriad practices of daily life through which emissions are generated, from eating to traveling to keeping warm and cool to making things and consuming them. These entail both highly specific interventions that reflect the diversity of these practices of daily life (to get someone onto their bicycle entails very different things from shaping how farmers cultivate their crops), but at the same time the cultivation of a general 'low-carbon' orientation towards all such practices. Simultaneously, these subjectivities are likely to become principal sites of contestation around climate change, as established regimes of practice and the subjectivities that they sustain are challenged ever more deeply.

The various concepts we have developed here from studies of governmentality are useful in advancing our understanding of the cultural politics of climate change in a number of ways. First, they displace our attention from the question of 'who' is governing – is it the state, or private sector actors, or NGOs? Instead it draws our attention to the 'how' of governing. Second, this shift in attention entails exploring the specific ways that climate change is problematized that then mobilize specific actors and rationalities to pursue climate governance. For example, a 'climate change as a problem of over-consumption' sort of framing underpins many of the carbon dieting practices we discuss, while a 'climate change as mal-development' frame may be seen to underpin the focus on urban planning and transport policy. Third, it draws our attention to the means by which governance is attempted, specifically to the technologies through which shifts in practice are organized, and to the complicated processes by which such technologies succeed, or fail to succeed, in shaping the daily practices that generate GHG emissions. Overall then, governmentality is an important conceptual and analytical device to explore emerging and arguably growing aspects of climate change politics.

Notes

1 We would like to thank Jeremy Kirouac for research assistance in the preparation of this chapter. Johannes Stripple would like to thank Eva Lövbrand, Linköping University, for creative discussions and joint writings on Foucault, governmentality, and climate change over the last years. Furthermore, financial support from BECC (Biodiversity and Ecosystem Services in a Changing Landscape), the Swedish government's strategic focus on climate change hosted by the Faculty of Science at Lund University and the Low-Carbon Energy and Transport Systems (LETS) project, financed by the Swedish Environmental Protection Agency (among others) is gratefully acknowledged. Matthew Paterson acknowledges support from the Social Science and Humanities Research Council of Canada for research funding that helped finance the research.
2 Note here that the notion of technology is not to be restricted to specific devices or inventions, but includes also the rules and instruments by which government is pursued. A specific sort of negotiating system, or a set of rules around carbon trading, are in this conception, technologies.

References

Agarwal, A. & Narain, S. (1991). *Global warming in an unequal world: A case of environmental colonialism*. New Delhi: Centre for Science and Environment.
Aldy, J. & Stavins, R. (Eds.). (2007). *Architectures for agreement: Addressing global climate change in the post-Kyoto world*. Cambridge: Cambridge University Press.
Barnouin, K. (2010). *Skinny bitch: Ultimate everyday cookbook: Crazy delicious recipes that are good to the earth and great for your bod*. New York: Running Press.
Barrett, S. (2005). *Environment and statecraft: The strategy of environmental treaty-making*. Oxford: Oxford University Press.
Bridge, G. (2010). Resource geographies 1. *Progress in Human Geography*, 35(6), 820–834.
Busby, J. W. (2008). Who cares about the weather? Climate change and US National Security. *Security Studies*, 17(3), 468–504.
Clark, B. & York, R. (2005). Carbon metabolism: Global capitalism, climate change, and the biospheric rift. *Theory and Society*, 34(4), 391–428.
De Goede, M. & Randalls, S. (2009). Precaution, preemption: Arts and technologies of the actionable future. *Environment and Planning D: Society and Space*, 27(5), 859–878.
Dean, M. (1999). *Governmentality*. London: Sage.
Dean, M. (2007). *Governing societies: Political perspectives on domestic and international rule*. Maidenhead: Open University Press.
Dean, M. (2010). *Governmentality: Power and rule in modern society*, 2nd edition. London: Sage.
Delpeuch, F., Maire, B., Monnier, E., & Holdsworth, M. (2009). *Globesity: A planet out of control?* New York: Routledge.
Dillon, M. (2003). Culture, governance, and global biopolitics. In F. Debrix & C. Weber (Eds.), *Rituals of mediation: International politics and social meaning* (pp. 135–153). Minneapolis, MN: University of Minnesota Press.
Dowling, R. (2010). Geographies of identity: Climate change, governmentality and activism. *Progress in Human Geography*, 34(4), 488–495.
Edwards, P. & Roberts, I. (2009). Population adiposity and climate change. *International Journal of Epidemiology*, 10(1), 1–4.
Egger, G. (2008). Dousing our inflammatory environment(s): Is personal carbon trading an option for reducing obesity – and climate change? *Obesity Review*, 9(1), 456–463.

Foucault, M. (1977). *Discipline and punish. The birth of the prison.* London: Penguin.

Foucault, M. (1982). Afterword. In H. Dreyfus & P. Rabinow (Eds.), *Michel Foucault: Beyond structuralism and hermeneutics* (pp. 208–226). Chicago, IL: The University of Chicago Press.

Geagan, K. (2009). *Go green get lean: Trim your waistline with the ultimate low-carbon footprint diet.* New York: Rodale Books.

German Advisory Council on Global Change. (2008). *Climate change as a security risk.* London: Earthscan.

Gordon C. (1991). Governmental rationality: An introduction. In G. Burchell, C. Gordon, & P. Miller (Eds), *The Foucault effect* (pp. 1–51). Chicago, IL: University of Chicago Press.

Griffiths, J. & Stewart, L. (2008). *Sustaining a healthy future: Taking action on climate change.* London: Faculty of Public Health.

Gupta S., Tirpak, D., Burger, N., Gupta, J., Höhne, N., Boncheva, A. I., Kanoan, G. M., Kolstad, C., Kruger, J., Michaelowa, A., Murase, S., Pershing, J., Saijo, T., & Sari A. (2007). Policies, instruments and co-operative arrangements. In B. Metz, O. Davidson, P. Bosch, R. Dave, & L. Meyer (Eds.), *Climate change 2007: Mitigation. Contribution of Working Group III to the Fourth Assessment Report of the Intergovernmental Panel on Climate Change* (pp. 745–807). Cambridge and New York: Cambridge University Press.

Hargreaves, T. (2013). Smart meters and the governance of energy use in the household. In J. Stripple & H. Bulkeley (Eds.), *Governing climate: New approaches to rationality, power and politics.* Cambridge: Cambridge University Press.

Hargreaves, T., Nye, M., & Burgess, J. (2010). Making energy visible: A qualitative field study of how householders interact with feedback from smart energy monitors. *Energy Policy*, 38, 6111–6119.

Harrington, J. (2008). *The climate diet: How you can cut carbon, cut costs, and save the planet.* New York: Routledge.

Heyhoe, K. (2009). *Cooking green: Reducing your carbon footprint in the kitchen.* Boston, MA: Da Capo Lifelong Books.

Hulme, M. (2010). The idea of climate change: Exploring complexity, plurality and opportunity. *GAIA – Ecological Perspectives for Science and Society*, 19(3), 171–174.

Lövbrand, E. & Stripple, J. (2011). Making climate change governable: Accounting for carbon as sinks, credits and personal budgets. *Critical Policy Studies*, 5(2), 187–200.

Luke, T. (1994). Green consumerism: Ecology and the ruse of recycling. In W. Chaloupka & J. Bennett (Eds.), *In the nature of things* (pp. 154–172). Minneapolis, MN: University of Minnesota Press.

Maibach, E., Steg, L., & Anable, J. (2009). Promoting physical activity and reducing climate change: Opportunities to replace short car trips with active transportation. *Preventive Medicine*, 49(1), 326–327.

Miller, P. & Rose, N. (2008). *Governing the present: Administering economic, social and personal life.* Cambridge: Polity Press.

Newell, P. & Paterson, M. (2010). *Climate capitalism: Global warming and the transformation of the global economy.* Cambridge: Cambridge University Press.

Okereke, C. (2010). *Global justice and neoliberal environmental governance: Sustainable development, ethics and international co-operation.* London: Routledge.

O'Malley, P., Weir, L., & Shearing, C. (1997). Governmentality, criticism, politics. *Economy and Society*, 26(4), 501–517.

Panitch, L. & Leys, C. (Eds.). (2007). *Socialist register 2007: Coming to terms with nature.* London: Merlin Press.

Paterson M. & Stripple, J. (2010). My space: Governing individuals' carbon emissions. *Environment and Planning D: Society and Space*, 28(2), 341–362.

Pelling, M., Manuel-Navarrete, D., & Redclift, M. (Eds.). (2012). *Climate change and the crisis of capitalism*. London: Routledge.

Reisch, L. A. & Gwozdz, W. (2011). Chubby cheeks and climate change: Childhood obesity as a sustainable development. *International Journal of Consumer Studies*, (35), 3–9.

Rice, J. L. (2010). Climate, carbon, and territory: Greenhouse gas mitigation in Seattle, Washington. *Annals of the Association of American Geographers*, 100(4), 929–937.

Roberts, J. T. & Parks, B. (2007). *A climate of injustice: Global inequality, north-south politics, and climate policy*. Cambridge, MA: MIT Press.

Rose N. (1996). Governing 'advanced' liberal democracies. In A. Barry, T. Osborne, & N. Rose (Eds.), *Foucault and political reason* (pp. 37–64). London: UCL Press.

Rose, N. & Miller, P. (1992). Political power beyond the state: Problematics of government. *British Journal of Sociology*, 43(2), 173–205.

Rutland, T. & Aylett, A. (2008). The work of policy: Actor networks, governmentality, and local action on climate change in Portland, Oregon. *Environment and Planning D: Society and Space*, 26, 627–646.

Skoglund, A. (2011). *Homo clima: Climate man and productive power – Government through climate change as bioaesthetic frame*. PhD thesis, KTH Royal Institute of Technology, Stockholm. Retrieved November 8, 2013: http://urn.kb.se/resolve?urn=urn:nbn:se:kth:diva-34285.

Sprinz, D. & Luterbacher, U. (Eds.). (2001). *International relations and global climate change*. Cambridge, MA: MIT Press.

Stec, L. & Cordero, E. (2008). *Cool cuisine: Taking a bite out of global warming*. Layton, UT: Gibbs Smith.

Walters, W. (2012). *Governmentality: Critical encounters, critical issues in global politics*. New York: Routledge.

Woodiwiss, C. (2012). *Carbon fasting: Christians give up CO_2 for Lent*. Center for American Progress. Retrieved January 8, 2013: http://www.americanprogress.org/issues/religion/news/2012/03/05/11217/carbon-fasting.

World Bank. (2012). *Turn down the heat: Why a 4°C warmer world must be avoided*. Washington, DC: World Bank.

10

MAKING CLIMATE-SCIENCE COMMUNICATION *EVIDENCE*-BASED

All the way down

Dan M. Kahan

Introduction

It would be incorrect to say that social scientists have been studying the dynamics that constrain public comprehension of climate science for as long as climate scientists have been trying to communicate what they know to the public. Social scientists began studying the relevant science-communication dynamics much earlier.

The impetus for the scientific study of science communication was the divide between the public and experts on nuclear power in the late 1970s and early 1980s. In that case, members of the public were more worried than scientists rather than less. The nation's most preeminent scientists assured the public that nuclear power was quite safe – in fact saf*er* for the environment than use of fossil-fuel energy sources such as coal (Bethe, 1976). The failure of widely accessible and seemingly compelling science to quiet public conflict over nuclear power (and a variety of other environmental risks) motivated Paul Slovic, Daniel Kahneman, Baruch Fischhoff, and other collaborators to invent the psychometric theory of risk perception (Kahneman et al., 1982; Slovic, 1987; Slovic et al., 1976), the common ancestor of today's decision sciences. Far from social scientists beginning to study science communication in response to public conflict over climate science, it was the intensity of public conflict over climate change that seems finally to have shocked scientists, policy analysts, and a whole lot of other people into discovering the existing science of science communication.

One might say 'better late than never,' except the situation is not yet nearly as good as it should be. At this point, many more scientists, government officials, and public advocacy groups recognize that a science of science communication exists and that it has generated knowledge relevant to understanding and resolving problems like political conflict over climate change. But mere familiarity with the science of science communication is not sufficient. For genuine progress to be made, it is necessary for these actors and others to proceed scientifically in making *use* of such knowledge.

Decision science comprises a rich array of concepts and mechanisms. Any creative person can easily use them to construct an account – or two or three – of why the public is divided on climate change and what to do to about it. Plausible-sounding communication strategies informed by 'heuristics and biases,' 'tipping points,' 'nudges,' 'framing,' 'narratives,' 'fMRI neurocorrelates,' and the like abound in newspaper op-eds, blog posts, and animated 'how to' climate-communication guides.

The number of plausible accounts of any complicated phenomenon will always be larger than the number that is actually true. The primary mission of social science is to help extricate the latter from the vast sea of the former. A style of analysis that treats decision science as a grab bag of story-telling templates necessarily can't do that. Only the disciplined forms of observation, measurement, and inference distinctive of science can (Watts, 2011).

It's fine – essential, even – to engage in imaginative conjecture informed by valid decision science. But the results must be recognized for what they really are – not genuine "scientifically established" conclusions but rather plausible hypotheses that merit testing by valid empirical means.

Moreover, when such tests have been carried out, the evidence they yield must actually be used. Assessments of the relative likelihood of competing conjectures must be updated in light of such evidence. As accounts that seemed plausible at one point are shown to be less so, those accounts shouldn't be endlessly recycled and dumped back into the stream of information being directed to practitioners looking for guidance on how to communicate in real-world settings.

Nor should general insights derived from laboratory experiments be oversold. They identify mechanisms of consequence, but they do not in themselves furnish meaningful, determined guides to action. If they are valid and skillfully designed, they tell communicators where to train their attention and stimulate them to formulate concrete hypotheses about how the results obtained in the lab might be reproduced in the real-world setting in which they are working. Social scientists should help them *test* those hypotheses in field studies designed to determine which plausible conjectures about which real-world strategies actually work and which don't.

What I am advocating is an approach to science communication that is genuinely *evidence*-based from beginning to end. I will try to make the nature of this approach more vivid by displaying it. In successive parts, I will identify one commonplace hypothesis about the source of public conflict over climate science that is not empirically supported, and another hypothesis that is. I'll then outline the sort of field testing that should be done to convert the knowledge generated by the sorts of laboratory studies used to test these hypotheses into effective real-world strategies for communicating climate science.

A common but unsupported conjecture on climate change conflict: public irrationality

I will call the first hypothesis the 'public irrationality thesis' or 'PIT.' PIT attributes public controversy over climate change, in effect, to a deficit in public comprehension.

The public, on this view, doesn't really know much science. As a result, it can't understand what climate scientists are telling them, or are easily misled about what the state of the scientific evidence really is.

In addition, members of the public don't think the way that scientists do. Whereas scientists reason in a conscious, deliberate, and highly analytical fashion – what Kahneman (2011) calls 'System 2' in his deservedly popular book *Thinking: Fast and Slow* – members of the public form perceptions of risk in a largely unconscious, affect-driven fashion – what Kahneman calls 'System 1' reasoning. Forlorn polar bears drifting on shrinking patches of ice are less emotionally gripping than an airliner fuselage embedded in a flaming highrise. Members of the public thus end up predictably underestimating the hazard posed by climate change relative to more dramatic but actuarial remote risks, such as terrorism.

PIT is widely espoused, even among social scientists engaged in synthetic or interpretive assessments (Sunstein, 2007; Weber, 2006; Weber & Stern, 2011). Indeed, what makes this account plausible is that it is rooted in valid social science. But PIT is still only a conjecture – a hypothesis about the nature of public controversy over climate science.

It has also been tested. In one study (Kahan et al., 2012b), my colleagues and I asked a large, nationally representative sample of US adults to indicate 'how much risk' they believe 'climate change poses' on a scale of 0 (for 'no risk') to 10 ('extreme risk'). Responses to this item are known to be highly correlated with the ones ordinary members of the public will give when asked whether they believe the earth is heating up, whether humans are causing it, whether such warming will cause particular catastrophic results – or pretty much any other more particular question that members of the public can understand. So it makes for an efficient single-item indicator of what amounts to a generalized latent disposition that members of the public have toward climate change and other risks.

The point of using a measure like this isn't to see how close people generally are getting to the 'right answer' (who knows what that would be on this scale) but to explore variance in climate-change risk perceptions. By correlating responses with individual characteristics, we can see what sorts of people tend to be more concerned and which ones less. That information can be used to test hypotheses about why the 'average' member of the public is not *as* concerned as climate scientists think he or she should be.

PIT generates a testable predication. If the reason that the average member of the public doesn't take climate change risks as seriously as she should is that she doesn't understand enough science and doesn't think the way scientists do, then

"How much risk do you believe climate change poses to human health, safety, or prosperity?"

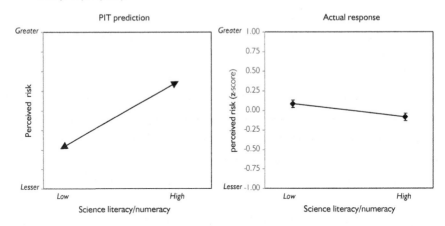

FIGURE 10.1   PIT prediction vs. actual impact of science comprehension on climate-change risk perceptions. Contrary to PIT's predictions, higher degrees of science literacy and numeracy are not associated with an increase in the perceived seriousness of climate-change risks but instead with a small decrease. Score on 11-point Likert measure (*M* = 5.7, SD =3.4) transformed to *z*-score. CIs reflect 0.95 level of confidence.

we should expect perceptions of risk to increase as people become more science literate and more adept at systematic or so-called System 2 reasoning (Figure 10.1).

Accordingly, we also measured our subjects' *science literacy* and *numeracy* as well. For the former, we used the National Science Foundation's 'Science Indicators.' We also used standard items to measure numeracy, which has been shown to be a valid predictor of individuals' disposition to rely on the conscious and deliberate form of information processing that Kahneman labels System 2 and to avoid the cognitive biases that are the signature of over-reliance on the affect-driven form of information processing that Kahneman labels System 1. Science literacy and numeracy, it turned out, cohered very nicely with each other, allowing them to be combined into a valid scale, which can be regarded as measuring a latent 'science comprehension' aptitude (which is in fact distinct from how educated a person is).

This science comprehension measure, we found, was *not* positively correlated with climate-change risk perception. On the contrary, it was negatively correlated with it, although only to a very slight degree (Figure 10.1).

We did not observe the strong positive correlation one would expect to if PIT were correct. On this basis, then, someone with a genuinely evidence-based orientation would reduce downward her estimation of the likelihood that a deficit in science knowledge or a tendency to over-rely on heuristic-driven System 1 reasoning explains the failure of the US public to converge on a perception of risk that reflects the concern scientists believe they ought to have.

The study, it turns out, furnishes still more reason to discount PIT, and to an even stronger degree. But it will be easier to appreciate the significance of this additional evidence in connection with my discussion of the next plausible and more amply supported account of the source of public controversy over climate change.

An evidence-based account of climate change conflict

The second plausible hypothesis can be called the 'motivated reasoning thesis' (MRT). Motivated reasoning refers to the tendency of people to conform their assessment of information – whether empirical data, logical arguments, the credibility of information sources, or even what they perceive with their own senses – to some goal or interest extrinsic to forming an accurate belief. The classic study, from the 1950s, showed that students from Ivy League colleges formed diametrically opposed perceptions of the correctness of certain disputed officiating calls made in a game between their schools' respective football teams: the emotional stake the students had in experiencing solidarity with their peers had unconsciously affected what they *saw* in viewing a film of the game (Hastorf & Cantril, 1954). MRT asserts that the same thing is happening when ordinary members of the public form perceptions of climate change risks: that is, they selectively credit or discredit evidence in patterns that reflect their commitments to important or self-defining social groups – again, a plausible conjecture in need of testing by empirical studies.

One such study tested the hypothesis that MRT explains the failure of expert consensus to dispel public controversy on disputed risks (Kahan et al., 2011). In the study, subjects (a large, nationally representative sample of US adults) were asked to indicate whether they viewed the featured scientists as 'knowledgeable and credible experts' on climate change, nuclear wastes, and gun control. Each scientist, the subjects were told, had received graduate training in a field related to the specified topic, was on the faculty of an elite US university, and was a member of the National Academy of Sciences (Figure 10.2). For each scientist, half the subjects were shown a book excerpt (patterned on writings from actual scientists) that took the 'high risk' position on the relevant issue: anthropogenic climate change is real and unless arrested will impose catastrophic consequences; deep geologic storage of nuclear wastes is unacceptably dangerous; or permitting ordinary citizens to carry concealed handguns in public increases the crime rate. The other half were shown an excerpt that took the 'low risk' position: the evidence on climate change is inconclusive; deep geologic isolation of nuclear waste is safe; permitting citizens to carry concealed handguns deters violent predation.

We picked these three issues because they were ones known to divide members of the public on *cultural lines*. In research that examines 'cultural cognition' – a version of MRT that posits individuals will form perceptions of risk that connect them to others who share their cultural values (Kahan, 2012b) – subjects'

Is this a knowledgeable and credible expert on …?

Robert Linden	**Oliver Roberts**	**James Williams**
Position: Professor of Meteorology, Massachusetts Institute of Technology	**Position:** Professor of Nuclear Engineering, University of California, Berkeley	**Position:** Professor of Criminology, Stanford University
Education: Ph.D., Harvard University	**Education:** Ph.D., Princeton University	**Education:** Ph.D., Yale University
Memberships: • American Meteorological Society • National Academy of Sciences	**Memberships:** • American Association of Physics • National Academy of Sciences	**Memberships:** • American Society of Criminologists • National Academy of Sciences

Global warming	**Nuclear power**	**Gun control**

FIGURE 10.2 Featured scientists: Subjects were instructed to indicate whether they viewed the featured scientist as an expert on the issue of climate change risks, disposal of nuclear wastes, and the consequences of permitting citizens to carry concealed handguns. The positions of the featured scientists were experimentally manipulated: each was represented to one-half of the subjects as having taken the 'high societal risk' position, and the other half as having taken the 'lows ocietal risk' position, on the relevant issue.

'worldviews' or preferences for how to organize society or other collective enterprises are characterized along two orthogonal dimensions. 'Individualism-communitarianism' (or simply 'Individualism') reflects their relative preference for social orderings that treat individuals as responsible for securing the conditions of their own well-being versus ones that assign such responsibility to the group or collective. 'Hierarchy-egalitarianism' (or simply 'Hierarchy') reflects their relative preference for social orderings that are pervaded with rankings that tie authority to social roles versus ones that deny that who can tell what to do can depend on any sort of socially stratified system of classifications. In previous studies, we and other researchers had found that individuals with simultaneously 'hierarchical' and 'individualistic' worldviews and those with simultaneously 'egalitarian' and 'communitarian' ones tend to hold opposing perceptions of environmental risks, including ones associated with climate change and nuclear power, and risks associated with guns and gun control (Kahan, 2010).

Now we were, in effect, asking individuals whose cultural worldviews varied along these lines to assess whether scientists who had reached conclusions on these issues were genuine 'experts.' The answer, we found, depended strongly on the fit between the position the scientist was depicted as taking on the indicated risk issue and the position that predominates within the subjects' own cultural groups (Figure 10.3). Thus, where the relevant scientist endorsed a 'high risk' conclusion on climate change, an 'egalitarian communitarian' subject was (all else equal) 72 percentage points more likely than a 'hierarchical individualist' one to designate him an 'expert' on that issue. But where the same scientist endorsed a 'low risk' conclusion on climate change, the hierarchical individualist subject was

Featured scientist is a knowledgeable and credible expert on ...

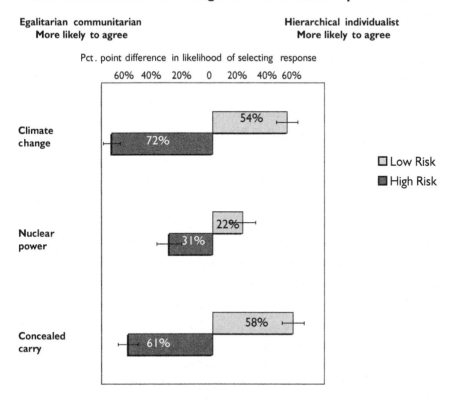

FIGURE 10.3   Impact of cultural cognition on perceptions of scientific expertise. Bars indicate how much more likely a subject with the indicated worldview is to agree than is a subject with the opposing worldview that the author is a 'knowledgeable and trustworthy expert' when that author is assigned a particular position ('high' or 'low risk'). Confidence intervals reflect .95 level of confidence.

54 percentage points more likely to identify him as an expert than an egalitarian communitarian. Subjects with these values also formed radically divergent perceptions of the relevant scientists' expertise conditional on the position they were depicted as endorsing on the safety of the disposal of nuclear wastes and the effect of concealed-carry laws.

The position of 'experts' is generally regarded as highly relevant on disputed risk issues like these. But when shown a highly accomplished scientist who had reached a conclusion on such an issue, subjects in the experiment were unlikely to perceive that he *was* an expert unless he took the position consistent with the one that predominated in their cultural group. This is exactly what MRT would predict: like the students viewing the tape of the disputed officiating calls, the subjects unconsciously adjusted the weight they afforded the evidence in patterns that reflect their commitments to others with whom they share a strong social bond.

If people are similarly selective in crediting evidence on what 'experts' believe when they encounter it outside the laboratory, then they will end up culturally polarized about what expert 'scientific consensus' is on such issues. In another component of the same study, we found exactly that: subjects with hierarchical and individualistic values, on the one hand, and ones with egalitarian communitarian values, on the other, had highly divergent beliefs about what scientific consensus is on the risks of climate change, on the safety of deep geologic isolation of nuclear wastes, and on the impact of permitting citizens to carry concealed weapons.

Indeed, the point of the study was to test MRT in relation to competing conjectures about why scientific consensus on climate change has not quieted public conflict over it. A popular surmise was – and continues to be – that climate skeptics either reject the authority of science or are members of a benighted ideological or cultural group whose members are uniquely disabled from forming reliable perceptions of what scientific consensus is.

However plausible these hypotheses might have been, the study results strongly undermine them. Neither of the cultural groups that are polarized on climate change, nuclear power, and gun control says it doesn't care what scientists believe. Rather, members of each believe that the position their group espouses is *consistent* with scientific consensus.

Moreover, they are all poorly attuned to what scientific consensus actually is. Another reason why we picked the risks posed by climate change, the safety of deep geological isolation of nuclear wastes, and the impact of concealed-carry handgun laws is that each of these issues has been addressed in a National Academy of Sciences 'expert consensus' report. At least if we use these reports as the benchmark, members of each group are right about scientific consensus about one-third of the time.

Neither group is very reliable, in other words, in discerning what scientists believe on issues like these because they both are unconsciously motivated to fit evidence of expert opinion to their cultural predispositions. Or at least this is the conclusion most supported by the study results.

One thing individuals with these cultural outlooks apparently *do* agree on is that personal observation of local weather is a good indicator of whether climate change is occurring. Or in any event, whether they perceive climate to be changing is predicted by their perception of recent weather conditions.

What they perceive the weather to have *been*, however, is not predicted by what it actually *was* (Akerlof et al., 2012). It is predicted instead by their cultural worldviews: individuals with an egalitarian predisposition perceive that recent temperatures in their area have been warmer than usual, while those with an individualist predisposition perceive that it has in fact been cooler (Goebbert et al., 2012).

This is consistent with MRT – one might expect individuals selectively to notice and recall aberrant weather in patterns supportive of the position that predominates in their cultural group – and strongly inconsistent with another PIT-related popular surmise, namely, that the public concerns have been impeded by the lack of any personal experience with the effects of climate change but can be expected to grow as individuals 'feel' the impact of climate change for themselves (Weber, 2006).

For more evidence still, I want to return to the study with which I started. In the study in which we examined how science comprehension relates to variance in climate-change risk perceptions, we measured subjects' cultural worldviews, too (Kahan et al., 2012b). Unsurprisingly, we found that subjects with hierarchical individualist worldviews and those with egalitarian communitarian ones were highly polarized. The reason we measured the subjects' worldviews, however, wasn't so that we could observe this pattern for the fiftieth time. It was so that we could see how cultural cognition – the form of motivated reasoning that features the influence of cultural worldviews on information processing – *interacts* with the subjects' science comprehension.

By itself, cultural cognition might seem perfectly compatible with PIT. Individuals who have acquired a significant degree of scientific knowledge and who are able to reason in the reflective manner associated with science, according to PIT, can be expected to recognize and make sense of the best available scientific evidence on climate change risks. But those who don't possess very much scientific knowledge and who can't engage in the sort of technical reasoning necessary to understand scientific evidence must necessarily rely on imperfect heuristics to figure out what is known to science. One of these might involve finding out what others who share their values think and basically deferring to them. If cultural cognition is essentially a heuristic substitute for science comprehension, then cultural polarization over climate change risks can itself be viewed as reflecting the sort of deficit in reason associated with PIT (Leiserowitz, 2006; Sunstein, 2006; Weber & Stern, 2011).

Such an account generates another set of testable predictions. If cultural cognition is a heuristic substitute for science comprehension, then subjects with hierarchical and individualistic values ought to become more concerned with climate change risk as their level of science comprehension increases. In addition, because they will now be basing their perceptions to a greater extent on the best available evidence, culturally diverse individuals who enjoy greater science comprehension ought to converge in their risk perceptions.

The evidence doesn't support these predictions (Figure 10.4). Subjects who are more egalitarian and communitarian in their values do become slightly more concerned about climate change risks as their level of science comprehension increases. But for subjects whose values are hierarchical and individualistic, an increase in science comprehension predicts less concern with climate change risks, not more. As a result, the already sizeable gap between subjects of opposing cultural worldviews who are low in science comprehension only becomes larger as people with those values become more science literate and more numerate. Greater scientific knowledge and a stronger disposition to use System 2 reasoning, in other words, magnify the MRT effect reflected in cultural cognition.

This evidence, then, simultaneously increases the likelihood that MRT explains public conflict over climate change risk and decreases the likelihood that

"How much risk do you believe climate change poses to human health, safety, or prosperity?"

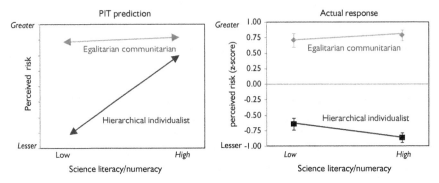

FIGURE 10.4 PIT prediction vs. actual impact of interaction between science comprehension and cultural worldviews. Contrary to PIT's predictions, highly science-literate and numerate Hierarchical Individualists are more skeptical, not less, of climate-change risks. CIs reflect 0.95 level of confidence.

PIT does. It doesn't 'settle the issue'; nothing ever does, because if one adopts an evidence-based stance, one always regards one's current best understanding as just a 'prior' subject to revision in light of any new, valid evidence. But if one does want to adopt this evidence-based orientation toward the science of science communication, then it would be a mistake not to take account of the strength of the evidence for MRT and the paucity of evidence for PIT in advising communicators and in designing further research.

What is to be done by whom and where

The point of trying to figure out why there is public controversy about climate change is to guide efforts to figure out what to do to dispel such conflict. The evidence I've reviewed so far suggests that the source of public conflict over climate change is not a deficit in public rationality but an excess of it. Cultural polarization is a consequence of how proficient individuals are in extracting from the science communication environment the information on climate change that matters most for their own lives. Nothing any ordinary member of the public personally believes about the existence, causes, or likely consequences of global warming will affect the risk that climate changes poses to her, or to anyone or anything she cares about. Nothing she does as a consumer, as a voter, as a contributor to political campaigns and causes, or as a participant in public conversation will be of sufficient consequence on its own to have any impact. However, if she forms the wrong position on climate change relative to the one that people with whom she has a close affinity – and on whose high regard and support she depends on in myriad ways in her daily life – she could suffer extremely unpleasant consequences, from shunning to the loss of employment.

Because the cost to her of making a mistake on the science is zero and the cost of being out of synch with her peers potentially catastrophic, it is indeed *individually* rational for her to attend to information on climate change in a manner geared to conforming her position to that of others in her cultural group.

One doesn't have to be a rocket scientist, of course, to figure out which position *is* dominant in one's group, particularly on an issue as high-profile as climate change. But if one *does* know more science and enjoys a higher-than-average technical reasoning capacity, one can do an even better job seeking out evidence that supports, and fending off or explaining away evidence that threatens, one's persistence in the belief that best coheres with one's group commitments (Kahan, 2013).

As much as it suits the interest of any individual to form his or her perception of climate change risks this way, however, it frustrates their collective interests when all individuals do this simultaneously. For in that case, democratic institutions of government are less likely to adopt policies that reflect the best available evidence on the risks culturally diverse citizens all face. This consequence, however, doesn't change the incentive that any individual faces to engage information about climate change or other disputed risks in a manner that is better suited to connecting her to her cultural group's position than to the truth – because again, nothing she believes, says, or does is going to have any meaningful impact on the level of risk she or her community faces from climate change or what democratic institutions of government do about that.

Dispelling controversy over climate change, then, requires overcoming this 'tragedy of the science communication commons.' We need science communication strategies that make crediting the best available evidence compatible with membership in the diverse cultural groups that comprise our pluralistic liberal society. If we can rid the science communication environment of the toxic partisan resonances that transform positions on climate change into badges of loyalty to contending factions, then we can be confident that ordinary members of the public, using the normal and normally reliable faculties that they use to discern who knows what about what, will converge on the best available scientific evidence on climate change as they do on the vast run of other questions for which science supplies the best answer.

What are those strategies? I *refuse* to answer.

The reason is not that I have no ideas about how to counteract the influences that generate motivated reasoning of the sort that figures in cultural cognition. Decision scientists, including ones using the methods of the science of science communication to address climate-change risk perceptions have done lots of work that I think helps to identify plausible lines of attack (Hart & Nisbet, 2011; Kahan et al., 2012a; Myers et al., 2012).

But here too the number of strategies that it is plausible to believe will work exceeds the number it's reasonable to believe will actually work. If I were to say, "Here's the answer: do this!" I'd be engaging in the very form of story-telling that it is the central aim of this chapter to discredit.

I can't tell those engaged in the mission to improve public engagement with climate science what to do but I can tell them *how* to do it: by engaging in a genuinely evidence-based approach to science communication. To make this prescription responsibly more concrete, I'll say one thing about the methods that should be employed for this purpose, and another about where to use them.

Methods

In my view, both making use of and enlarging our knowledge of climate science communication requires making a transition from *lab models* to *field experiments*. The research that I adverted to on strategies for counteracting motivated reasoning consists of simplified and stylized experiments administered face-to-face or online to general population samples. The best studies build explicitly on previous research – much of it also consisting in stylized experiments – that have generated information about the nature of the motivating group dispositions and the specific cognitive mechanisms through which they operate. They then formulate and test conjectures about how devices already familiar to decision science – including message framing, in-group information sources, identity-affirmation, and narrative – might be adapted to avoid triggering these mechanisms with communicating with these groups.

But such studies do not in themselves generate useable communication materials. They are only *models* of how materials that reflect their essential characteristics might work. Experimental models of this type play a critical role in the advancement of science communication knowledge: by silencing the cacophony of real-world influences that operate independently of anyone's control, they make it possible for researchers to isolate and manipulate mechanisms of interest, and thus draw confident inferences about their significance, or lack thereof. They are thus ideally suited to reducing the class of the merely plausible strategies to ones that their communicators can have an empirically justified conviction are likely to have an impact. But one can't then take the stimulus materials used in such experiments and send them to people in the mail or show them on television and imagine that they will have an effect.

Communicators are relying on a bad model if they expect lab researchers to supply them with a bounty of ready-to-use strategies. The researchers have furnished them something else: a reliable map of where to look. Such a map (it is hoped) will spare the communicators from wasting their time searching for nonexistent buried treasure But the communicators will still have to *dig*, making and acting on informed judgments about what sorts of real materials they believe might reproduce in the real-world contexts the effects that researchers elicited in their models.

The communicators, moreover, are the only ones who can competently direct this reproduction effort. The science communication researchers who constructed the models can't just tell them what to do because they don't know enough about the critical details of the communication environment: who the relevant players are, what their stakes and interests might be, how they talk to each other, and to whom they listen. If researchers nevertheless accept the invitation to give 'how to' advice, the best they will be able to manage are banalities – "Know your audience!"; "Grab the audience's attention!" – along with Goldilocks admonitions such as, "Use vivid images, because people engage information with their emotions ... but beware of appealing *too much* to emotion, because people become numb and shut down when they are overwhelmed with alarming images!"

Communicators possess knowledge of all the messy particulars that researchers not only didn't need to understand but were obliged to abstract away from in constructing their models. Indeed, like all smart and practical people, the communicators are filled with many plausible ideas about how to proceed – more than they have the time and resources to implement, and many of which are not compatible with one another anyway. What experimental models – if constructed appropriately – can tell them is which of their surmises rest on empirically sound presuppositions and which do not. Exposure to the information that such modeling yields will (if the models are elegant) activate experienced-informed imagination on the communicators' part, and enable them to make evidence-informed judgments about which strategies they believe are most likely to work for their particular problem.

At that point, it is time for the scientist of science communication to step back in – or to join alongside the communicator. The communicator's informed conjecture is now a hypothesis to be tested. In advising field communicators, science of science communication researchers should treat what the communicators do as experiments. Science communication researchers should work with the communicator to structure their communication strategies in a manner that yields valid observations that can be measured and analyzed.

Indeed, communicators, with or without the advice of science of science communication researchers, should not just go on blind instinct. They shouldn't just read a few studies, translate them into a plausible-sounding plans of action, and then wing it. Their plausible surmises about what will work are likely to be more plausible, more likely to work, than the ones dreamed up by less worldly laboratory researchers. But the researchers' plausible surmises are still just that. They are still only hypotheses. Without evidence, we will not learn whether policies based on such surmises did or didn't work. If we don't learn that, we won't really have learned anything, including how we can do even better next time.

Genuinely evidence-based science communication must be based on evidence *all the way down*. Communicators should make themselves aware of the existing empirical information that science communication researchers have generated (and steer clear of the myriad stories that retail consumers of decision-science work like to tell) about why the public is divided on climate science. They should formulate strategies that seek to reproduce in the world effects that have been shown to help counter the dynamics of motivated reasoning responsible for such division. Then, working with empirical researchers, they should *observe* and *measure*. They should collect appropriate forms of pretest or preliminary data to try to corroborate that the basis for expecting a strategy to work is sound and to calibrate and refine its elements to maximize its expected effect. They should also collect and analyze data on the actual impact of their strategies once they've been deployed.

Finally, *they should make the information that they have generated at every step of this process available to others so that they can learn from it too.* Every exercise in evidence-based science communication itself generates knowledge. Every such exercise itself furnishes an instructive *model* of how that knowledge can be intelligently used. The failure to extract and share the intelligence latent in *doing* science communication perpetuates the dissipation of collective knowledge that it is the primary mission of the science of science communication to staunch.

Local adaptation

Consider this paradox. If one is trying to be elected to Congress in either Florida or Arizona, it is not a good idea to make 'combating global climate change' the centerpiece of one's campaign. Yet both of these states are hotbeds of local political activity focusing on climate adaptation. A bill passed by Florida's Republican-controlled legislature in 2011 and signed into law by its tea-party Governor (Laws of Florida, 2011) has initiated city- and county-level proceedings to formulate measures for protecting the state from the impact of projected sea-level rises, which are expected to be aggravated by the increased incidence of hurricanes. Arizona is the site of similar initiatives (Arizona Department of Energy Quality, 2013). Overseen by that state's conservative Governor (who once punched a reporter for asking her whether she believed in global warming (Wing, 2012)), the Arizona proceedings are aimed at anticipating expected stresses on regional water supplies.

Climate science – of the highest quality, and supplied by expert governmental and academic sources – is playing a key role in the deliberations of both states. Florida officials, for example, have insisted that new nuclear power generation facilities being constructed offshore at Turkey Point be raised to a level higher than contemplated by the original design in order to reflect new sea-level rise and storm-activity projections associated with climate change (Kenward, 2011). The basis of these Florida officials' projections are the same scientific models that Florida Senator Marco Rubio, now considered a likely 2016 presidential candidate, says he still finds insufficiently convincing to justify national regulation of carbon emissions (Bennett-Smith, 2013).

The influences that trigger cultural cognition when climate change is addressed at the national level are much weaker at the local one. When they are considering adaptation, citizens engage the issue of climate change not as members of warring cultural factions but as property owners, resource consumers, insurance policy holders, and tax payers – identities they all share. The people who are furnishing them with pertinent scientific evidence about the risks they face and how to abate them are not the national representatives of competing political brands but rather their municipal representatives, their neighbors, and even their local utility companies. What's more, the sorts of issues they are addressing – damage to property and infrastructure from flooding, reduced access to scarce water supplies, diminished farming yields as a result of drought – are matters they deal with all the time. They are the issues they have always dealt with as members of the regions in which they live; they have a natural shared vocabulary for thinking and talking about these issues, the use of which reinforces their sense of linked fate and reassures them they are working with others whose interests are aligned with theirs. Because they are, in effect, all on the same team, citizens at the local level are less likely to react to scientific evidence in defensive, partisan ways that sports fans do to contentious officiating calls.

Nevertheless, it would be a mistake to assume that local engagement with adaptation is impervious to polarizing forms of motivated reasoning. The antagonistic cultural meanings that have contaminated the national science communication environment could easily spill over into local ones as well. Something like this happened – or came close to it – in North Carolina, where the state legislature enacted a law that restricts use of anything but 'historical data' on sea-level in state planning. The provision got enacted because proponents of adaptation planning legislation there failed to do what those in the neighboring state of Virginia did in creating a rhetorical separation between the issue of local flood planning and 'global climate change.' Polarizing forms of engagement have bogged down municipal planning in some parts of Florida – at the same time as progress is being made elsewhere in the state.

The issue of local adaptation, then, presents a unique but precarious opportunity to promote constructive public engagement with climate science. The prospects for success will turn on how science is communicated – by scientists addressing local officials and the public, certainly, but also by local officials addressing their constituents and by myriad civic entities (chambers of commerce, property owner associations, utility companies) addressing the individuals whom they serve. These *climate-science communicators* face myriad challenges that admit of informed, *evidence*-based guidance, and they are eager to get guidance of that kind. Making their needs the focus of field-based science communication experiments would confer an immense benefit on them.

The social science researchers conducting such experiments would receive an immense benefit in return. Collaborating with these communicators to help them protect their science communication environment from degradation, and to effectively deliver consequential scientific information within it, would generate a wealth of knowledge on how to adapt insights from lab models to the real world.

There are lots of places to do science communication field experiments, of course, because there are lots of settings in which people are making decisions that should be informed by the best available climate science. There is no incompatibility between carrying out programs in support of adaptation-science communication simultaneously with ones focused on communicating relevant to climate policymaking at the national level.

On the contrary, there are likely to be numerous synergies. For one thing, the knowledge that adaptation-focused field experimentation will likely generate about how to convert laboratory models to field-based strategies will be relevant to science communication in all domains. In addition, by widening the positive exposure to climate science, adaptation-focused communication is likely to create greater public receptivity to open-minded engagement with this science in all contexts in which it is relevant. Finally, by uniting on a local level all manner of groups and interests that currently occupy an adversarial relation on the climate change issue nationally, the experience of constructive public engagement with climate science at the local level has the potential to clear the air of the toxic meanings that have been poisoning climate discourse in our democracy for decades.

Conclusion

A central aim of the science of science communication is to protect the value of what is arguably our society's greatest asset. Modern science has conferred on us the *knowledge* necessary to live healthier, safer, and more prosperous lives than our forebears could even have imagined, much less lived. But the same conditions of political liberty and cultural pluralism that have nourished the advancement of science have multiplied the competing number of certifiers of what is collectively known (Kahan, 2012a). Our prospects for actually making effective *use* of what science has taught us about the workings of nature demands that we use *science* to improve our understanding of how to enable culturally diverse citizens to converge on the best scientific evidence as they deliberate over how to pursue their common ends.

The imperfect state of the science of science communication is part of the explanation for cultural polarization over climate science. But it is no more than a *part* of it. Another, perhaps even larger one is the failure for decades to have made effective use of what had already been learned as a result of the scientific study of risk perception and communication.

Now, many public-spirited citizens and institutions are turning to the knowledge associated with the science of science communication to try to dispel the fog of cultural conflict that obscures the best available scientific evidence on climate change. But unless we use *evidence-based* methods, this decisive opportunity to integrate the science of science communication with the practice of science will end up wasted, too.

References

Akerlof, K., Maibach, E. W., Fitzgerald, D., Cedeno, A.Y., & Neuman, A. (2012). Do people 'personally experience' global warming, and if so how, and does it matter? *Global Environmental Change*, 23(1), 81–91.

Arizona Department of Environmental Quality. (2013). Arizona Climate Change Initiatives. Retrieved November 13, 2013: http://www.azclimatechange.gov.

Bennett-Smith, M. (2013). Marco Rubio not convinced climate change an actual problem. *Huffington Post*, February 6. Retrieved: http://www.huffingtonpost.com/2013/02/06/marco-rubio-climate-change_n_2630930.html.

Bethe, H. A. (1976). The necessity of fission power. *Scientific American*, 234(1), 21–31.

Goebbert, K., Jenkins-Smith, H. C., Klockow, K., Nowlin, M. C., & Silva, C .L. (2012). Weather, climate and worldviews: The sources and consequences of public perceptions of changes in local weather patterns. *Weather, Climate, and Society*, 4(2), 132–144.

Hart, P. & Nisbet, E. C. (2011). Boomerang effects in science communication: How motivated reasoning and identity cues amplify opinion polarization about climate mitigation policies. *Communication Research*, August 11.

Hastorf, A. H. & Cantril, H. (1954). They saw a game: A case study. *The Journal of Abnormal and Social Psychology*, 49(1), 129–134.

Kahan, D. (2010). Fixing the communications failure. *Nature*, 463(7279), 296–297.

Kahan, D. M. (2012a). *Cognitive bias and the constitution of the liberal republic of science*. Yale Law School Public Law Working Paper No. 270.

Kahan, D. M. (2012b). Cultural cognition as a conception of the cultural theory of risk. In R. Hillerbrand, P. Sandin, S. Roeser, & M. Peterson (Eds.), *Handbook of risk theory: Epistemology, decision theory, ethics and social implications of risk* (pp. 725–260). London: Springer.

Kahan, D. M. (2013). Ideology, motivated reasoning, and cognitive reflection. *Judgment and Decision Making*, 8,(4) 407–424.

Kahan, D. M., Jenkins-Smith, H., & Braman, D. (2011). Cultural cognition of scientific consensus. *Journal of Risk Research*, 14(2), 147–174.

Kahan D. M., Jenkins-Smith, J., Taranotola, T., Silva, C., & Braman, D. (2012a). *Geoengineering and the science communication environment: A cross-cultural study*. CCP Working Paper No. 92, January 9.

Kahan, D. M., Peters, E., Wittlin, M., Slovic, P., Ouellette, L. L., Braman, D., & Mandel, G. (2012b). The polarizing impact of science literacy and numeracy on perceived climate change risks. *Nature Climate Change*, 2(10), 732–735.

Kahneman, D. (2011).*Thinking, fast and slow*. New York: Farrar, Straus and Giroux.

Kahneman, D., Slovic, P., & Tversky, A. (1982). *Judgment under uncertainty: Heuristics and biases*. Cambridge and New York: Cambridge University Press.

Kenward, A. (2011). Sea level rise brings added risk to coastal nuclear plants. *Climate Central*, March 23. Retrieved November 13, 2013: http://www.climatecentral.org/news/sea-level-rise-brings-added-risks-to-coastal-nuclear-plants.

Laws of Florida. (2011). *Community Planning Act*. Ch. 2011--2139.

Leiserowitz, A. A. (2006). Climate change risk perception and policy preferences: The role of affect, imagery, and values. *Climatic Change*, 77, 45–72.

Myers, T., Nisbet, M., Maibach, E., & Leiserowitz, A. (2012). A public health frame arouses hopeful emotions about climate change. *Climatic Change*, 113(3–4), 1105–1112.

Slovic, P. (1987). Risk perception. *Science*, 236(4799), 280–285.

Slovic, P., Fischhoff, B., & Lichtenstein, S. (1976). Cognitive processes and societal risk taking. In J. S. Carroll & J. W. Payne (Eds.), *Cognition and social behavior* (pp. 165–184). New York: L. Erlbaum Associates.

Sunstein, C. R. (2006). Misfearing: A reply. *Harvard Law Review*, 119(4), 1110–1125.

Sunstein, C. R. (2007). On the divergent American reactions to terrorism and climate change. *Columbia Law Review*, 107(2), 503–557.

Watts, D. J. (2011). *Everything is obvious: Once you know the answer: How common sense fails*. New York: Atlantic Books.

Weber, E. (2006). Experience-based and description-based perceptions of long-term risk: why global warming does not scare us (yet). *Climatic Change,* 77(1).

Weber, E. U. & Stern, P. C. (2011). Public understanding of climate change in the United States. *American Psychologist,* 66(4), 315–328.

Wing, N. (2012). Jan Brewer 'slugged' reporter who asked climate change question. *Huffington Post,* December 5. Retrieved November 13, 2013: http://www.huffingtonpost.com/2012/12/05/jan-brewer-reporter_n_2247350.html.

COMMENTARY ON PART IV

Rethinking climate change communication

Alison Anderson

We are undoubtedly entering a crucially important period in the history of climate change communication. The scale and complexity of structural-level changes that are needed to address climate change (political, regulatory and economic) cannot be underestimated (Cox, 2013). Over the past decade climate change has become more prominent on local and national policy agendas across the globe and yet government leaders have been slow to act and public attitudes concerning the reality, scale and urgency of the issues have dipped and wavered (Moser & Dilling, 2011). While the seriousness of the threat, the rate of change and the links to the frequency and intensity of extreme weather events is the subject of much debate, there is a clear scientific consensus that the mean global temperature has increased significantly since pre-industrial times and human activity is the main cause (see Anderson, 2009; Brulle et al., 2012). Yet in the US and, to a lesser extent in the UK, organized groups of climate skeptics and right-wing think tanks have used a variety of communication channels to steadily trickle-feed seeds of doubt and to attack individual scientists. It is evident that over the past ten years significant ideological and partisan polarization has occurred on the issue of climate change among the American public (see McCright & Dunlap, 2011; Rolfe-Redding et al. 2011). People who think that scientists disagree on climate change tend to be less certain that climate change is happening and are less likely to support climate policy (see Ding et al., 2011).

It is increasingly accepted that science communication scholars have failed to effectively convey the findings of their research and that there is an urgent need for communicators to apply their models to real-world situations, rather than rely on outdated intuitive approaches. As Pidgeon and Fischhoff observe: "Given its critical importance, public understanding of climate science deserves the strongest possible communications science to convey the practical implications of large, complex, uncertain physical, biological and social processes" (Pidgeon & Fischhoff, 2011, p. 35). The 'one size fits all' model is clearly inadequate. Communication about climate change needs to be informed by the latest research evidence based upon a very clear understanding of the demographics of the target audience, their media preferences and opinion-leaders, their political ideologies and cultural worldviews, and the issues that most closely resonate with them (Moser & Dilling, 2011). People's views are often closely linked to their direct experience, demonstrated by the way in which concerns often rise in response to locally experienced changing weather patterns (e.g., heatwaves or flooding) and observable impacts further afield, such as melting ice. At the same time they may be influenced by broader structures such as shifting media frames and agendas, and the perceived well-being of the economy (Anderson, 2009; Lakoff, 2010).

But there are a number of significant barriers to public engagement with climate change beyond simply providing people with greater knowledge and awareness (Lorenzoni et al., 2007; Ockwell et al., 2009). These two chapters have usefully drawn attention to the tensions posed by top-down versus bottom-up approaches to climate governance, and raise important questions concerning the extent to which publics can be viewed as rational citizens and the limits of state control. Kahan calls for a new 'evidence-based' approach to climate science communication. Having debunked the 'public irrationality thesis' he concludes that, rather than there being a deficit in rationality among the public, there is actually an excess of rationality. He argues that individuals make very rational choices about their perceptions based on their attachments to their cultural groupings, and the consequences that may follow if they adopt a position counter to the one that is dominant within their circle. In the past it was often assumed that all we needed to do was relay the 'facts' to people and they would accept the evidence and controversy would go away (Nisbet, 2010). The information deficit model has long been widely critiqued within science policy studies for its simplistic and highly linear view of communication processes and its failure to problematize the relationship between 'experts' and 'lay publics.' However, as Kahan rightly observes, it has taken a long time for scientists and policymakers to catch up (see also Moser & Dilling, 2011; Nisbet & Scheufele, 2009).

The motivated reasoning thesis posits that people tend to assess information on the basis of an extrinsic goal or belief. This suggests that people tend to judge evidence (including the credibility of sources of information) in ways that reinforce the worldviews that are most widely accepted in their cultural group. A range of experiments undertaken by Kahan and colleagues suggest that our positions on an array of issues (including climate change, nanotechnology, and gun control) fundamentally reflect our need to belong and identify with our particular social groupings. In the US context, this roughly translates into communitarian/egalitarian worldviews tending to be adopted by Democrats (who mostly accept the risks of climate change) and individualist/hierarchical worldviews tending to be held by Republicans (who mostly doubt the risks). Cultural identity, then, becomes key to understanding how the climate change debate has become so deeply polarized. Yet understanding public attitudes to climate change is extraordinarily complex and often does not simply reflect a desire to conform to underlying political ideologies/belief systems that are predominant within one's social group. An important difference between the US and the UK is that in terms of attitudes to climate change the former is sharply polarized on right–left party political lines, whereas the latter is not so clearly divided (Dunlap & McCright, 2008). While political ideology has clearly become an important factor, there are multiple 'publics' who may belong to a variety of different networks at any one time. Other key intervening variables include age, gender, education and religion. Studies suggest that climate skepticism tends to increase with age, and men are more likely to doubt the scientific evidence compared to women (Pidgeon, 2012). Also it is important to take into account intra-party heterogeneity, given that a variety of competing goals and ideologies exist within a political party and these shift over time (see Rolfe-Redding et al., 2011). In addition to Kahan's call for more experimental studies I believe there is also a need for more qualitative work to inform communication strategies. Such work reveals ambivalences and contradictions around people's attitudes and suggests there is a considerable amount of diversity of opinion among those that might be labeled as individualists versus communitarians (see Smith & Joffe, 2013).

Efforts to make public engagement about climate change more informed by research evidence and more reflective by conducting evaluation, by itself will not achieve the desired outcome. As the chapter by Paterson and Stripple makes clear, it is vital that structural barriers are also addressed. Governments have increasingly become key actors in engaging publics with climate change and a proliferation of communication plans have been developed, though sometimes giving off conflicting messages. In the UK these have involved a number of attempts to introduce individualized incentives to cut carbon footprints, such as offering financial help to householders to introduce energy efficiency measures, or the introduction of carbon-offsetting. As Moser and Dilling argue:

> Clearly, communication on climate change is only part of the picture. Raising awareness and discussing an issue does not directly result in behavior change or policy action. Other factors, especially policy options, windows and barriers, come into play. Thus for communication to be effective in leading to active engagement it must be supported by policy, economic and infrastructure changes that allow concerns and good intensions to be realized.
>
> (Moser & Dilling, 2011, p. 169)

Yet direct state intervention in the private sphere tends to result in resistance, or feelings of disempowerment. Governments tend to be reluctant to regulate on green behavior since they fear losing votes and there is a fundamental mismatch between the timescale of short electoral cycles and the long timescale of environmental issues (Ockwell et al., 2009). Also external interventions (through providing economic incentives for example) may not achieve long-lasting impacts once they are removed and may lessen an individual's intrinsic motivations to act. One alternative is to take a more bottom-up approach by using communication to foster demand for climate change regulation via lobbying and advocacy. As Ockwell et al. (2009) maintain, this involves communication strategies that are informed by state-of-the-art political science research and audience segmentation approaches. The deficiencies of top-down climate change communication are increasingly being recognized and more emphasis has been placed on communication from peer to peers (Nerlich et al., 2009). The role of opinion-leader and face-to-face communication can be very effective. Mass communication is not necessarily the best way to reach audiences, as it is often not tailored towards specific audience segments.

Paterson and Stripple usefully draw attention to the role of problematization and issue framing – for example, carbon dieting, or health and well-being. It needs to be linked to concrete local issues that people can relate to, such as health or the economy, rather than abstract issues that are perceived to have little relevance or impact on daily life. Of course, these are not separate issues but they are often perceived to be unconnected. They may also be linked to other intrinsic goals such as community belongingness, well-being, and quality-of-life. At the same time communicators need to be open and honest about the benefits of taking action. Engendering a sense of collective purpose through people's social networks by embedding pro-environmental social norms via, for example, faith groups, mother and toddler groups, or student societies, can play a key role in spreading social change and building bottom-up demand for government regulation but policymakers and the media also have a critical role to play. As Pidgeon and Fischhoff acknowledge, there is "no simple recipe for climate change communication" but we need cross-disciplinary teams skilled in sustained strategic listening and strategic organization.

Science communication scholars are not always very good at meaningfully translating scholarly research so that it is accessible to wider audiences both within and outside academia. More energy needs to be directed towards outreach and interdisciplinary collaboration. This involves more active engagement with policymakers, scientists, think tanks, and advocacy groups. As Kahan points out, scientists, government officials and NGOs have generally made little use of the findings generated by scholars working in the science communication area. Field experiments provide an opportunity for models to be tested in the real world, evidence applied, and lessons learned. There are myriad opportunities to work alongside communicators on particular campaigns targeting specific social and cultural groupings in order to develop their communication strategies in ways that can be observed and measured. Looking ahead to the future there is a need for rigorous empirical analysis of source-media relations including more systematic analysis of the strategic and tactical action of news sources (e.g., scientists, NGOs, policymakers, industry) in relation to the media. Research also needs to explore how these connect with public interests and concerns, particularly in an increasingly information saturated, sound-bite celebrity-focused culture. The role of imagery in climate change communication has increasingly been given serious attention (e.g., Doyle, 2007; Hansen & Machin, 2013). Future research could usefully explore in more depth how different audiences interpret a range of widely circulated images of climate change; this would help to establish their usefulness and highlight how messages about climate change could best be developed and targeted in the future.

One of the most significant challenges that we face is getting to grips with the complex new media landscape, where information flows more readily across societal and geographical boundaries, and developing conceptual frameworks and methodologies that are sophisticated enough to capture this. Over recent years there has been a growing number of internationally comparative studies on climate change and analyses of global communications networks. Future research could usefully explore the reasons for different levels of coverage among countries, their different emphases, and why the perspectives of developing countries tend to rarely be given prominence (Painter, 2007; Shanahan, 2007). Further work in this area could develop our understanding of complex information flows between countries and their wider socio-political contexts. Within the increasingly international, multi-digital, and fragmented media environment, we need to analyze how competing rationality claims are inflected through different media given that they are complexly differentiated and governed by their own distinct internal and external constraints (Anderson, 2009). The decline of traditional news and the proliferation of news sources, including the growing importance of blogs and online social networking forums, have important implications for the communication of climate change. Such developments raise questions about who controls access to news and how far the media are becoming dependent upon international news agencies, corporate sources, and public relations companies. Future studies need to reflect changes in media consumption including the declining influence of the newspaper press and the growing use of digital media, particularly among young people in the west. New modes of analysis and theoretical approaches are needed that are capable of addressing the complex ways in which media are intermeshed within political and economic structures of power. There is a lack of studies that focus upon the different kinds of effects of online and offline media, and social network analysis could shed new light on how flows reciprocally impact on one another in non-linear ways. Whilst much useful work has been undertaken over recent years, we need to move beyond the media-centric focus that has tended to dominate the field. Too often previous research has focused on media content alone, ignoring the politics of news production and how publics variously make sense of the issues (see Anderson, 2006). While such studies clearly have value in their own right there is now an urgent need to step up a scale and widen the lens to consider the complexities and contingencies of social processes and the wider play of political power.

References

Anderson, A. (2006). Media and risk. In S. Walklate & G. Mythen (Eds.), *Beyond the risk society* (pp. 114–131). Milton Keynes: Open University/McGraw Hill.

Anderson, A. (2009). Media, politics and climate change: Towards a new research agenda. *Sociology Compass*, 3(2), 166–182.

Brulle, R. J., Carmichael, J., & Jenkins, J. C. (2012). Shifting public opinion on climate change: Assessment of factors influencing concern over climate change in the US 2002–2010. *Climatic Change*, 114(2), 169–188.

Cox, R. (2013). *Scale, complexity, and communicative systems*. Panel session on 'Organizing and Integrating Knowledge about Environmental Communication', International Communication Association Conference, London, June 21.

Ding D., Maibach, E. W., Zhao, X., Roser-Renouf, C., & Leiserowitz, A. (2011). Support for climate policy and societal action are linked to perceptions about scientific agreement. *Nature Climate Change*, 1, December, 462–466.

Doyle, J. (2007). Picturing the clima(c)tic: Greenpeace and the representational politics of climate change communication. *Science as Culture*, 16(2), 129–150.

Dunlap, R. E. & McCright, A. M. (2008). A widening gap: Republican and democratic views on climate change. *Environment*, 50(5), 26–35.

Hansen, A. & Machin, D. (2013). Researching visual environmental communication. *Environmental Communication*, 7(2), 151–168.

Lakoff, G. (2010). Why it matters how we frame the environment. *Environmental Communication*, 4(1), 70–81.

Lorenzoni, I., Nicholson-Cole, S., & Whitmarsh, L. (2007). Barriers perceived to engaging with climate change among the UK public and their policy implications. *Global Environmental Change*, 17(3–4), 445–459.

McCright, A. M. & Dunlap, R. E. (2011). The politicization of climate change and polarization in the American public's views of global warming, 2001–2010. *The Sociological Quarterly*, 52(2), 155–194.

Moser, S. C. & Dilling, L. (2011). Communicating climate change: Opportunities and challenges for closing the science-action gap. In R. Norgaard, D. Schlosberg, & J. Dryzek, (Eds.), *The Oxford handbook of climate change and society* (pp. 161–174). New York: Oxford University Press.

Nerlich, B., Koteyko, N., & Brown, B. (2009). Theory and language of climate change communication. *Climate Change*, 1(1), 97–110.

Nisbet, M. C. & Scheufele, D. A. (2009). What's next for science communication? Promising directions and lingering distractions. *American Journal of Botany*, 96(10), 1767–1778.

Nisbet, M. C. (2010). Framing science: A new paradigm in public engagement. In L. Kahlor & P. A. Stout (Eds.), *Communicating science: New agendas in communication* (pp. 40–68). New York: Routledge.

Ockwell, D., Whitmarsh, L., & O'Neill, S. (2009). Reorienting climate change communication for effective mitigation – forcing people to be green or fostering grass-roots engagement? *Science Communication*, 30(3), 305–327.

Painter, J. (2007). *All doom and gloom? International TV coverage of the April and May 2007 IPCC Reports*. Retrieved August 4, 2013: http://www.eci.ox.ac.uk/news/events/070727-carbonundrum/painter.pdf.

Pidgeon, N. F. (2012). Climate change risk perception and communication: Addressing a critical moment? *Risk Analysis*, 32(6), 951–956.

Pidgeon, N. & Fischhoff, B. (2011). The role of social and decision sciences in communicating uncertain climate risks. *Nature Climate Change*, 1, 35–41.

Rolfe-Redding, J. C., Maibach, E. W., Feldman, L., & Leiserowitz, A. (2011). *Republicans and climate change: An audience analysis of predictors for belief and policy preferences.* Working paper. Retrieved August 4, 2013: http://ssrn.com/abstract=2026002, http://dx.doi.org/10.2139/ssrn.2026002.

Shanahan, M. (2007). *Talking about a revolution: Climate change and the media: An International Institute for Environment and Development Briefing.* IIED, December.

Smith, N. & Joffe, H. (2013). How the public engages with global warming: A social representations approach. *Public Understanding of Science*, 22(1), 16–32.

INDEX

CPSIA information can be obtained at www.ICGtesting.com
Printed in the USA
BVOW06s0949221115

427965BV00003B/10/P